DEATH'S LONG SHADOW

Richard Brinsley Sheridan Mysteries

Book Two

R M Cullen

Also in the Richard Brinsley Sheridan series:
Harlequin Is Dead
The Thirteenth Apostle

DEATH'S LONG SHADOW

Published by Sapere Books.

24 Trafalgar Road, Ilkley, LS29 8HH

saperebooks.com

Copyright © R M Cullen, 2025

R M Cullen has asserted her right to be identified as the author of this work.
All rights reserved.

No part of this publication may be reproduced, stored in any retrieval system, or transmitted, in any form, or by any means, electronic, mechanical, photocopying, recording, or otherwise, without the prior written permission of the publishers.
This book is a work of fiction. Names, characters, businesses, organisations, places and events, other than those clearly in the public domain, are either the product of the author's imagination, or are used fictitiously.
Any resemblances to actual persons, living or dead, events or locales are purely coincidental.

ISBN: 978-0-85495-689-0

For Ellen,
the best of friends

ACKNOWLEDGMENTS

My thanks as ever go to my family and their continued support; it was always a pleasure to read my first drafts aloud to my late mother and to receive her thoughtful opinions.

I am forever grateful to belong to the South Manchester Writers and to have received their invaluable feedback over many years. I am also blessed with some stern critics, in particular Carole Thomson and my old colleague Jan Weddup.

My thanks go to Giles Milburn for his invaluable suggestions and also to Jonathan Ruppin.

The support and encouragement of friends like Ellen Fox, Olly James and Maggie Mackay has helped to sustain my efforts.

There are some splendid biographies of Sheridan, by Fintan O'Toole and Linda Kelly to name a few, which have helped to colour in my portrait of him, but given the fictitious elements he will always be my own version and any historical inaccuracies are to be laid entirely at my door.

Lastly, I owe a debt of gratitude to Sapere Books for taking on my Sheridan series. My editors, Amy Durant, Matilda Richards and Natalie Linh Bolderston, have applied their sharp eyes to keeping the manuscript focused and succinct and all the better for it.

CHAPTER ONE

Stafford, England, 1792

The weather had turned unbearably hot even for that time of the year. After so much poor weather in June and July, this sudden appearance of summer at the end of August was unexpected. They were all a-sweat, the men with handkerchiefs at the ready to mop their brows and the women with their fans constantly to hand. Richard Brinsley Sheridan had journeyed up to Stafford on constituency business. Although elections were some time off, Sheridan knew that he had neglected to attend sufficiently to his interests in the borough. There had been reasons, of course, his wife's last illness and her recent death not least amongst them.

Eliza. It took very little to set his mind springing back to those last days in Southampton at the end of June. The helpless wretchedness he had felt as he had watched her life ebb away. Weakened by childbirth, she had fallen at last to the tubercular tendency of the Linley family, which had already claimed her younger sister. In company with Eliza's dear friend, Mrs Canning, Sheridan had been glad to have been with Eliza at the end, for all the heartbreak. She had endured much throughout their marriage: his neglect as he pursued ambitions in theatre and politics, and of course his string of infidelities. She had forgiven and tolerated; he could not but take upon himself the blame for driving Eliza into her liaison with young Lord Edward Fitzgerald — an affair which had led to the birth of a daughter, Mary, in March. Sheridan had insisted on claiming the child as his own, not only for the sake of Eliza's reputation but also in some measure as a means to find his own redemption.

Sheridan stayed at The Stafford Arms as usual. His supporters in the town were full of understanding and solicitudes for his bereaved state. His loyal Mr Dudley was most reassuring as to the respect he commanded in the neighbourhood, despite his absence. It was important that Sheridan be seen to have a care of the local petitioners. Stafford was an independent borough not in the gift of any one patron. It was a matter of pride to him, given his constant calls at Westminster for electoral reform, that Stafford was counted amongst the most democratic seats in the country. That day of his first election twelve years previous, in 1780, he had declared to be one of the happiest of his life.

It was a relief nevertheless to accept the invitation from Lord Cannock to stay for the weekend at his estate at Sandbourne and to leave the tradesmen and petitioners of the town behind. His carriage trundled through the close cobbled streets of the town and out onto the rural thoroughfares that led towards Cannock Chase. In no time at all his vistas were of hedgerows full of the song of the yellowhammer and meadows where cattle grazed amongst a swathe of buttercups. He was in every sense a man of the city, but Sheridan conceded that on such a summer's day there was no finer scene than this. The perfect blue of the sky allowed his spirits to lift and to contemplate the possibility of future joys after a time of so much grief.

The sweep up the long and imposing drive through the parkland of the estate towards the grand house further lightened his mood. The façade of Sandbourne presented a glorious prospect. It was a house which had been built by Christopher Stretton, the first earl, and then added to substantially by his successors. He had been granted the title and estates following the Restoration of Charles II, having fought valiantly in the Royalist cause.

With a welcoming nod, Lady Cannock greeted Sheridan from the top of the steps as he alighted from his carriage. He had not seen the countess for some years and he noted how she had filled out and become altogether more matronly. The bloom of youth might have faded, but her energy and enthusiasm were as infectious as ever and as he climbed the steps to join her, Sheridan found himself charmed once again by her warmth of expression.

'We are so delighted that you are able to tear yourself away from pressing matters in Stafford, Mr Sheridan. Your company is most welcome. And please, dear, dear Richard —' she placed a hand on his arm and squeezed lightly — 'do not think we mean you to entertain us, as many do, I fear. I know the grief you must be feeling, and your child so young to lose her mother. You have our deepest sympathies.'

He bowed. 'Thank you, madam.'

After a suitable pause to cement those sentiments, Lady Cannock drew Sheridan indoors with a broad smile.

'We are all informal here. My uncle, Sir Humphrey Barclay, joins us later this afternoon with his daughter, Mrs Smethurst, and her young son. We expect Dr Burton for dinner and perhaps our cousin Edward, but that is never certain. So, you see we are scarcely a party at all.'

On the threshold she turned to a factotum, who bowed imperceptibly. 'Here is our Mr Hanley — Samuel. He will see that you are shown to your room and ensure that your needs are attended to whilst you stay.'

Lady Cannock led Sheridan into the cool and elegant vestibule.

'My husband is in his library. He looks forward to greeting you himself when you have refreshed.'

It was an excellent library. One of the finest that Sheridan had ever seen. He breathed in the pleasing aroma of leather-bound volumes. The present earl's father had been renowned as a scientist and a man of letters, and his son clearly favoured scholarly pursuits over the military achievements of earlier ancestors. Sheridan had always found Cannock a rather dry old stick. Although at forty he was not particularly old, having been born in the same year as Sheridan himself, he was not a man who relished society. In fact, he was seldom seen abroad and considered something of a recluse amongst his peers. He had been educated entirely at home and despite his evident learning had for the same reasons of ill health been unable to attend at university.

Looking at the 4th Earl, Sheridan could well imagine that he had been a frail boy. With his slight build and the pallor of the scholar, there was nothing rugged about him. There was something closed and contained about the earl. Sheridan could think of no one within his own circle who would have considered Cannock a dear friend or to be more than a passing acquaintance.

Tea was served. Sheridan could have wished for something a little stronger, but the beverage was refreshing, he had to admit. There had been a momentary awkward exchange of pleasantries and then Sheridan had recovered his usual garrulous self, jabbering about nothing of any particular substance. Cannock was now standing near to the window; the curtains had been drawn back, affording a view down to the sun-drenched lake, landscaped for Cannock's father by Capability Brown himself. Sheridan observed him. The earl was short of stature, which he did not attempt to increase with heels, for he was not a man of fashion. He eschewed powder and wigs, his fair hair trimmed and framing smooth features. The earl favoured sombre colours and long waistcoats; not for him the tight breeches of the dandy. He reminded Sheridan of nothing so much as a country doctor or parson, and one might never imagine him one of the wealthiest landowners in the county.

Cannock withdrew a volume from the bookshelf at his side and held it up. Sheridan paused in his ramblings.

'Your play, Mr Sheridan, *The Rivals*.'

'I trust you have found it entertaining in some small way, sir.'

Cannock sighed. 'I have often mused at the waste of talent.'

Sheridan's mouth fell open for a moment before he recovered his composure. 'It must seem a frivolous piece to a man of your tastes, I am sure.'

The earl frowned and then laughed, a light, tinkling sound. 'Oh, my dear Sheridan, you misunderstand. It is quite the most delightful play. A favourite of mine and of Lady Ann. No, I have wondered why you have abandoned your greatest gift.' He riffled through the pages. 'Here is a talent at once prodigious and fertile, and all achieved when you were in the hot flush of youth.'

'Needs must, you know. I married with little to my name.'

'Ah yes, I recall. Quite the romantic sensation of the time.'

'My wife was the celebrity then.'

'How pleasing it must have been for you then to know your own success.'

'I own it has been very welcome.'

'*The School for Scandal* seems never to go out of fashion.'

'If it pleases the audience, I am grateful.'

'The draw of Westminster must have been very strong for you?'

'I felt it was in me, sir, and damned if I wasn't going to bring it out.'

'These are challenging times to be a Reformer. I admire that you remain so steadfast, Sheridan.'

On his first visit to Stafford, some twelve years previous, Sheridan had been surprised to discover that Lord Cannock was ardent for progress, almost a *Leveller*, with a passion for reforms of many different hues. On electoral rights he could be provoked from his usual silence to speak in a manner quite radical and heated, his otherwise soft and low voice rising to a fervent squeak. On matters of education he exhibited a most enlightened outlook, espousing the controversial views of Mary Wollstonecraft.

They were interests shared by his wife. Lady Cannock was well known for her efforts to improve the provision of education in the locality, in particular to encourage girls to read and write. However, it was medicine and the medical welfare of his tenants which were the true focus of Lord Cannock's own intellect and endeavours. Sheridan had observed that the great majority of the books on display were scientific, both ancient and modern.

Cannock shook his head. 'More's the pity the Whigs are in such disarray and Mr Pitt, it would appear, will not be dislodged from government.'

Sheridan's eyes flashed. 'Pitt uses the current volatile situation in France to his own ends.'

A sound of running footsteps came from the corridor and in pursuit a man's voice in sharp injunction. The handle of the library door rattled and then it was thrust open, and a child of five or six hurtled across the Persian carpet.

To Sheridan's surprise, the earl crouched to one knee and the boy flung himself into his waiting arms.

'Master Sempronius!' A young man halted in the open doorway. 'Sir.' The tutor bowed when he saw his employer.

Cannock addressed the laughing boy. 'Come, my fine fellow, do you run from your lessons?'

'Papa!'

'What will Mr Cray imagine? That you care nothing for Latin or poetry?'

The boy clung tightly to his father.

'Mr Sheridan, you must pardon my boy's poor manners. We have few guests here at Sandbourne and I fear Sempronius is become like one of Rousseau's noble savages, although perhaps not so noble.'

Sheridan nodded and smiled. This fatherly indulgence was unexpected and, in some way, pleasing.

The earl disentangled his son and rose with a hand on the boy's shoulder, guiding him in Sheridan's direction.

'Sempronius, here is Mr Sheridan, a great man of letters, who will be known when we are both long forgotten.'

'Sir.' The boy extended his hand and Sheridan shook it with a slight bow.

'I am pleased to make your acquaintance, young sir, and I have no doubt that your brilliance will outshine us all.'

'Hmm. But only if you will attend to your lessons, boy. Now, Mr Cray…' The earl turned to the tutor. 'Perhaps you could consider a lesson out of doors?'

The boy's face brightened.

'In the gardens, say, where Sempronius might learn the names of our plants in both Latin and French — what say you?'

'You are too indulgent, John, is what we say.' Lady Cannock appeared behind the young tutor, the merriment in her eye belying the sternness of her tone. 'Come, Sempronius, we must not disturb your father and Mr Sheridan.'

The child hesitated and then dutifully retreated from the room, followed by his tutor. Moments later he could be heard running and whooping down the corridor.

Lady Cannock sighed. 'And now I must see to preparations for Uncle Barclay's arrival — you know how he likes to settle himself.'

Cannock groaned in sympathy.

Sheridan had dismissed the valet and was completing his toilet in preparation for dinner when a commotion outside drew him to the open window of his room in the West Wing. From this position he held a partial view of the final approach to Sandbourne. He had heard a galloping horseman and could now see that the rider had pulled up at the point where the path widened for carriages to turn. His way was blocked by another man also on horseback and in the uniform of the Light Dragoons. Both men were shouting and Sheridan strained to catch the sense amongst the barrage of oaths.

'What the devil, Harding!'

'Stretton, you filthy coward!'

Sheridan edged the window further ajar the better to catch the unfolding drama.

'Why won't you fight like a man?'

'With a pimply boy like you! Go home to your mewling sister. I promised her nothing, God's blood!'

He took the man to be the earl's cousin, Edward Stretton. His accent confused him at first, until Sheridan recalled that this cousin had been born and bred in the Americas.

Edward urged his steed forward.

The cavalry man wheeled about and continued to block the way.

Sheridan recognised the conflict. It had been the talk amongst the regular drinkers at The Stafford Arms. Young Lieutenant Harding had recently returned home on furlough to his widowed mother and sisters, swearing to avenge the slight on the eldest Miss Harding. She claimed that Stretton had proposed marriage and taken advantage of her acceptance only to throw her over in his pursuit of another, a wealthier heiress in Shrewsbury.

'Wouldn't be the first time!' one of the drinkers had guffawed.

'Nor the last! Handsome rogue. Likes to have his way,' his companion had added, winking broadly.

'Devil, like his father — he had to marry in Americky after ruining half the young ladies of this county!'

'They say Harding's a young hothead and he'll not have his sister insulted.'

Lieutenant Harding unsheathed his sword. Stretton's grey backed and reared in the face of the brandished blade.

'Do the honourable thing, Stretton, and accept my challenge.'

'Damn and blast you, Harding!'

Stretton tried to control his terrified mount, but to no avail. The horse reared up again, spooked by the sweeping sword, and he lost his seat, tumbling to the dust. The grey took flight, bolting across the sward.

Harding dismounted. He re-sheathed his sword and stood resolute in the path of the older man. 'Accept my challenge, you blackguard!'

Puce with rage, Edward Stretton staggered to his feet and ran at Lieutenant Harding, lashing out at his face with his horse whip.

Sheridan gasped as he saw the dragoon fall back and grasp at his cheek. There would be blood now, surely. Someone must stop this. And almost as if in answer, men appeared in his line of sight. A couple of grooms and Cannock's man, Samuel Hanley, were racing to the scene. The latter attempted to place himself between the assailants.

'Sirs, I beseech you!'

Stretton raised the whip again and seemed about to turn his wrath on the servant when an elderly gentleman hastening to the fray called out to him.

'Edward! Edward, this must stop!'

Stretton paused, holding himself still in violent attitude.

Cradling his cheek, Harding backed away and grabbed at his horse's reins. 'You haven't heard the last of this, Stretton. I demand satisfaction, in front of these witnesses. Dr Burton, you know what the scoundrel has done!' He turned back to Stretton. 'Name the day or I will surely make you regret it!'

'You're a fool, Harding!' Stretton shoved past Samuel, nodded briefly to the old man dressed in sombre black, and strode towards the house.

Sheridan stepped back from the window as he caught the glare in Stretton's eyes. So much for the quiet life of the country. The evening's dinner party might be more entertaining than he had supposed.

CHAPTER TWO

The claret was excellent. Sheridan must commend Cannock on his cellar. Although the earl himself was abstemious and seemed to take little relish in even the finest wine, his cousin, Edward Stretton, made up for that and more. Stretton's glass was emptied and then a refill demanded from the attendant. His mood had not improved since the earlier fracas on the driveway and he seemed disinclined to enter into any attempt at politesse. On first introduction to Sheridan, he had merely sneered.

'Ain't you a player's son?'

Sheridan had bridled at the old insult but hid behind his usual charm. 'We all may have our parts to play upon the stage.'

'And an Irishman?'

'To be sure.' Sheridan affected a jaunty brogue. 'As proudly as you are of being an Englishman — or American, I believe.'

'We are all proud to be His Majesty's subjects,' Cannock interjected.

Sir Humphrey Barclay was announced at that moment. A portly old gentleman entered with his daughter on his arm, Mrs Smethurst, the wife of a wealthy sugar merchant in Birmingham, and the pleasantries of introductions continued.

Lady Cannock greeted her uncle warmly and then drew her cousin Harriet aside to exclaim how fine her boy Robert looked, tall for nine years and of a jolly disposition.

'Sempronius is beside himself with the excitement of a companion in play.'

'There will be mischief, Ann, I can assure you. Robert is full of pranks.'

'And I am glad of it!'

Sheridan found himself drawn into the local politics by Sir Humphrey, who it became clear favoured Pitt and the government in almost every instance. Despite his own radical views, Cannock seemed to humour the old gentleman with a show of genuine fondness. Sheridan took this cue, charming the older man and finding common cause and complaint against the mining interest in the borough. Cannock turned his attention to Dr Burton and the two were soon heard to be discussing the latest surgical techniques.

Edward Stretton had turned his back on the company to gaze out across the lawns to the lake beyond. He seemed preoccupied, occasionally tapping his glass in apparent irritation with whatever thoughts were troubling him.

When dinner was announced, Lady Cannock took Mrs Smethurst's arm and led the party across the entrance hall to the dining room, followed by her uncle and Dr Burton, who were discussing the vicissitudes of the insufferable heat. Her husband made to follow but was swiftly detained by his cousin. As he exited, Sheridan caught a snatch of low and urgent conversation in his wake and lingered by the doorway out of natural curiosity.

'This is urgent, John.'

'Enough, Edward…'

'Dammit, Cannock, I am being threatened!'

'There is nothing new in that, Cousin.' The earl sighed.

'This man Greaves is not to be played with; he wants a thousand now! You must help me!'

Sheridan's eyes widened with interest. Acton Greaves. A dangerous name to conjure with. And not a man to be indebted to. Stretton had clearly been losing heavily at the racetracks.

'I have done all I can to help you. For years. But here is an end.'

Edward snorted. 'Is this about that old harridan Mrs Harding?'

'You have insulted and abused our neighbours, Edward. But no. That is simply a final straw.'

Sheridan perceived that Cannock had turned away. Quickly he set his own foot in motion.

'We will speak later, Cannock!' Stretton called after his cousin.

Sheridan flew across the entrance hall and skidded to a halt in front of a portrait of the 3rd Earl and his countess, striking a stance as if caught up in reflective perusal.

'Ah, Sheridan —'

'Sir, I was admiring Mr Reynolds' portrait of your parents. I was honoured to sit for that most esteemed artist myself. He is a great loss. You bear a strong likeness to the 3rd Earl.'

'And my mother, too, I think.'

'A most charming lady.'

'I never knew her. She died at my birth.'

'I did not know. I am sorry to hear of it.'

'My father was a scholar, as you know. His marriage was unexpected, as was mine, and equally a great joy. My mother's untimely passing left him broken.' Cannock gazed sadly at the portrait.

'You must have been some comfort to him, sir.'

Cannock hesitated. 'I wanted only to do his bidding.'

Dinner was a display of the natural bounty of the estate, green goose, leverets and a magnificent carp from the lake. There was much earnest discussion of the new hospital which the Cannocks had endowed in the village nearby. Dr Burton had taken charge at the opening the week before. It was not a large establishment but sufficient for the needs of the estates and villages in the surrounding countryside. Sheridan struggled to find anything witty to remark. Edward sat in sullen silence and continued to drink his fill whilst the rest of the party all expressed their utmost interest in the facilities which the hospital boasted and the new procedures of which Dr Burton spoke with unrestrained enthusiasm.

Cannock nodded his approval and turned to his guests. 'Perhaps tomorrow morning, after church, we might stay on in the village and take a tour of the new hospital — if Dr Burton would not object to our intrusion?'

'I would be honoured, sir.'

'We will not tarry long, Doctor, and may then make our return stroll through the woods.'

'Splendid!' Sheridan concurred enthusiastically, and rather hoped that Cannock's support at the next election might now be thoroughly relied upon.

The visit to Sandbourne must pay some dividends. It must be worth the effort to overcome his general boredom with the countryside. Eliza had always preferred rural retreats, but he was a man for the hustle and bustle of the city. Clubs and coffee houses and theatres — they were his true domain. Trips to Parliament and to the prince at Carlton House for dinner, where one might be sure of laughter and games and a pretty woman to charm. Oh, but he would be ready to return to London soon.

He looked around the table. Two matrons, an old squire, a bachelor doctor and an earl who cared more for his tenants than for throwing parties where one might dance and jape. His eyes rested momentarily on Lady Cannock. He recalled that he had flirted with her on first acquaintance, some seven years previous, soon after she had married the earl. He had assumed that like many marriages amongst the aristocracy, it had already lost its juices, if it ever really had them in the first place. Sheridan had acted the gallant and made gestures of love to her, which were playfully reciprocated.

The countess had been a handsome woman then of thirty or thereabouts, with a fine figure and that winsome smile which she could still bestow to some effect. They had amused each other. How thoroughly motherhood seemed to have dulled her. Sheridan stifled a yawn and scooped the last of his syllabub.

Edward looked around the party and spread his arms. 'Strange, is it not, how a man's life can turn on the head of a pin?'

The conversation in the room subsided and the attention shifted uneasily to Stretton.

'All for a matter of minutes. Two minutes, three minutes and a fortune is decided. What say you, Sheridan? Would that be subject for a tragedy? Or a comedy?' He drained his glass and waved it impatiently at the servant in attendance.

What the devil was Stretton on about? 'I should say that would be a daily occurrence at the Newmarket races.'

'An accident of birth. Had my father been the first to enter the world, then Sandbourne would all be mine!' Edward laughed, but without humour. 'My father swore it was his kick from within the womb that catapulted his brother out into the world to take that first breath. Francis Stretton was ever the more vigorous twin, much good it did him.'

'Edward…' Lady Cannock's tone held an edge of warning.

'By that same reckoning, neither Francis nor my father John would have inherited,' the earl explained to the company. 'There was a real tragedy. Their older brother, Christopher, was drowned in the lake at only ten years. It was a skating accident — the ice was too thin in parts.'

Sheridan sat up straight and attempted to lighten the mood. 'In Ireland it is said that we are all descended from kings. I gather my ancestor was one Niall of the Nine Hostages, a brute but he had the gift of the gab — and that's about the sum of my inheritance!'

Edward Stretton would not be deflected. 'What a curse it was for a man of appetite.' He stared across the table at his cousin. 'The 3rd Earl would have been as happy to have remained poring over books at his college in Oxford as enjoying the hunting and shooting at Sandbourne.'

'There are many who would say that fate favoured the better man,' Dr Burton responded, and Sheridan caught a note of ice in his tone.

'My father was a true Stretton,' Edward countered, slapping his hand on the table. 'They have always been fighting men! Our grandfather fought against the Spanish at Gibraltar, and my father died with great valour in the war against the American Rebels.'

'In a reckless assault that saw half his men go down with him,' Dr Burton returned, not to be cowed.

'The little you know of military strategy, Doctor...' Edward glowered. 'I could wish that I had taken up a commission. I think we will soon be at war with the French, and then what a chance there shall be to show those pie-faced revolutionaries our mettle.'

'Let us have no talk of war, gentlemen,' Mrs Smethurst pleaded. She turned to Sheridan. 'Mr Sheridan, it is an age since

I have been to the theatre in London. Tell me, what may be worth seeing? Mrs Jordan, I hear, is deliciously comic.'

'Mrs Jordan is a delight in all she does.'

'I suppose Clarence would agree with that!' Edward leered.

Lady Cannock pursed her lips at this reference to the relationship of King George III's third son with the renowned comedienne.

'Come, Harriet, let us leave the men to their politics and billiards.'

'Oh, well, indeed.' Harriet nodded with a hint of reluctance, for here was an opportunity to gather court gossip and she had rather hoped that Mr Sheridan would regale them with some amusing titbits about the royal brothers.

Sheridan had to admit that Cannock had the edge when it came to billiards. If the earl had been a gambling man, he might have fleeced the room. As it was, they were the only players. Dr Burton had made his excuses and left after dinner. Sir Humphrey was comfortably dozing in an armchair. And whilst Edward slammed a few shots around the table, he seemed more intent now on demolishing the brandy.

Clearly, the younger man wished for the opportunity to speak alone again with his cousin, no doubt to continue pressing his desperate straits. Sheridan almost enjoyed the evident fury which his own continued presence occasioned. He did not much like Edward Stretton. He was a handsome man to be sure, and no doubt could charm the ladies when he saw his interest might profit, but he was not amiable. Sheridan was inclined to poke at him whenever the opportunity might arise. A loud, lengthy snore came from Sir Humphrey in the corner and Sheridan missed his shot.

'I think you may fairly take that one again, Sheridan.' Cannock smiled wryly and rang for a servant.

When the footman arrived, he was asked to fetch Sir Humphrey's man.

'Yes, sir, at once, sir. And a note has come for Mr Stretton.' A salver was proffered.

'Lieutenant Harding, no doubt!' Edward snorted and stuffed the note into his pocket. 'Devil take his sister! I had a narrow escape there.'

'You made promises, Edward.'

'I did not, Cousin. Yes, I whispered sweet nothings. The sort of romantic things women like to hear, but the prospect of marriage was all Miss Harding's imagination. On my honour. I will not be drawn into a duel on her account.'

Cannock sighed. 'Well then, we must do our utmost to smooth the ruffled feathers.'

Stretton softened his tone. 'I would be grateful for your intercession, John. In other matters too,' he added lightly.

A sharp rap came at the door.

Sheridan was taken by surprise when a young brown-skinned servant entered — to see a black man in the countryside was still a rarity.

'Emmanuel, it would seem Sir Humphrey is ready to retire.'

Another stentorian snore underlined the earl's observation.

The youth, for he seemed no more than twenty or so years, moved with an elegant grace towards the old squire and placed a hand gently on his shoulder.

'My, how you have grown. How old were you when I had you? A skinny scrap of eight or nine? Your master must feed you well. Perhaps I should have kept you after all. You would fetch a very good price now.'

Emmanuel stiffened and looked across to the figure emerging from the shadows at the far side of the room. From where he was positioned, Sheridan took note of the look of pure hatred which passed between the servant and Edward Stretton.

'We have no slavery here, thank God!' Cannock exclaimed. 'Emmanuel was free from the moment you gave him to Sir Humphrey to discharge your debt. And that was a fortunate day for him indeed. He stays because he chooses to do so, because he has been treated with kindness and dignity. He is no man's possession to sell now, and least of all yours, Cousin.'

'Well, well, Cannock, why so hot under your Abolitionist collar?' Stretton laughed and raised his hands. 'I make jest.' He turned to Emmanuel. 'Do I not? Or is that all the province of Mr Sheridan this evening?'

'It is in poor taste, Edward.'

Cannock moved to the armchair to help rouse the old man and get him to his feet.

'What, what — I have dozed? You must pardon me, gentlemen.'

'It is no matter, Uncle; the day has been long for you. Emmanuel is here and will help you upstairs.'

'Come, sir, take my arm,' the young servant offered, and Sheridan recognised a faint burr of the West Indies.

When they had departed Sheridan waved his cue. 'Well, I shall take my cue from Sir Humphrey. I too will retire, my lord. All the better to enjoy the morning's expedition.'

In the corridor he caught sight of Samuel Hanley and hastened towards the factotum to request that a bottle of brandy might be sent to his room, for medicinal purposes. Hanley nodded with the merest hint of a smile.

'Certainly, sir.'

Sheridan had scarce reached the upstairs landing when he heard voices coming from below. He peered over the rail.

Stretton was striding unsteadily across the marble floor with Cannock in pursuit.

'Edward, stay the night. You have drunk far too much.'

'I'll not stay where I am not welcome!'

Cannock came to a halt. 'Very well, then. I bid you goodnight, Cousin.'

The front door slammed shut.

Sheridan whistled beneath his breath. 'Good for you, Cannock, good for you.'

CHAPTER THREE

Was there ever anyone so dull as a country parson? Sheridan doubted it very much. Certainly not one who relished the chance to sermonise in front of a larger than usual audience from the principal estate of the area. Oh, how the good Reverend Grayson could drone on and on, with lengthy injunctions to covet not the wealth of one's neighbours but to nurture the promise of riches to come in the afterlife. All well and good, Sheridan mused, but most people were in need of some riches in this one. Without unlimited resources it was an easy matter to fall into debt. Only think of the Prince of Wales, who lived so far beyond his means that should a reckoning be made at this very moment, he might be deemed poorer than the most miserable pauper in the land. Sheridan himself was forever juggling one debt against another; it was wearisome. Cultivating the promise of the afterlife might be no amelioration from the tribulations of this one.

Then there was the importunate Edward Stretton, who, Sheridan observed, was not in attendance at church, and who must beg his cousin to bail him out, clearly for the umpteenth time, until the earl had lost all patience. During another sleepless night — even with the window ajar, the heat was unrelenting — Sheridan had had time to reflect on the information he had gleaned the previous day. He was minded to have a quiet word with Cannock. He would apologise for having overheard a private conversation but, despite his dislike of Stretton, he would urge the earl to leniency for one last time. The earl would not be aware that Acton Greaves was a very dangerous man indeed and likely to make good on any threat. Yes. He resolved that he would speak with Cannock. Perhaps as they strolled back to the house through the woods there might be an opportune moment.

From the corner of his eye Sheridan could see young Sempronius and his cousin Robert fidgeting, with the occasional stifled titter from the younger boy. He almost sniggered himself when he caught sight of the reason for their mirth. Robert had a little mouse in his pocket, which he now brought forth cupped in his hands, the little whiskered head sniffing at the air. Then, very discreetly, the boy let the creature loose. Moments later their anticipation was rewarded with a series of shrieks as Mrs Smethurst leapt to her feet, dancing about and looking as though she might actually jump up onto the seat of the pew. The boys were doubled over now, desperately clutching at their sides so as not to squeal themselves for a very different reason. Sheridan hid his face behind his hymnal. It was just the sort of prank he might have played himself as a boy. And oh, what joy! The congregation was all in fits. Ladies a-jitter and their menfolk grabbing hopelessly for the verminous culprit. The Reverend Grayson, sensing that his time was up, hurried the service to an end and watched forlornly the wave of exodus.

Outside, whilst a number of the ladies were having frayed nerves soothed, an air of hilarity prevailed and perhaps some relief at having been released from their instruction. From the fierce looks which Mrs Smethurst threw towards her son from behind her fan, she clearly had her suspicions as to the source of this unexpected diversion, but she was not about to draw attention to his misdemeanour amongst this company. The boys were dispatched with the tutor, Mr Cray, and were to go fishing at the lake. The rest of the party proceeded with Dr Burton to visit the new hospital.

It was a small but well-proportioned building which had been built for the express purpose of serving the medical needs of the surrounding countryside. Sheridan admired the architectural restraint. So many of these charitable endowments were an outward showcase for the philanthropy of some landed family and festooned with crests and embellishments to remind all who entered of their munificence. Sheridan felt certain that no expense had been spared on the hospital, but all was within, to fit the hospital with the latest in medical advancement. There was a long-term ward, short-term facilities, and a small but well-equipped operating theatre.

Lord and Lady Cannock's enthusiasm for the advancement of medicine and the care of their tenants in both the village and the farms around the area was infectious, Sheridan considered and chuckled at his own choice of word. Infectious. Yes, it really was as if the Cannocks were infected with a shared passion, and for the first time it occurred to him that here was a happy marriage.

Praises were heaped upon Dr Burton and that sober gentleman fairly brimmed with pride and pleasure in all that had been accomplished.

'Without the continuing support of His Lordship, none of this would have been possible. It is the realisation of plans begun many years ago and I am very glad to see this day.'

'As are we, Dr Burton,' the countess concurred.

Lady Ann and Mrs Smethurst had then parted from the gentlemen to visit with an ailing spinster who had been a friend to Harriet's late mother. A maid accompanied them, carrying a basket of summer fruits and berries from the Sandbourne kitchen garden.

'Miss Hinckley is most fond of gooseberries.'

'The good spinster having been one herself, no doubt,' Sheridan could not help but quip.

Lady Cannock slapped his arm playfully. 'Now, Richard, she is a kind and Christian woman.'

Harriet Smethurst laughed gleefully. 'Who could not help the size of her nose!'

Sheridan almost wished that he might join them to marvel at this prodigious proboscis. Did it compare to the renowned Cyrano de Bergerac, he enquired?

'No, Mr Sheridan, you may not have that entertainment. We will leave you gentleman to talk of pheasants and the like.'

Cannock was solicitous of Sir Humphrey and wanted to be reassured that he was up to the length of the walk. A gig was still standing by for the purpose of transporting him back to the house, but the squire insisted on the expedition.

'I am not so decrepit yet, Cannock, that I cannot bear a short stroll through your woods.'

'At least the way is shaded. This remarkable heat shows no sign of abating yet,' the earl observed, placing his straw hat on his head. 'After all those grey days of July we should not complain, but we are never satisfied, I fear, with our weather.'

'On the contrary, sir, I should say we are very satisfied with our weather — it provides the most reliable topic of conversation.'

The gentlemen set off along the shaded woodland path which would bring them out near to the lake and to the rear of Sandbourne. Sheridan dawdled behind whilst the two men did indeed discuss the pheasants on the estate and the shooting season. There was something to be said for the peace and tranquillity of these dappled woods, Sheridan mused. Soothing to the nerves, and Sheridan lived on his nerves, he knew. People sometimes thought him idle. There had been that piece of wit posted to his door by some of the opposition when the Whigs had briefly held the reins of government under Rockingham. What was it that those devilish fellows had written?

No application to be received here on Sundays, nor any business done during the remainder of the week.

He had to admit it was rather amusing. Of course, the insult had hurt at the time. Even some of his own party had ribbed him. They did not understand that he was never at rest. His mind was a constant whirr and buzz. He might appear indolent, but all within was utter turmoil. That, he recognised, was to be a writer. A writer of plays, a writer of pamphlets, a man of letters living constantly in his mind. And then with great bursts of energy applying that inner industry to some outer project, be it the writing of a play or a parliamentary speech or the pursuit of business in the theatre. Here he was walking under this canopy of trees and he could not simply think about the leaves or the blue sky above.

'Sheridan, how do you like our woods?'

The earl had fallen into step beside him.

'I find them very soothing, sir, as far as I can be soothed.'

'Naturally … I know you have had many cares this year,' the earl added, solicitous.

'It is another matter that at present troubles me…'

'Oh? May I be of any assistance?'

Sheridan halted and Cannock followed suit with a look of enquiry.

'I hope that you will forgive my impertinence, Cannock. I do not intend to interfere. But I cannot unhear what I overheard.'

'You intrigue.'

'It is your cousin…'

'Ah.'

'I know that he has tried your patience and your generosity. But —'

'But?'

'This man, Acton Greaves, he is truly a very dangerous sort.'

Cannock stopped, a flash of anger in his eyes. 'Has my cousin asked you to intercede with me on his behalf? If he has, I apologise — it is he who is impertinent!'

'No. No, nothing of the sort. I overheard, as I say. I only speak, sir, because you will not know this fellow Greaves and what he is capable of.'

'And what is that?'

'Ruin. Destruction.'

Cannock's face hardened. 'My cousin is a man of thirty-two. What he brings upon himself I cannot help. Not anymore.'

'I understand. I should not have spoken. It was not my place, sir.'

Cannock relaxed. 'You are a kind man, Sheridan. And I admire you for it.'

Sir Humphrey was waiting for them by a fork in the path.

'Cannock, does this path not lead to the folly which Lady Ann has commissioned?'

Cannock smiled. 'My wife would not like to hear her temple described as a "folly"; it is a shrine to Calliope and Euterpe, the muses of epic and lyrical poetry.'

'Is it far?'

Cannock shook his head. 'Only a slight diversion.'

They took the path and emerged into a small clearing on a rise, a miniature temple in the classical Greek style crowning the height.

'Lady Ann comes here to read and to commune with nature.'

Sir Humphrey grunted in concurrence. 'I remember when she came to us as a girl, always had her head in a book.

Nothing like Harriet at all, who has never had any time for reading. Fashion, gowns and other frippery has always been my daughter's sort of thing. But they were company for each other.'

'And very fond.'

Sir Humphrey turned to Sheridan. 'Tragedy — my wife's sister and her husband returning from a visit to his family, some island…'

'The Isle of Man,' the earl offered.

'Man, that's it — bit of a backwater, I believe. Anyway, ship goes down. All lost, including Mr Cooper's investment in the cargo. Only decent thing to do was offer young Ann a home. Always reading, I remember that. Thought she might be an instructress. But my wife, you know, tubercular. Ann cared for her until she passed away, God rest her. Harriet married, you see. Got tired of waiting for His Lordship here and married Mr Smethurst instead. Decent enough fellow, tremendously rich. Some compensation for living in Birmingham. Then His Lordship ups and marries Ann. Took us all by surprise.'

'Myself included, Sir Humphrey.' Cannock made a playful attitude of surprise.

'I've come to realise that Lady Cannock is a woman who knows what she wants and tends to get it.'

Cannock laughed. 'That is very true, Uncle.'

'True of all women, I find,' Sheridan contributed as he set his foot upon the incline.

'If you don't object, gentlemen, I'll admire the edifice from here below.' Under the shade of a young oak, Sir Humphrey leant against the trunk and mopped his brow.

'We will be but a moment,' Cannock reassured. 'There is little to see, in truth — a place to sit with a pleasing outlook.'

As they approached the temple, Sheridan admired the carvings above the portico, the lyre and the Greek flute. It was indeed a pleasant retreat. He drew level with the entrance and saw immediately that there was something within. Or rather, someone, it would appear. A man. Lying across the floor. Edward Stretton, he was sure from his costume, although his face was turned away. Had he come here in his drunken state the night previous and chosen to lie within instead of in his own bed?

'There is something?' Cannock asked from behind.

And then they were both drawn level with the pillars and gazing down at the prone body of Edward Stretton. After a moment of shock, the earl moved swiftly to his cousin's side and, kneeling down, turned him onto his back and shook him.

'Edward!' He slapped gently but firmly at his cheek as though to rouse him from a deep slumber, although his eyes gazed vacantly into nothingness. 'Edward!' Loosening the cravat and opening Edward's shirt, the earl placed an ear to his chest.

Sheridan watched with bated breath.

Cannock sat back on his haunches, clearly stunned. 'He is gone.' He looked up at Sheridan. 'He is gone,' he repeated, as though to give the words more substance.

Sheridan took in the extended scene for the first time. There were no immediate signs of violence. No pool of blood or stain upon the floor. No indication that Stretton had been struck or robbed; he noted a fine pocket watch still in his hand.

'Edward...' A sob escaped from the earl.

'Some fit or apoplexy?' Sheridan conjectured.

'It would seem so.' The earl gently touched the dead man's face. 'His features suggest that he may have struggled to breathe at the last. His heart has given out.'

Sheridan nodded. 'I have known a young man, an actor in his prime, drop quite dead in the wings.'

They stayed in this attitude for a few moments longer before Cannock rose to his feet.

'Our poor cousin. But perhaps there is some comfort that the end was swift and he may scarce have suffered long.'

Sheridan felt his own heart flutter at the notion and shook his head. 'How thin is that line between this world and the next.'

'Come. We must call for assistance.'

It was then that Sheridan observed a mark towards the back of Stretton's neck, above his loose cravat. A prick of some kind? But no trace of blood. Odd?

'Cannock. There is something. On his neck.'

The earl bent forward, his brow creased at the sight of the small dark circle. 'You are right, Sheridan.' He crouched again and removed his cousin's wig to examine the mark more closely. 'It is a puncture wound…'

'Deliberately done?'

Cannock probed about his cousin's face, opening his mouth and peering within. He raised his eyelids further and looked into his dead, staring eyes.

The earl looked aghast. 'Sheridan, I believe this may be murder.'

Sheridan felt the ground shift beneath him.

CHAPTER FOUR

After their initial shock the earl gathered himself quickly and was all composure and purpose.

'Let me not jump to distressing conclusions. In all probability I am wrong. I am not a qualified medical man.'

Sheridan would have disputed that. There may have been no formal training, but he was certain that Cannock was at least as knowledgeable as any country quack.

'This mark may be some stinging insect. It is the time of year for hornets, wasps and bees. I have read of cases where such stings may be fatal even to a healthy man. There is some reference in ancient Greek medical literature to this very topic.'

Sheridan felt a wave of relief. Here was a simple explanation. They were not to imagine that assassins roamed these woods with deadly darts after all.

'But I will send for Dr Burton. There is something that still troubles me. He might confirm the cause of death.'

As one they moved to the pillars at the entrance and looked down towards Sir Humphrey, who smiled and waved up to them. Standing at his side was his servant, Emmanuel.

Cannock exhaled. 'That is some relief. Emmanuel will help Sir Humphrey back to the house. A most considerate young man, come to meet us when he heard that his master had joined our walk.' He looked at Sheridan. 'That Edward is dead will be shock enough for my uncle, whose constitution is not so strong as he would have us believe. For the moment, can I beg your discretion on our various speculations?'

'Of course, sir.'

On learning the news of Edward's apparent fatal collapse, Sir Humphrey paled, unsteady on his feet. Emmanuel took his arm at once, his face creased in concern.

'If you will pardon me, gentlemen, I will go on ahead. There is much to be done.' The earl bowed curtly and strode swiftly in the direction of Sandbourne.

The body had been brought back and placed in the icehouse. Lady Cannock and Mrs Smethurst returned soon after. Mrs Smethurst's concerns were all for her father, who had been taken to lie down in his rooms. She hastened to his care. Ann took the news of Edward's sudden death with commendable equanimity. She immediately constructed a version of events which made some sense for her. Edward had drunk far too much; he had decided to walk it off and taken the shortcut through the woods to his own house. It was a warm, moonlit night. He felt unwell and thought to rest a moment in the temple. He had perhaps even lain down, but then all at once his heart had failed. It was both tragic and shocking but somehow comprehensible. Death could come in this way — suddenly and without warning.

Cannock did not disabuse his wife of these notions.

It appeared, however, the earl confided to Sheridan, that Stretton had taken his grey from the stables on leaving the house the evening before. He may, nevertheless, have decided to walk or possibly been thrown again, his mare still nervous and frisky after the earlier confrontation with Harding. Neither the earl nor Sheridan had seen any sign of the horse near the temple.

The searing sun had risen to its highest point in the afternoon sky when Dr Burton arrived and went straight to the icehouse. His arrival was followed shortly after by the local

Justice of the Peace, Sir Anthony Peake, and a watchman of the parish. As these latter were announced, Lady Cannock turned to her husband with a note of alarm.

'You think there is something amiss, John?'

He took her hand. 'Such a sudden and unexpected death — we must be certain that there is nothing suspicious, Ann.'

'Of course. You are right.'

Cannock exchanged a look with Sheridan.

'Everything is so topsy-turvy. You have eaten nothing, gentlemen. And our visitors must be attended. I will arrange a luncheon table.'

'Thank you, my dear. I shall go to meet Sir Anthony and acquaint him with all we know. Dr Burton may have completed his examination by now.'

Lady Cannock hurried away to organise the provision of refreshment.

'Might I join you?' Sheridan asked the earl.

Cannock hesitated. 'As you wish, Sheridan. Though there is no need.'

'I have long been interested to see more of the business of the shire and to meet Sir Anthony.'

He would indeed be interested in cultivating a closer acquaintance with the ageing Tory squire who held such political and judicial sway in the locality of Sheridan's parliamentary seat. Sir Anthony had developed a reputation as one of those prone to magisterial imperiousness. The poorer sort, abused by his draconian sentencing and fondness for the noose, had little or no recourse. Very few Staffordshire magistrates, Sheridan knew all too well from his petitioners, were brought before the King's Bench and then never punished. He would keep an eye on Sir Anthony's conduct in this matter.

*

The corpse had been stripped and laid out on a trestle table. Dr Burton looked up from his examination of the body and nodded a curt greeting as Cannock and the officers of the law arrived. The earl had acquainted Sir Anthony with the circumstances of discovery that morning. Then, although he wished it proven otherwise, he had voiced his concern that there were intimations of foul play. Hence the summons.

'You are right to be cautious, Cannock.' Sir Anthony tapped his cane on the stone flags, then added in his forthright manner, 'Given your late cousin's unsavoury reputation in this neighbourhood, hey what?'

Sheridan noted a slight flush of embarrassment rising on Cannock's face.

'Nevertheless, I hope that I will soon have cause to apologise for disturbing the peace of your Sabbath, Sir Anthony.'

'Believe me, sir, in a household of women I count it a blessing to be called abroad on a Sunday.'

Dr Burton proceeded to establish the facts as he could thus far determine them. 'You will see that the process of rigor mortis is underway but not entire.' The doctor demonstrated the rigidity in the upper part of the body. 'When His Lordship found the body at the temple, that process had not yet taken hold, although he observed some stiffness around the face. We can tell little from the body temperature. Given the unusual heat of the day, the corpse will not have begun to cool as one would expect if we were at a more temperate time of the year. You may also observe the livor mortis, these patchy discolorations, which are still increasing.'

Sir Anthony interjected. 'And does this give you a notion as to when Mr Stretton might have met his end?'

The doctor spread his hands. 'I can only conjecture, Sir Anthony. Nevertheless, with some reasonable surety I can say that it was in the early hours of this morning. We are now past two o'clock, say some seven or eight hours since.'

'And cause?'

Dr Burton nodded solemnly. 'There are signs of asphyxia; the heart has given out. Mr Stretton struggled to breathe. Death would have been fairly rapid.'

Sir Anthony nodded. 'Such attacks of the heart are not uncommon, gentlemen. But His Lordship believes there is something unnatural here.' He turned to Burton. "Is that your opinion, my good man?'

Dr Burton pursed his lips. 'There is every appearance of some natural cause, were it not for the evidence of this puncture wound.'

The Justice brought forth his wig spectacles and leant in towards the small puncture. 'Looks like a bee sting to me, sir.'

'That was my first thought. And I have observed a case where such a sting proved fatal, bringing on a violent reaction of the heart.'

Sir Anthony stood straight again. 'Cut and dried then, I should say.'

'Would that it were so, Sir Anthony. But I tend to agree with His Lordship. This seems no natural death. See, the puncture itself is larger and appears to me more jagged than an insect sting. Of more significance, I note there is not the usual raised rash or pronounced swelling of throat and tongue that I would expect to see.'

'What else might have caused this fatality?' Sheridan ventured. 'A poisoned dart?'

Sir Anthony guffawed. 'Are we to imagine some native of the jungles inhabiting your woods, hey what, Cannock? Not many hereabouts using bows and arrows anymore!'

Dr Burton stiffened at the levity. 'I do believe Mr Stretton may have been poisoned, Sir Anthony. When I touched the wound I felt a tingling heat in my fingertips, suggesting there was some residue of unknown substance. Given the confined space of the temple, I am also inclined to think that the assailant was close, perhaps very close…'

The earl lightly touched the site of the wound. 'I think you begin to suspect, as I do, Doctor, that the poison has been injected?'

Burton nodded curtly. 'An injected poison would have been very fast-acting.'

'And might have been delivered with the aid of a piston syringe.'

Burton blew out his cheeks. 'That would make sense, my lord.'

'And what the devil might that be?'

Cannock turned to the Justice. 'That, Sir Anthony, is an instrument of my own devising.'

'What are you saying, Cannock?'

'Gentlemen, you will know that I have a scientific and a medical interest. Dr Burton and I have long speculated on and experimented with the development of new methods to more efficiently administer potions and opiates to his patients. One possible method may be the development of the piston syringe. I have here at Sandbourne a laboratory which I use for various experiments, including the development of just such an instrument.'

Sir Anthony stared at Cannock with increasing bewilderment.

The earl continued in his explanation. 'I confess that when Mr Sheridan first indicated the puncture on my cousin's neck, I thought it remarkably like the kind of wound which my syringe would inflict. Naturally, I wanted to believe otherwise, that some stinging insect had brought about my cousin's demise rather than a human hand intent on murder. But nature is more refined than this instrument currently. No doubt in time the needle will become so advanced that one may not even feel the prick or see the puncture, save for some small vibices, a little discolouration around the entry.'

'My lord, are you suggesting that the proposed weapon used to assassinate your cousin has come from your own house?' The Justice looked aghast.

'I think that most probable, Sir Anthony.'

'Well, here's a fine to-do.' Sir Anthony rapped his cane on the flag stones.

'I might also add that my laboratory is used for various experiments involving the medicinal use of plants, many of which are grown in the gardens and the new orangery. As you know, there are many plants with toxic properties, which given in sufficient dose may fatally poison a man.'

Sir Anthony grunted and nodded towards the corpse. 'So, Cannock, you argue that this is no hornet's sting? That we are to deal with murder?'

'I very much fear that to be the case.'

It was clear that Sir Anthony was displeased at this outcome and the conjectures presented to him. 'And you, Dr Burton? Is there room for doubt? Or are you in full agreement?'

The doctor looked grave. 'I believe I am, Sir Anthony.'

They could all sense where these speculations were leading. If the earl was correct, then Edward Stretton's killer had in all probability come from within the Sandbourne household itself.

Sheridan shivered, and it was not merely from the chill of the icehouse.

They left Dr Burton to finish his examination of the corpse and crossed the courtyard to the outbuildings, which had once been used as a brewery for the estate. It was the earl's father who had initiated the conversion into a place of scientific research and the laboratory had been completed by his son. Whereas the 3rd Earl's interest had been largely alchemical, the present Lord Cannock's scientific experiments were directed to medical application, he explained, as they toured the premises.

In the main laboratory were rows of shelves containing bottles and jars of various shapes and sizes whose contents, both powdered and liquid, presented an array of arresting colours. A workbench along one wall made use of the natural light available and was covered in the contraptions of preparation and distillery. At the far end a desk was stacked with ledgers recording the details and measurements of various experiments. Another room had been set aside for fashioning instruments and blowing glass to the specific requirements of the earl's experiments, and it appeared that his man Samuel, who acted as an assistant, was adept at this art. In yet another space Cannock kept a number of caged animals — rats and mice. Their whiskers twitched and they scurried about their enclosures, unsettled no doubt by the arrival of so many curious observers.

The earl led them to a cabinet and opened a drawer which contained a number of rectangular boxes. He took one of the boxes and placed it on the workbench. Opening the lid revealed the components of the syringe. The earl withdrew a slender cylindrical element with a plunger, which had been fashioned from glass and metal. Next, he brought out a long, thin metal dart, which he affixed to the cylinder to create the instrument.

'The needle is made with a fine hollowed tube of glass, such as those I imagine were crafted by the Arab physician Ali al-Mawsili in the eleventh century and which he used to suck cataracts from his patients' eyes. My innovation has been to thinly encase it in metal to thereby provide a sharp point with which to pierce the skin, so that liquid may also be injected as well as extracted. It is a little crude, I own.'

He opened a large glass container containing a clear substance.

'This is merely purified water,' Cannock explained as he inserted the needle point into the jar. From the other end of the instrument he pulled back a piston and the liquid was sucked up into the cylinder.

'Now one may deliver the contents of this tube by pricking the patient with the point which has been sharpened for that purpose.' The earl then pushed in the plunger, so that the liquid squirted from the instrument's end.

'By this device the liquid may immediately enter the bloodstream and circulate around the body, greatly increasing the efficacy of any medicinal treatment. Likewise, the surgeon might pierce an abscess and suck out the pestilence, or strike a vein and draw blood.'

Sheridan was fascinated and horrified in equal measure. He sincerely hoped that he would never personally need to encounter such an evil-looking implement.

'It has been used for these various purposes?'

Cannock shook his head. 'Not as yet on men. My experiment has been on the animals you see within. But this is the instrument which I believe has been applied against my cousin as a weapon.'

'This very instrument?'

Cannock hesitated for a moment. 'More likely the other. This is the early, clumsier, prototype.' He returned to the drawer and extracted another box. 'This later model is an improvement…'

He opened the lid and they could all see at once that it was empty of contents.

'It has been stolen?' the Justice snapped.

The earl looked disconcerted. 'I have not removed it, Sir Anthony, so yes, that would be my conjecture.'

'When did you last see it, Cannock?'

'I was here yesterday morning working on some preparations, before the arrival of my guests.' He indicated the workbench. 'The syringes were both in the cabinet.'

'Who has access here?'

'I confess it has never occurred to me that the laboratory presented any interest beyond my own. There are two sets of keys. One I keep about my own person, as I am frequently here.' He withdrew a key from his waistcoat pocket. 'The other is kept on a hook in the servant hall and may be freely taken, though usually it is by Samuel.' He indicated his factotum, who had followed from the icehouse. 'Samuel has acted as my assistant for many years. Do you have the second key about you, Hanley?'

'No, my lord. The animals were fed last night, I believe. It should be on the hook.'

'Any of the servants who clean the place or tend to the animals would know where to find the keys.'

Sir Anthony grunted. 'Well, we must question all your servants and also hope to find the weapon itself.'

Cannock nodded and then turned to Samuel, who bowed and took leave to arrange the gathering of all the servants in their hall.

The earl squinted and perused the rows of jars in one section of the shelf. 'I cannot swear to it, but I would say that the contents here have diminished.' He pointed out a container not quite a third full. 'A tincture of Aconite.'

'And what the devil's that?'

'You may know it as monkshood or wolfsbane, Sir Anthony.'

In an instant Sheridan called to mind Laertes. He had tipped his sword in wolfsbane to be sure of killing Hamlet.

'In small quantities one may use it in ointments to alleviate inflammation and pains in the joints or to stimulate the circulation of blood — it is readily absorbed through the skin. This tincture made from boiling the tubers is for that purpose. In a pure dose it is one of our most deadly plants.'

'This is a damnable business, Cannock. D'you have any notion who might want your cousin assassinated, and in so perverse a fashion?'

'Sir Anthony, I am at a loss.'

The Justice scowled and tapped his cane. 'There is much talk in the neighbourhood regarding Mr Stretton.'

'Small communities are wont to gossip.'

'Only this morning I learnt that that young hothead Harding has been pursuing your cousin and demanding satisfaction. Believes his sister's reputation has been besmirched.'

Here Sheridan stepped forward. 'Sir, Lieutenant Harding does not strike me as a man who would choose the low means of poison. He challenged the earl's cousin to a duel; I myself can speak witness to that, and as a soldier and a man of honour he would seek that recourse or otherwise feel free to defame Mr Stretton wherever he chose.'

'In the ordinary way of such matters, I would agree. But I am informed that Stretton thrashed young Harding with his whip and refused to face him.'

'That is so,' Sheridan conceded.

'Might turn the temper of any man.' Sir Anthony looked about the laboratory. 'And the means were close to hand to exact a humiliating and fatal vengeance.'

'You know the man's character better than I, sir,' Sheridan deferred.

'Well, well, but you may be right, Mr Sheridan. These actions do not speak to Harding. There is something sly and devious in all this.'

'Which suggests an assailant who doubted that they could match Stretton in a fair fight. He was a well-proportioned man, not above thirty-three.'

Sir Anthony turned back to the earl. 'No signs of robbery at the temple, I think you said, my lord?'

Cannock shook his head. From his pocket he withdrew a gold-cased watch, finely tooled. 'Edward still had his timepiece, which belonged to his father, Colonel Stretton. Indeed, it was clutched in his right hand.'

'As though he were waiting on an appointment?' Sheridan conjectured.

At this moment came a light rap at the door.

'Enter,' Cannock called out.

A young boy tentatively pushed the door open and, clutching his cap, entered the laboratory.

'Ah, Walter, come closer.'

The boy bowed and edged into the room, his eyes wide. 'Is it true, milord?'

'Yes, sadly it is so.'

The boy's face dropped in horror.

'Your master has met a cruel fate. But tell me, Walter, did Mr Stretton return to his house last night?'

The boy nodded. 'Why, yes, sir. I took Lady from him; she was ever so skittish.'

'Edward's grey,' Cannock explained. 'And did you see your master this morning?'

Walter shook his head. 'I was woken before first light by Mr Dodson. He said the master wanted me to ride into Stafford with an urgent message.'

'Who for, boy?' Sir Anthony demanded.

'A gentleman at The Stafford Arms.'

'His name?' Sir Anthony pressed.

The boy flushed. 'I do not know, sir. I cannot read. I was to hand the note to the landlord.'

'Edward's man Dodson will know. I shall send for him.'

Sheridan stepped forward. 'Please, allow me to be of some assistance. There are so many in the Sandbourne household for Sir Anthony and his officer to question. Let me undertake to go to Edward's house and see what I might find there.'

Sir Anthony eyed Sheridan with momentary hesitation.

'You know I have been a magistrate in Westminster, Sir Anthony, and I'll hardly make a blunder of this small errand.'

'Very well then.'

CHAPTER FIVE

Sheridan had in part volunteered to make the journey to Edward Stretton's house so that he might have the time to collect his thoughts. He was very much disquieted by the events and revelations of the day. Lurid fancies tugged at his mind. They were devilish notions and reminded him far too readily of the current taste for gothic literature: the horrors of *The Castle of Otranto*, or some Jacobean plot, *The Duchess of Malfi* or *The Changeling*, overwrought with intrigue and nefarious doings orchestrated by a fiendish mind. It was the use of poison that had sparked such imaginings.

He shuddered at the recollection of that evil-looking syringe. He had a vision of someone approaching Edward Stretton without seeming to be a threat. Calculating that he would not be on his guard. Approaching so closely that the deadly syringe might not have been seen by the victim until the moment of that fatal sting.

And Sheridan had dared to cast Lord Cannock in that role.

Who else was so familiar with this implement? Who else might boast such necessary knowledge of the various toxic elements kept in the laboratory? Who else would have the medical understanding to know precisely where to prick the victim in order to ensure a swift fatality? A man of slight build whom Edward Stretton would not consider in any way a physical threat. Someone from whom he sought help and assistance. And whose appearance he might then welcome and embrace.

All through his journey, as Sheridan skirted the rise of woods where Stretton had breathed his last and then followed the old cart tracks which led down through pastureland and into a shallow valley, he tumbled through one murderous scenario after another. For who would have more cause to want Edward Stretton dead? The earl's cousin had ruptured the peace and tranquillity of this estate. He was in debt beyond any hope of repayment and no doubt in constant need. A drain on resources of every kind.

Stretton had been taken in and housed by the earl and presented, Sheridan was certain, with every opportunity to establish himself in the locality and to make a good match. He was a man of handsome swagger. Women were all too frequently charmed and duped by such braggadocios. But his seductions had only succeeded in affronting Cannock's neighbours. Worse still, he had struck a man across the cheek with a horse whip. It had been apparent to Sheridan the previous evening that this was behaviour the earl could no longer countenance. The never-ending debts, the insults to friends, his treatment of the servant Emmanuel, all of this might have tipped the earl over the edge of tolerance. Edward Stretton was a parasite. Cannock wanted to be rid of him. And he had accomplished it with clinical efficiency.

Then, the murder done, here was the fiendish mind at work — to draw attention to it! To find the sad corpse in the company of others, to be first to raise suspicion of foul play, to call for the Justice, point readily to the perverse and peculiar means of assassination, provide no obstacle to investigation but rather encourage all speculation — surely this was the daring of a man of superior intellect? The contrary means by which to deflect any suspicion from himself? Cunning indeed.

Too cunning, Sheridan decided as he gazed upon sheep grazing in sun-drenched pastures and felt a faint breeze stirring across the languid rural landscape. Where was the benefit in raising the spectre of assassination? And how could Sheridan suspect his host of such devilry? Lord and Lady Cannock were kind and gentle people, if a little dull and worthy. It was he, Sheridan, who had first pointed to the deadly mark, else Stretton's demise, albeit sudden, might have been accounted natural and the body unexamined. He looked about. Here was a real world of summer earth and trees and sky that seemed too ordinary to encompass Sheridan's flights of dark fancy. And yet, close by in this pastoral idyll, there had indeed been gruesome murder.

It was a squat building of the Tudor period, by its oak-beamed façade, with some remnants still of its medieval history. The original manor house of Sandbourne and for centuries the demesne of an ancient family until one ancestor had chosen the wrong side in the civil war and lost all title. Sheridan drew up in the gig with the young groom Walter trotting alongside. A stooped man emerged, whom Sheridan took to be the butler Dodson, followed by a small rotund woman who might be his wife.

The man looked anxiously from the distressed face of the boy, Walter, to the new arrival.

'Has something ill happened to the master?'

Sheridan nodded soberly.

'I had an ill feeling this morning. Did I not say, Mrs Dodson?'

'That you did, Husband.' She looked up at Sheridan. 'An accident, sir? Or worse?'

Sheridan sensed that the housekeeper already anticipated the worst. 'Sadly so.'

Mrs Dodson shook her head and stifled a sob.

'I am sent by His Lordship and Sir Anthony Peake to seek any information that might assist in the enquiry.'

Mr Dodson nodded sadly. 'Come within, sir.'

After introductions and Sheridan acquainting the Dodsons with the bare outlines of their master's death, the good wife retreated from the parlour amid more fulsome sobs to fetch refreshment.

'Your master returned here last night?'

'Why yes, sir. I had not expected to see him return quite so early. It was before midnight.'

'What did he do? Did he go straight to his bed?'

'Oh no, sir. He seemed much agitated. I had two messages that had been delivered for him, and then when I came back with his claret he was pacing about in a most excitable fashion.'

'Distressed?'

'Why no, sir. He was grinning from ear to ear.'

Sheridan could scarce keep the surprise at this revelation from his features.

'I reckoned the master had received some pleasing news. He had been out of sorts of late. My wife will hear no word against him, he had that way with women, but he was never a man of even temper. Then after a while I was sent for again and he bade me deliver a sealed message to The Stafford Arms at first light. I immediately sent young Walter by horse. Mr Stretton had said that it was urgent.'

'To whom was the message addressed?'

'A gentleman by the name of Mr Greaves.'

Acton Greaves. Sheridan took a deep breath. So, Greaves was staying nearby in Stafford. The viper had arrived, no doubt, to personally call in his debt. The dead man had not been lying to his cousin when he had pressed the desperate urgency of his need for funds.

'And your master was still in possession of his recent good humour when he handed you this note?'

'I would say so, sir. I asked if he wanted help to undress; the hour was very late. But he shook his head, saying he had no thought of sleep and he ordered then an early breakfast. After which he left the house.'

'When he ventured out in the morning, it was on foot?'

'Yes, sir.'

'About what hour was this, Dodson?'

'I reckon it was a little before seven o'clock.'

'Did he speak of an appointment?'

'No, sir.'

Sheridan grimaced.

'He did ask that his grey be made ready for nine o'clock. When he did not return at that hour, I did not at first think much on it. The master was ever changeable. I assumed he might have walked to the big house. Then when he was not back in the afternoon, I thought I should send Walter to enquire if he needed the grey brought up to him there.'

'I see.'

'Well, he has no need for it now. Skittish creature. Walter only said this morning, "That grey has got all flighty, Mr Dodson." Poor beast must have known what was become of his master; they have a sense for such things.'

Sheridan nodded. So, Stretton had gone out early with some purpose, a meeting? Which he might arrive at on foot and yet expect to be returned before nine o'clock. That venue, it would appear, was Lady Cannock's temple. But later he planned to ride further afield. With whom were these appointments? That information might lie in the notes received the previous evening. There might be the signature of the assassin himself.

'I would like to view the messages which you gave to your master last night.'

Dodson hesitated.

'There can be nothing that is private now, Dodson, not if we are to find out your master's killer.'

'Follow me, sir.'

The manservant brought Sheridan to Stretton's chambers and indicated a large bureau with a writing table and numerous drawers and pigeonholes which were stuffed with papers.

'You might find them amongst his correspondence here, sir.'

'Thank you, Dodson.'

Sheridan pulled out the seat and prepared to examine the detritus of Edward's life. The servant lingered a moment and then tactfully withdrew.

Sheridan recognised many of the creditors. Here was a London tailor with whom he too was in a regular one-way correspondence. The desk was fairly covered in similar pleas and invoices.

In the tray of a candle holder he saw the remnants of a letter which had clearly been burnt in the flame. Well, that might be one of the messages, all gone up in smoke — save for one corner only scorched, seemingly held by the fingertips until the last. Sheridan fished it out of the tray and peered closely. A partial word was faintly discernible: —*ding*

A missive from Lieutenant Harding? Another attempt to call Stretton out, burnt in derision? No. Here was not the cause for Edward's apparent excitability and change of humour, but perhaps a signal that Harding was still in desperate pursuit. He should discover the extent of the young lieutenant's furlough. His return to the Dragoons might be imminent and his actions therefore urgent and un-tempered.

And then he caught sight of a correspondence which he had expected and hoped to find: the letter from Acton Greaves, dated the day before and sent from The Stafford Arms. Sheridan scanned the contents.

I have been a patient man, Mr Stretton, but that credit is all spent. You must honour the amount requested — or face the consequences and I'll play the Devil with you. We meet tomorrow morn at 9 o'clock at The Stafford Arms. I am not a man who should be kept waiting.
Acton Greaves Esq.

Edward Stretton had failed to keep that appointment. If he did not have the means to satisfy Mr Greaves, that would hardly be surprising. In which instance Stretton would have been best advised to flee at once as far from the tentacles of that man's reach as was possible. Abroad — to the Continent at the very least. He had not flown. He had grinned from ear to ear. Did Edward Stretton have an expectation that his fortunes were changing? He had kept another appointment instead. With whom? Sheridan continued to scour the desk. A Herculean task amongst so many papers. After a half hour nothing came immediately to hand which would throw light on Edward's actions. Sheridan surrendered. He had done his duty. He would return to Sandbourne and impart the little he had learnt.

On the approach to the big house Sheridan caught sight of the tutor, Mr Cray, and the two young boys crossing the lawns and converging in the same direction. He waved a greeting, which was returned, and little Sempronius ran towards him waving a fishing rod.

'Mr Sheridan! Come, you must see our fish! We have caught a great many and mine is this big!' The boy spread his arms to their utmost and laughed.

A groom had appeared and Sheridan stepped down from the gig.

'Let me see this monster of the deep. This leviathan of the lake.'

Mr Cray was bringing up the rear carrying a pail, water sloshing from the sides.

'Robert, I think you may carry our catch now to the kitchens. Cook will be well pleased and there will be a fish pie for supper, I should think.'

Robert sprang forward to take the bucket, his muscles straining to make light of the weight, and together the boys hurried ahead to show cook the results of their angling prowess.

Once out of earshot, Mr Cray drew up to Sheridan.

'Sir, what has happened? A message came to keep Sempronius and Robert away until late afternoon. On the earl's instruction the fellow would not say more.'

Sheridan looked after the racing boys. 'They will know soon enough, Cray. Mr Edward Stretton has been murdered. Early this morning. We discovered his body in the woods, at the temple.'

Cray smirked.

'You do not look surprised, sir?'

'Nor am I, Mr Sheridan.'

'You have reason to suspect someone?'

Mr Cray sneered. 'Half of Staffordshire, I should say. He has either insulted or deceived anyone of worth.' The tutor eyed Sheridan. 'Of course, it is nothing for milords and miladies to run up a fortune in debts. I have been witness in other great houses. But the creditors may keep their patience when they expect some eventual return from one who has lands and estate.'

Sheridan inclined his head in acknowledgement of this truth.

Cray continued. 'When Mr Stretton first arrived in the district some eleven years ago as His Lordship's heir, he traded on that expectation. There are those in the county who foolishly extended their credit to him or invested in his harebrained ventures. Her Ladyship's uncle, Sir Humphrey, being one such.'

'That is news to me.' Sheridan shook his head. 'I had not sensed any friendship between them.'

'Not anymore, by God. Stretton had to give up his servant in part repayment.'

'Ah yes, Emmanuel.'

The tutor was warming to his subject. 'Mr Stretton relied too heavily on the commonly held belief that my Lord Cannock would not marry; His Lordship had never shown any inclination, apparently. But Lord Cannock did marry and has a son. And so, Mr Stretton's great expectations were scuppered, but his tastes and gambling did not economise.' Cray laughed without mirth; he was clearly relishing this opportunity to denigrate the earl's cousin and rattled on. 'His only hope was to marry an heiress. That was his sole object. Only his reputation was sullied you see, sir; no woman was safe with him, whatever her station, and he had a known taste for the lower orders.'

Sheridan's interest was piqued. 'Any of this household?'

Mr Cray pulled up and then continued nervously, 'I should not like to name. I would not be responsible for a servant that might lose employment.'

Sheridan nodded. 'I understand. Quite right. Even a maid must keep her reputation beyond reproach.'

Mr Cray flushed vehemently. 'He has cruelly toyed with the affections of one such.'

Sheridan appraised the pimpled tutor. He suspected that the young scholar was enamoured of this self-same girl but his hopes, honourable or otherwise, had foundered in the face of an altogether superior and more dashing rival for her affections, Edward Stretton.

CHAPTER SIX

They found Sir Anthony, his constable and the earl with the servants of the household assembled in the servants' hall below stairs. A number of facts had been ascertained during Sheridan's absence. He drew the young officer aside to be swiftly apprised of them. The kitchen servants were able to vouch for each other through the previous evening and in the morning from the earliest hour. Cook had returned to her duties, muttering about the interruptions to her work. Others who had insufficient witnesses to their presence had nevertheless the outcome of their labours to point to. The horses and carriages which had been readied for the outing to church. The maids and valets busy with their masters' and mistresses' needs. No one, it appeared by their reports, would have had time to visit the temple in the woods and to return.

A number of the servants were absent, however. The head gardener was away visiting relatives; a lady's maid and a scullery girl had Sunday for their day off. All three had departed between six and seven or thereabouts that morning. All were to be questioned on their return as to whether they had observed anything of suspicion.

The second key to the laboratory was missing, and none could recall seeing it past Saturday evening when the animals had been fed. The stableboy, whose job it had been to clean their cages and provide fresh straw and feed, swore that he had replaced the key soon after eight o'clock. He looked about anxiously to his fellows for corroboration, but after much scratching of heads none was forthcoming. It was a busy hour and no one had taken note of the boy's return from his task or the return of the key to its hook. Sir Anthony was certain its discovery would be damning.

There was also the missing syringe. The Justice voiced his opinion that the assassin had not found the time to replace either of the incriminating objects. The constable would conduct a search of the servants and their rooms. In this he was to be aided by Mr Hanley and his mother, Mrs Hanley, an upright and dignified lady, who was housekeeper. The prospect of a search occasioned ripples of discontent and murmurs of protest around the servants' hall.

It soon became apparent why. Although there was no sign of the key or syringe, there had been other finds. A small truckle of cheese. Two silver buckles. And a strip of Her Ladyship's lace. Sheridan had arrived on the scene in time to witness Sir Anthony's beetle brows raised in triumph.

'Well, Cannock, seems you have a household of thieving rogues! You may dismiss the villains at once and I shall see that they are all dealt with forthwith. The buckles will be a hanging offence, you may rest assured.'

Cannock wrung his hands. 'Sir Anthony, I am certain there has been no villainy amongst my servants.' He looked about the servants' hall anxiously. 'There will be explanations forthcoming. My memory is poor for such things, but I do seem to recall the buckles needed repair and polishing, and the lace most likely mending.'

Sir Anthony stiffened at the lost prospect of prosecution. 'And the cheese? Did that need to be sliced in an attic bedroom?'

A young maid sniffled loudly into the apron she clutched to her face.

'I should not be surprised if it was a gift from my wife for young Hephzibah's grandmother. Is that not so, Hephzibah?

Mrs Gough worked here in my father's time. She is very partial to cheese.'

The girl quivered and nodded her head.

Sheridan smiled inwardly. Cannock might be a dry old stick who spent his life in his books and potions, but he had a heart and would not see his servants in Sir Anthony's legal clutches. As he observed the earl, he felt more certain than ever that this mild man could not possibly be the fiendish assassin of his recent gothic fancy. It was a reassuring conclusion.

The Justice tapped his cane impatiently. 'Well, let us to the business in hand.' He looked about the servants with a face of thunder. 'Are there any more still to be questioned and searched?'

Samuel inclined his head. 'Only the visiting servants, sir. The coachmen for Mr Sheridan and Sir Humphrey. Mrs Smethurst's maid and her father's valet. Lady Cannock's maid, who has been out all day visiting her mother is not yet returned, although it is past that hour,' he muttered with dissatisfaction.

Hephzibah, having recovered a little of her composure, piped up. 'Please, sir. Lucy come back hours ago. I myself told her of poor Mr Stretton's misfortune. It did make her go pale. She may be in her room if you did not think to call her.'

The girl was dispatched to fetch the lady's maid before the Justice.

Samuel continued, 'Mr Moore the gardener is gone to Birmingham for three days on family matters. His brother is unwell. The scullery girl should be here this evening; she has a further distance to walk.' Samuel paused a moment and then looked enquiringly at Sir Anthony. 'And I did not know if you wished to include Mr Cray in the number of our enquiry, sir?'

At mention of his name the tutor looked about in affronted consternation. He had been thrust suddenly from the role of fascinated observer to that of potential suspect.

'I am sure that will not be necessary,' Cannock interjected quickly.

'I have nothing to hide, Sir Anthony!' the young tutor announced, jutting his chin forward and standing on his dignity.

Hephzibah returned at that moment, wide-eyed and breathless from her haste. 'Lucy is gone! She is missing!'

'What do you mean?' Sir Anthony snapped.

'Well, the room is empty of her possessions, sir.'

Ripples of astonishment surged around the hall at the announcement of Lucy's evident and hasty flight, and Sir Anthony had to raise his voice and beat a tattoo with his cane to restore order and attention.

'She has packed up and flown? Who is the girl?'

'Lucy Webster, maid to Lady Cannock,' Samuel supplied.

No one had witnessed this second departure. It was speculated that Lucy had heard the call to assemble and chosen the very moment that the household were here gathered to slip away from Sandbourne unobserved and unobstructed.

As Sir Anthony questioned, the servants began to paint a picture of Lucy Webster. A young woman of twenty-one years and numbered amongst Lady Cannock's local prodigies. Her widowed mother lived in the village of Sandbourne, took in mending work, and was a devout Methodist. Lucy had been quick to read and write. Pretty and with a flair for the dressing of hair, needlework and other such tasks as befitted a lady's maid. She had been raised up by all accounts because she was a clever little madam, was an opinion supplied from one quarter.

'Who knows of any reason why this girl might have flown?' the Justice demanded.

He was met with shaking heads and bemused silence.

'Come, some amongst you must be privy to her actions? It will not go well for you if justice is thwarted! Mr Stretton has been cruelly assassinated. If this girl has anything to do with this business and you don't speak up, there'll be the devil to pay!'

Samuel stepped forward. 'Sir Anthony, I have observed that Miss Webster has been very secretive of late. She avoids the company she formally enjoyed in this household.'

'That's right, sir,' Hephzibah offered brightly, her confidence now fully restored in the wake of her acquittal. 'Begging your pardon, me and Lucy used to share a room, sir, and were always at a blether. But these past six months she is like one struck dumb. I had it down to her new position as Her Ladyship's maid and that she felt herself above speaking with me anymore, sir.'

There were mutterings of agreement amongst other of the servants.

'Only I have known Lucy these many years and I did have a suspicion…'

'A suspicion? Of what, girl?'

'That she has a sweetheart, sir.'

'A sweetheart?'

'There was that smile about her. Like when the cat's got the cream. It was not unusual for her to flit from the house in her hours of leisure, and I did believe it was to meet with someone.' Hephzibah was warming to her moment. 'And now I do remember, sir, one time Mrs Hanley —' she paused to bob a curtsey to the housekeeper — 'had given her some instruction and I could see Lucy took it ill. I made some jest and she fairly snapped at me and says how one day she will be the one with servants. Well, that did make me laugh even more, which put her in a fury.'

'Are we to imagine then that this maid has eloped with her swain?'

The earl nodded. 'That may be a plausible explanation for her flight, Sir Anthony. I hazard it might be someone of whom her mother may not have approved. Mrs Webster is a stern character.'

'There may be other cause for the girl's flight on a day that has seen vile murder, Cannock.' The Justice's eyes gleamed at the prospect of a suspect at last.

The earl grimaced. 'I cannot credit that little Lucy would have either the cause or the wherewithal to bring Mr Stretton to so violent an end.'

'Mr Sheridan, what do you make of this?' Sir Anthony blustered. 'Romance. Tragedy. Might as well be one of your damn theatricals. How should this end?'

Sheridan was tempted to say, 'In comedy, sir,' to make light of this strange day, but he refrained. Instead he bowed and said, 'In justice, I trust, Sir Anthony.'

In truth he felt uneasy. He could sense that Sir Anthony was now losing all patience with this enquiry. The Justice longed for a villain, plain and simple. A blood-stained dagger. Well, it would be that infernal syringe in this case. Sir Anthony wanted an obvious motive for the crime. Revenge. Greed. He wanted the assassin to be of the lower orders. Barring a poacher or a highwayman, then it must be a servant. He had not even considered anyone above stairs. What the Justice did not want on any account was a mystery. In these circumstances, where there was no obvious suspect upon whom to fix, someone might quite easily get away with murder.

'This is a damnable business, my lord.'

The earl nodded. 'It is, Sir Anthony, and we should perhaps leave off enquiry until the morrow. Like Mr Sheridan, I am certain that justice will be done.'

'Of that you can be assured, sir. But let us complete the search.' The Justice looked across to Samuel. 'There are these few others, the coachmen and so forth. If you will be so good as to conduct the parish officer to them.'

'I am sure you are ready for refreshment, gentlemen.' Cannock looked from Sir Anthony to Sheridan.

'Believe you have a decent claret, Cannock, eh what?'

Sheridan concurred. 'Rather better than decent, I should say.'

The earl smiled. 'Mr Sheridan is a connoisseur of fine wine, so I will take his word.'

Something above thirty minutes later the polite conversation in the Drawing Room was interrupted. There had been a discovery in the guest servants' quarters. Sir Humphrey's man was being held by the constable and Mr Hanley.

Lord Cannock started and looked concerned. 'Emmanuel?'

Sir Anthony grinned broadly, beating his fist into his palm. 'I knew we would find the fellow!'

Sheridan frowned. This was not a direction he had in any way anticipated.

As Sheridan followed Sir Anthony and the earl into the simple but neat attic room, they were met with the sight of Emmanuel standing tall and tight-lipped by his cot. His hands were held out in front of him, encased in metal cuffs. The officer stood by his side, a pistol at the ready. On the bed lay a cloth object.

Sheridan squinted to make it out. It looked like some kind of raggedy doll. The head was made from a soft wood which had been fashioned as a man.

'What is this abomination?'

'It appears to be some sort of doll, sir, an effigy of some kind. But see here —' Samuel picked up the small figure. 'A number of nails have been driven into the body, and one here at the neck.'

'Be damned!' The Justice glared at Emmanuel. 'What is this? What does it mean?'

'It is Edward Stretton, sir,' the manservant answered, almost spitting the words.

A moment of stunned silence followed. Sheridan stared in fascination at the young man. Here was hatred that was plain, without disguise.

'It is a puppet. You have made a figure of Mr Stretton?' he ventured.

Emmanuel nodded. 'It is Obeah.'

'And what the devil is that?' Sir Anthony spluttered, his gall rising.

'It is a religious belief of African origin, I believe, Sir Anthony, involving magic and sorcery.' The earl spoke quietly as he stepped further into the room. 'One that is practised in parts of the Indies.'

'Witchcraft, you mean? Well, here is your evil.' The Justice pointed at the disturbing effigy, which seemed to stare at them from hollow, empty eyes.

'Yes, Sir Anthony, it is a vile and ugly puppet, but is this a proof of murder?'

'And how else, Mr Sheridan, are we to interpret these nails, pray?'

Cannock nodded in agreement with Sheridan. 'The desire for harm is clear in this figure, but it is not the deed.' The earl turned to the young man. 'Emmanuel, did you murder Mr Stretton?'

'No, sir. I did not wish him dead. I wished him to suffer. As I did when I was torn from my mother's skirts and given to him.'

The fellow was admirably honest. That much Sheridan conceded.

Sir Anthony rapped his cane. 'And there you have the admission! You may not have intended to kill him, but kill him you did! And you will hang for it!'

Sheridan felt his breath stop and the earl too seemed frozen. Sir Anthony was not to be restrained. He commanded the room with the full force of his authority.

'Emmanuel...' Sir Anthony jerked his head to Samuel. 'Does the fellow have a second name?'

'Stretton.'

They turned to find Lady Cannock at the threshold.

'Emmanuel Stretton, late of Barbados. Former slave to our distant cousin James Stretton, plantation owner, from whom Edward won the boy in a game of chance.'

'Lady Cannock. Ah yes, I do believe it is the practice; slaves are given their master's surname — it denotes the estate from where they originate. Is that not right?'

Lady Cannock glared at Sir Anthony. 'Oftentimes their fathers too.'

The earl moved swiftly to take his wife's arm, whether to comfort or silence her, Sheridan could not tell.

She would speak nevertheless, her eyes boring into Sir Anthony. 'You have noted the lightness of Emmanuel's complexion? See, gentlemen, here is our cousin, Emmanuel Stretton. Son to James Stretton who is his grandfather also.'

'What mean you by these riddles, my lady?' Sir Anthony shifted uncomfortably.

'Only think on it.'

Sir Anthony's eyes narrowed and his features set hard. 'Pray, forgive me, madam. Whatever the blood — it is bad blood and that plain to see. We have found our villain.' He nodded to his officer, who took firm hold of the culprit. 'Emmanuel —' Sir Anthony paused, clearly finding the connection unsavoury — 'Stretton, you are arrested for the murder of Mr Edward Stretton Esquire.'

CHAPTER SEVEN

Thunder rumbled ominously in the near distance and the crack of lightning seemed ready to split the world in two. Darkness rolled over the bright skies. The late summer heat had come to an end. After Sir Anthony's departure with the accused, they had returned to the Drawing Room. Cannock poured them both a glass of claret.

'To my cousin Edward.' He raised his glass. 'Sadly, he was never at peace in life but may he rest so in death.'

'To Edward.' Sheridan downed the glass. Tonight, he would welcome the oblivion of a bottle of wine or two.

Much distressed, Lady Cannock had retired to her bedchamber. Sir Humphrey Barclay had taken his leave under the care of Mrs Smethurst. The events of the day and the dramatic outcome with the arrest of his manservant had exacted their toll on the old squire's constitution, and he thought only of the comforts of his own home and bed. Robert, however, was to stay on at Sandbourne as companion to Sempronius.

Cannock nodded towards Sheridan. 'This has been a day which has sadly diverted us from entertaining you as our guest.'

Sheridan shook his head. It had certainly been a day of tumult. He expressed his intention to return to Stafford that evening. He had no wish to intrude on the general grief. Cannock thanked him for his consideration.

The rains came as a flood. Clouds grey and roiling. Sheridan had to sprint from his carriage to the entrance of The Stafford Arms not to be fairly drenched by the deluge. The landlord greeted him as he entered and offered refreshment. Sheridan was knocking the rain from his hat as he entered the parlour and looked about for a seat. He stopped, frozen. In a far corner he was taken aback to recognise the features, familiar from so many race meetings, of Mr Acton Greaves sitting with another man. Sheridan hesitated and wondered whether he might take a late supper in his room. He did not wish to have Greaves for company. Too late. He had been spied.

Greaves rose to his feet. 'Sheridan. Just the fellow!' He bowed, flourishing a silk handkerchief.

Sheridan returned the bow. 'Greaves.'

'Do join us, Sheridan. We are about to have a cold collation.' Greaves smiled graciously.

Sheridan nodded and crossed the room, attempting to disguise his reluctance behind his own false smile.

Greaves turned to the gentleman across from him. 'Mr Swain, have you met your Member of Parliament? The Right Honourable Richard Brinsley Sheridan.'

The man rose and bowed; he looked a little uncomfortable in his frockcoat, as though he did not wear it often. 'I have not had that pleasure, sir. It is an honour indeed. You are highly thought of here, Mr Sheridan. And you do make us laugh from time to time. Tha' was a piece of rascality at the last election. When you sent tha' cart about the streets with the scarecrow hung on the gallows!' The man's grin was as broad as his local accent.

Sheridan flinched. The effigy had been a crude and tasteless joke on his part to embarrass Sir Elijah Impey, former Chief Justice in Calcutta and an ally of the Governor General Warren Hastings.

Sir Elijah had thought to unseat Sheridan by challenging him in the Stafford seat in the wake of Sheridan's triumph in

Parliament, when he had spoken to impeach Hastings. Many believed that Sheridan had almost single-handedly brought about the decision to bring Hastings to trial over his misconduct as Governor in India. The fame of Sheridan's five-hour speech on the outrageous abuse of the Begums of Oudh had reached far and wide. He had been hailed a hero. There had not been a dry eye in the House, even on the Government side. But he had made powerful enemies, including Sir Elijah Impey. Sheridan had resorted to cheap theatricals in that election. But the tableaux on the cart had served its purpose. Sir Elijah had withdrawn from the Stafford election forthwith. And Sheridan had counted it another small victory against entitlement.

'What brings you here, Mr Greaves?'

'I had business. But its nature has changed in a rather dramatic manner,' he added enigmatically.

'I see. And Mr Swain is a business acquaintance?'

'Of sorts.'

They sat. Greaves made a steeple of his fingers. 'But perhaps you can enlighten us, Sheridan. My business was with Mr Edward Stretton. Unfortunately, he has not been able to keep our appointment. I believe you have just come from Sandbourne. The whole of Stafford is agog, I am sure, to learn of what has passed there, and you are "hot foot" as they say.'

He was bold indeed.

'It has been a sad and distressing day at Sandbourne.'

'One can only imagine.'

The waiting man arrived then to disrupt the flow with a tray of drinks and some plates of cheese and meats. Sheridan had to find a way to extract himself from this conversation. It was altogether distasteful.

'I gather that someone has been arrested. A black servant. The arrest must be of some comfort to His Lordship,' Greaves continued.

'Slight comfort, I would say.'

'You came across the scene, did you not?'

'You are remarkably well-informed, Greaves. But that is your forte, I understand, the collection of information. I may have little to add to what you already know.'

'The devil is in the detail, Mr Sheridan. As I say, my business with Mr Stretton is not yet concluded.'

'Let us not make pretence, Greaves. You held a substantial part of Edward Stretton's debts. He is dead. There is nothing. All he had is gone. He lived on the charity of his cousin.'

'I would not be so sure of that. Our interests have shifted in another direction.'

Greaves smiled again, as a snake would smile if it could, Sheridan imagined. He frowned. Was Greaves making play with him? Something in what he said made Sheridan feel uneasy.

Greaves leaned back in his chair. A roll of thunder rumbled loudly overhead.

'Damnable turn in the weather! We may be stuck in this backwater another day.'

Sheridan endured the light supper with Greaves and Swain as they talked inconsequentially of horses and races and when the Prince of Wales might next be at Newmarket. Sheridan then begged to be excused from the table. He asked the landlord for a bottle of his best wine to be sent upstairs, and hoped it would aid him to sleep.

It was a small gathering at the Stretton family plot in the churchyard bordering Sandbourne. Edward Stretton, it appeared, did not have many friends. Aside from the family, Sir Anthony Peake, and a number of older notables from the neighbouring estates, the service had been attended by a handful of curious locals, but none had been so bold as to intrude on the interment. The roads being mired in mud on the Monday following the storms, Sheridan had extended his stay in Stafford, and it was but the matter of another day's sojourn in order to attend the funeral. He was anxious to return to London but had felt conscious of his duty not only to Lord and Lady Cannock, but as a local dignitary himself. And so it was he must endure that country parson for the second time within the week. The Reverend Grayson spoke fulsomely of the deceased in terms which no one present would recognise, Sheridan felt certain. There was no prospect of a comic relief on this occasion. Robert Smethurst had clearly been impressed with the solemnity of the service and was of an age to understand that death was no laughing matter.

The year had tipped into September and with it, intimations of autumn. Heavy overcast skies loomed on the horizon. A suitably dismal mood pervaded the proceedings. Sheridan had found himself standing beside an elderly squire, Sir Toby Moxley.

'Believe you too are an old Harrovian, Mr Sheridan?'

'I am indeed, sir.'

'I was there myself with the old 3rd Earl and his brother. Twins, don't you know. Chalk and cheese. Francis, who was father to this fellow we are burying today, was an utter scoundrel. A bully, sir. Thrashed me on more than one occasion. Fine figure of a man, have to say. Young Edward and his father were like as two peas. Same could be said of the earl and his father. Remarkable. Two sons. Two fathers. So different. Makes you wonder. Where's the blood in it all, heh?

Might have had a repetition of such diverse natures if the present earl's twin had survived.'

Sheridan, who had not been taking a great deal of notice of the old man's burbling, now became attentive.

'A twin?'

'A girl. Of course, girls can go to the bad too.'

'I have heard no word of a sister.'

'Died at birth. Taking her mother with her, sadly. Dr Burton over there delivered them. Managed to save Cannock, thank the Lord, and as I say, as like his late father as a son can be. Scholarly, retiring type.' Sir Toby shook his head and glanced towards the earl. 'Lovely woman, his mother — Henrietta Fairley, her name was. Rather had a fancy for her myself. Old Cannock never got over losing Henrietta, poor fellow. One reason I think he kept his son at home. Feared to let him abroad, in case any harm should come to him. Don't hold with that. A boy needs the horseplay, don't you think?'

'There is something to be said for it.'

Beyond the cemetery Sheridan spotted his carriage waiting to take him back to London. That moment could not come too soon. It was a long and tiresome journey. The service finally came to an end, the coffin interred, and the mourners began to disperse. Sheridan reiterated his condolences to the Cannocks and was taking his leave when Lady Ann grasped his arm and took him to one side. She was clearly upset. Sheridan was surprised. He had not imagined she had any great feeling for Edward Stretton.

'Richard. If there is anything you can do… Please, you must!'

'In whatever way I can help you, Lady Cannock, I will. Be assured. What would you have me do?'

'Emmanuel.' She squeezed his arm. 'He must not hang.'

'I see.' Sheridan nodded and sought to offer some small comfort. 'I can imagine how distressing it might be to you, Ann, if Emmanuel were to hang. I can try and make argument for the new prison colony —'

'No. You do not understand me. He is innocent.'

Sheridan hesitated. 'My lady, there is the evidence and the fact that no one can verify his whereabouts at the time the murder took place.'

Lady Cannock shook her head vigorously. 'I do not believe it. It is all speculation. I know Emmanuel. I have known him since he was a small boy. I taught him to read and write myself. He is a bright and clever and good young man. This is not him.'

'I am sensitive to your feeling, Lady Cannock, believe me. This must be disturbing in every way. Murder is a violent end. And you do not wish to consider that someone you have nurtured and cared for might be responsible. I can understand that. But that strange doll — you must have seen it. His expressed and vehement desire to hurt Edward.'

He could see that there were tears brimming in Her Ladyship's eyes. He clasped her hand.

'If there is anything that I can do to argue for clemency, I will do it. It was clearly an act of insanity,' he attempted to reassure, 'and therefore, entirely out of character, one might argue.'

'My poor Emmanuel.'

Lady Cannock turned away from him. Sheridan could not help but think that he had somehow disappointed her, and he was surprised at how ill this made him feel.

CHAPTER EIGHT

Sheridan lurched down the steps of Brooks's Club and steadied himself on the railing. He pulled his greatcoat closer about his frame, already missing the warmth of the fires within and the unfinished bottle of claret which he had left at his seat. But he must get to Haymarket to catch the manager at The King's Theatre.

His company had taken up temporary residence whilst his new Theatre Royal on Drury Lane was under construction. In these makeshift premises he was beset with grumbles from his actors and complaints from the vast army backstage, not least from Mrs Petty, the formidable wardrobe mistress. In truth, however, there was another he hoped to see that evening at the theatre. A young woman, Pamela Syms. It had become his fancy that she might help to lift the blue devils which had consumed him since Eliza's death.

'Sherry,' a voice called to him from behind.

Sheridan turned. It was Major Hanger, who followed down the steps and clapped an overly familiar hand on his shoulder as he too disgorged from the club.

'I am to remind you that His Royal Highness will be expecting your company in Brighton tomorrow eve.' The equerry to the Prince of Wales grinned lopsidedly — he was well in his cups.

'I have not forgotten, Major.'

Hanger nodded. 'I never took you for a betting man, Sherry.'

Sheridan flushed. There were many failings he would honestly own, but gambling had not been one of them. He had always considered it a foolish vice and been open-mouthed at the vast sums which various friends squandered on the tables and at the track. Of course, Sheridan did not have the funds to risk his flimsy credit to chance, yet these past weeks he had become wild and reckless. He was out of kilter. He was not himself.

'You are not yourself, I think,' said Hanger kindly, giving voice to his thoughts.

Sheridan wondered why he and George Hanger were not better friends, for the man was quick of wit and game for any sort of jape. Well, he knew why: he had never entirely trusted the fellow after the business of the duel — a prank engineered by the prince. Sheridan had used some flimsy excuse to challenge Hanger. His Royal Highness then substituted blanks in the pistols, and when the shots were fired Sheridan dropped down dead. Amidst the panic, all acted as if the incident should be covered up with great haste. That evening, over a private dinner, Sheridan had emerged ghostlike into the dimly lit room covered in white powder. Poor Hanger near jumped out of his skin. Cause for great hilarity — but Sheridan could not easily forget that Hanger had not known it was a blank that he fired and that his aim had been to kill.

'We look forward to the pleasure of your company at the Marine Pavilion.' The major gave a short bow and stepped into a waiting hackney carriage.

As Sheridan headed into the fug belching out from London's chimneys and dived into the ginnels which would bring him to Haymarket by the shortest route, he mused on what the summons to the prince might mean. Whatever the reason, he would be called upon to entertain the party, of that he could be certain.

'God's blood!'

He was roughly shoved to one side. More savage oaths followed. Distracted by his thoughts, and cloaked in the miasma of the fog, Sheridan had stumbled into a thoroughfare amongst a group of steaming, beery men. His mind raced to determine their purpose. They were clearly riled. Propelled to what end? He looked about to get his bearings. The drunken mob surged in from passages on both sides to centre on a shop. A watchmaker, Sheridan construed from the signage.

'Hang the bloody traitors!' a thick-necked ruffian bellowed.

'And quarter and quarter!' squeaked another, waving his cudgel.

Alarmed, Sheridan strained to make out the name above the premises. Monsieur Bernard De Lubac. An old papist? Sheridan shuddered. The violent intent of the mob was palpable.

'Burn 'em out!' a fellow goaded.

Another, with a lighted torch gripped in his hand, stepped forward, but with hesitation.

Men had begun to tug and wrench at the cobbles.

'Kill our king, would they?'

A ruffian burst into song, full-throated, and others joined in.

'Come all honest Britons, assist me to sing;
Long Life and good Health, let us drink to the King.'

For certain they were a Church and King gang, Sheridan realised, their crude loyalties worked up by some government provocateur, no doubt.

'So take off your hats now and give him a Cheer,
Then down with the Paineites, if any be here!'

Sheridan recoiled from the sound of breaking glass. Violence and destruction were now clearly threatened. He must make haste away and raise the alarm.

'We'll give the papist French scum what for!'

'No popery!'

'But plenty of pokery — right up the arse!'

Coarse laughter assailed his ears as Sheridan tried to nudge and weave his way through the heaving body of men who were pressing in close. Then he was grabbed by the lapel and found himself being appraised by a sharp-eyed youth whose weasel face thrust into his own.

'Bugger — it's Mr Sheridan, ain't it?'

'Let me go, sir!' Sheridan tried to remove the hand that held him but the grip tightened.

'You for the Jacobin? I hear you're a regular Reformer!'

'Him a king-toppler, Ned?' An older, pockmarked companion looked on agog.

'Too right, Isaac, and I reckon it would be a service to top him instead.'

Sheridan took a deep breath. 'Sir, you are mistaken. If you would kindly release me.'

The youth sneered, gap-toothed and malicious.

Sheridan looked about for assistance, but all that he could see were men whose interest was now converting to himself, and their looks were not kind.

'What you got here, Ned?'

'Mr Fox's bootlicker, ain't he?'

'Who's that then?'

'One as writes plays and is in the Nobs House with them French-loving Whigs as would down our good King George.' Ned spat the last into Sheridan's face.

'Irish too! Them is all papists!' another growled.

Sheridan's mind thrummed with half a dozen cutting retorts, but he knew the dangers of adding fuel to their flame. He elected to smile at the bellwether.

'Well, you have had your entertainment. Now let me pass, good fellows.'

'What shall we, Ned?' The pockmarked man deferred to his weasel friend in a high wheedling voice.

'You shall desist!'

A voice of authority burst through the mob. With a swell of relief Sheridan recognised the Bow Street Runners wielding truncheons and cutlasses and the man who had shouted through the mob as his young friend, Constable Nicholls. Members of the night patrol set about dispersing the drunken gathering and few, it became immediately apparent, had the stomach for a real fight but slunk away through the passages on either side.

Ned hesitated momentarily before flinging Sheridan roughly to the ground with a fearsome oath and making good his own escape.

Sheridan lay on his back, much shaken but thankful that he had suffered no more than the indignity of his present position.

'Sir.' Nicholls leant over him with an outstretched hand. He was broad-shouldered and of a serious mien. 'Mr Sheridan.'

Sheridan took the proffered hand and scrambled awkwardly to his feet.

'Constable Nicholls.'

'Are you hurt, sir?'

'Much obliged. No... No ... but a dent here and there. A Church and King mob — worked up against the French Catholics in our city.'

Nicholls shook his head grimly and nodded towards the shop. 'Not Catholic, a Huguenot — but these fellows have no care of the difference.'

The door of the shop opened tentatively and a frail man poked his head into the street.

Nicholls immediately switched his attention and solicitude. 'Monsieur De Lubac…?'

'Louis-Pierre! *Sacré coeur*! *Merci. Merci…*' The watchmaker trembled.

The constable turned to Sheridan. 'Forgive me, sir, if you will allow…?' He nodded towards the old man.

'Of course, dear fellow. I am quite all right, I do assure you.'

Nicholls bowed curtly and then hurried to Monsieur De Lubac's side. He led him back inside the shop with reassuring words spoken in French.

Sheridan shook his head and dusted himself down, groaning at a patch of filth and manure on his coat.

'Mr Sheridan, sir? Am I correct?'

Sheridan looked to see a portly officer approaching on horseback now that the street was clear.

'You are, sir,' Sheridan acknowledged.

'Officer Biddulph, glad to be of service.' The man puffed himself up. 'I hope these ruffians have not harmed you, sir.'

'I am grateful for your intervention.'

'There will be more of this. Mark my words. Troubled days ahead, Mr Sheridan. Those French are like to murder their king!' The officer shook his head and pursed his lips. 'We are beset by revolutions all around.' He pointed to the shop. 'Monsieur De Lubac is no Jacobin in God's truth, but there are those amongst the French community that are. And then we have our own breed of Radical. In such times, who may we trust?'

The man's squinting eyes peered at Sheridan as though to search out the colour of his allegiance.

'The danger lies in the error of judgement, good officer. Particularly when a man may be a reformer and not a traitor. We must all be on our guard against King Mob!' Sheridan shook his head. 'That will be swayed first this way and then the other.'

Biddulph snorted. 'True, but the Runners have enough to deal with, sir, with plain murder and robbery.'

'You must excuse me, Mr Biddulph. I have an appointment.'

'I can send a man with you, Mr Sheridan; a member of our good parliament should not be waylaid by these drunken —'

'That will not be necessary.' Sheridan bowed. 'I am on my guard now.'

Sheridan strode into the thickening fog with a new alertness. These were troubled times to be sure, and he needed a good swig of brandy to steady his nerve.

CHAPTER NINE

An unusual hush gripped the audience for the finale as Sheridan slipped into the Duke of St Albans' box to pay his respects to one of his company's more esteemed patrons. Standing behind her seat, he observed that even the duchess and her otherwise rowdy family of young Beauclerks were mesmerised by the main attraction of the evening. Dr Cardonnet swirled his cape about him and glided across the boards whilst the ethereal notes of a glass harmonica sent ghostly shivers through the group assembled and seated on the stage.

Sheridan smirked. It was the usual flimflam of the showman. After so many years standing in the wings he was privy to their deceptions, misdirections and tricks of the light. But this fellow Cardonnet claimed to be a scientist using the healing powers of 'animal magnetism' and not, as his detractors insinuated, a purveyor of supernatural hokum-pokum. A victim of his own self-deception, Sheridan deduced, and was about to make some witty snipe when the duchess raised a silencing finger. Dr Cardonnet swept along the line of his volunteers, clicking his fingers, and each in turn dropped their head into an attitude of slumber.

The young Beauclerks gasped and leant over the edge of the box whilst murmurs of surprise rippled through the audience. Cardonnet waited pointedly for the hubbub to fade, his piercing eyes scanning the stalls and the boxes to either side. Sheridan noted with satisfaction that the entire audience had remained for the climax event of the evening. Below he spied Skiffy Skeffington and his cronies. In a box overlooking the stage there sat Sir John with Letitia, Lady Lade, and in the box directly opposite he locked eyes for a moment with Lord Cannock. They nodded briefly to each other.

The presence of the Cannocks made Sheridan start with remembrance of their last encounter at the end of the summer. He shuddered to recollect that horrifying discovery — the body of Edward Stretton sprawled on the floor of the temple. What strange events had then ensued. Sheridan had cast the murder and its disturbing aftermath to the far recesses of his mind, and the intervening weeks had been so hectic and all-consuming with the business of raising monies for the new theatre that he had almost succeeded in forgetting it. He grimaced, recalling Lady Cannock's plea on behalf of the servant, Emmanuel. But what could Sheridan do? All the evidence had pointed in that direction and he himself had been witness to the murderous hatred in Emmanuel's eyes on the night before the assassination. He rather wished that he might be able to evade the Cannocks at the end of the evening, so that he might avoid a repeat of that plea.

Dr Cardonnet's daughter emerged onto the stage carrying an enormous hoop whose diameter exceeded her height. Félicité skipped to the apron of the stage, exhibiting it to the assembled watchers with dancing swirls. Pretty and spry, she was airily light on her toes with flashing eyes and a disarming smile which might captivate as surely as any Mesmer passing of hands. A coquette, Sheridan reflected ruefully as he recalled the way in which the young mademoiselle had teased him whilst her imperious father pressed for an increase of fee.

In truth, Cardonnet should be paying *him* to appear. The demonstration was simply a window to advertise his wares. The real money lay in private audiences, one hostess after another competing for his presence. He could see that the charming Duchess of St Albans might soon be amongst that number. The man would make a small fortune.

Sheridan shook his head — would that he had such funds at his disposal. The costs of the rebuild at Drury Lane Theatre seemed to be ever rising and the project much delayed. He must constantly badger and cajole for support and investment. For all the success of his theatrical endeavours, he was forever chasing his tail. And what a year of upheavals. Sheridan was a man well used to chaos, but this year the world seemed truly turned upside down. The French in revolution, their king imprisoned. The Whigs dividing. He without his own theatre. His sweet Eliza passed away, leaving him to be father to the infant Mary, whilst their own son Tom turned wayward. And his personal finances… Sheridan despaired. When he put his mind to it, he could be as good a man of business as any, better perhaps than most, given his facility with the mathematical. But his mind was wanted in so very many different places.

A new play might be the answer. Sheridan had toyed with the notion of a comedy of mesmerism. A dashing and impoverished rake, Augustus Merriweather, seeks to use the services of a mesmerist to influence a young invalid heiress in his favour. The dramatis personae, including Lord Doubtmore, her intransigent father, the sexual hysteric Lady Fullalove — he might persuade Dora Jordan into that role — and the scheming Dr Pasdemain with his fiendish use of 'artificial somnambulism'. He had heard the practice of mesmerism referred to as 'juggling'; his title might be *The Jugglers*. As Sheridan watched Félicité prance about the stage, the idea came that here might be another character to create, a part for one of his promising ingénues — Miss Barrett, perhaps?

But this was all simply musing. His first duty must be to parliament. There lay his passion, the arena to voice his cries against corruption and express his yearning for electoral reform, that the men of merit and ability might govern in place of the privileged and venal. If he had been one to suffer bribes and preferment, where might he be now? The holder of some lucrative office? A baronet? It brought a tear to his eye to consider his honour and integrity; he was such a man that any son might be proud of, for he had never sold his principles to fortune.

Félicité gave a curtsey to the enraptured audience. At this cue Dr Cardonnet addressed himself to the assembly in his florid French accent.

'My lords, my ladies, mesdames, messieurs. You have witnessed the demonstration of the baquet, the vessel through which we may pass the healing properties of my animal magnetism.' Cardonnet indicated the contraption, a large, lidded cauldron, around the edges of which protruding rods bent outwards at different heights. 'You have perhaps doubted the efficacy of this method?' His eyes searched the crowd for any who would be brave enough to challenge.

'Balderdash, sir!'

Sheridan could not suppress a grin as a young man stood up from the middle of the pit, swayed a little until steadied by his fellows and barked again.

'Damn balderdash!'

His companions hooted their agreement.

Dr Cardonnet waited with patient disdain for the ensuing murmurs to fade away and then with a sweeping flourish turned to indicate the elderly slumbering gentleman to his right.

'You have noted that the gentleman has complained of a stiffness in his left knee. Allow me to demonstrate the magnetic effects of the baquet.' He approached the man. 'Monsieur, I will count to three and you will open your eyes. You will feel revived and full of the *joie de vivre* and you will follow my instructions. *Un … deux…*' The audience were once again hushed and attentive. '*Trois!*'

At once the man jerked up and grinned foolishly.

'Monsieur, if you will kindly come to the front of the stage.'

The man did as he was bidden.

Dr Cardonnet indicated the hoop. 'Here it is, a hoop, sir. When I touch your shoulder, you will jump through this hoop until I click my fingers, and then you will awake and the audience may witness with their own eyes —' he scanned the audience — 'the cure!'

Then with the most delicate of gestures he tapped the gentleman's shoulder.

At once the man leapt through the hoop which Félicité held aloft. Back and forth he went, as directed, in an absurd dance. At first uncertain, the audience soon began to cackle and urge the fellow on to an ever faster display of his agility. Sheridan had seen enough. He bowed toward the duchess and took his leave.

Amongst the notables in the audience Sheridan had been satisfied by the presence of Madame de Genlis with her charge, the fifteen-year-old Bourbon princess Mademoiselle Adèle, daughter of the Duc d'Orléans. And sitting beside them her own adopted daughter, Pamela Syms. Pamela's beauty caught and stopped his breath. At eighteen she was the very image of Eliza in the flower of her youth, with the same pale complexion, the same high forehead and dark curls. He experienced an urgent impulse to embrace her. Of late he had become quite feverish with desire — his carnal desire laced with other less tangible desires. What a chance it might be to start again, to wipe the slate clean of foolish errors and to be a worthy husband.

Sheridan felt the delirium of his passion. He must not miss this opportunity to apprehend Madame de Genlis and her daughter, who many discreetly asserted was her own natural child by the Duc d'Orléans. Orléans was one of the wealthiest men in Europe; he had been mooted as a future King of France before the declaration of a French Republic in September. He still held great sway in the Assembly and had changed his name to Philippe Égalité in keeping with his revolutionary ideals. Whilst Sheridan might be ill-advised to think of such exalted connections, nevertheless, the man who married Pamela Syms would be fortunate indeed.

He placed himself to greet the French party as the sounds of audience appreciation for the evening's entertainment died away and they began to spill from the auditorium into the foyer. He nodded to a number of acquaintances. Lord and Lady Cannock were not to be avoided. He bowed politely, but as he moved to greet them with an open smile his way was blocked by the enthusiastic approach of Mrs Buckberry and her portly niece. Sheridan groaned inwardly. Lady Cannock must have caught his expression, for she smiled knowingly and signalled their farewell.

'Gadzooks, Mr Sheridan!' Mrs Buckberry clutched his arm. 'Dr Cardonnet's speculatum is the very pineapple of tribulation. My niece is all aglimmer!'

'Mrs Buckberry, Miss Cressida, delighted that you find our entertainments so diverting.'

Cressida tittered, her jowls wobbling, as she cast her simpering eyes on him.

'Quite redoubtable,' Mrs Buckberry continued.

'Quite.' Over the ladies' shoulders Sheridan espied Madame de Genlis descending the stairs.

'You know, dear Mr Sheridan, that I will be hosting a little entertainment myself on Tuesday next.'

'You have always been an inspiration to me, Mrs Buckberry.'

'Darling Cressida will be our chatelaine; she has a very sweet voice.'

'I have no doubt —'

'Oh, but I touch on painful themes!' Mrs Buckberry turned to her niece. 'You must know, Cressida, that Mr Sheridan's late wife was counted the utmost soprano of her age — Miss Linley, as she then was. Such a tragic loss. You have already received my condiments, of course.'

Sheridan bowed sorrowfully. 'You will excuse me, I beg —'

'Naturally, dear man, you lead the way and we'll precede.' Mrs Buckberry indicated their path with a flourish.

Sheridan bowed again, resigned to the impossibility of speaking with Pamela on this occasion. He escorted the two ladies through the crowded foyer to the entrance. The fog was thickening and a light drizzle gleamed on the cobblestones. Instructing one of his regular urchins to fetch the Buckberry carriage, he turned inside once more to find Pamela before him. She cast a demure glance up to him but with what he took to be a twinkle in her eye.

'Monsieur Sherrie!' Madame de Genlis greeted Sheridan with an open smile. 'Our evening is complete in this encounter.'

'You are most gracious, madame.' From the corner of his eye Sheridan glimpsed Mrs Buckberry scowling at them with imperious disapproval. She would not be the only one in the foyer casting such looks at the French party, given their connection to Philippe Égalité and the Revolutionaries.

'I see you are gallant as ever with the ladies and minister to our every need.' Madame de Genlis inclined her head politely to Mrs Buckberry.

The good matron bridled whilst Miss Cressida quivered behind the fan which she had drawn forth for no particular reason.

Sheridan busied himself arranging carriages and with much ceremony led Mrs Buckberry and her niece to their conveyance, or 'convenience' as Mrs Buckberry so aptly put it.

He fully expected Madame de Genlis to have departed with her attendant footman when he returned to the foyer, but there she tarried.

'Monsieur Sherrie.' She took a motherly hold of his arm. 'How we have missed your company now we are residing in Bury St Edmunds. We are so dull without your amusements.'

'It would be my pleasure to wait on you, and your delightful charges.' He inclined his head to the young ladies and thought he caught again a glint in Pamela's eye. How his heart leapt.

'It must be soon, I fear. The duc has written, bidding us to return to Paris. I have refused, of course. It is unreasonable at such a time as this; it is all so —' she groped for the words — 'turbulent.' Madame lowered her voice almost to a whisper and Sheridan caught the whiff of real fear. 'I must confess I am in great terror of Paris and what these men, these Robespierre and Danton, may be capable of.' Her free hand fluttered to her neck.

Sheridan had a sudden image of bull-necked Monsieur Danton. His monstrous head and livid scars did inspire terror on first acquaintance, but Sheridan had discovered the French lawyer to be the most jovial and charming of men with an earthy relish of fine wine and good company. Despite never quite knowing whether he could trust him, Sheridan had been disappointed not to extend his friendship beyond the Jacobin's brief exile in England in the year before. It was true that on occasion the Paris mobs had been brutal and savage, but there were men of sense at the helm, which convinced Sheridan that a true constitutional monarchy in France remained not only desirable but imminent if the duc might be championed in the role.

'You know the duc, monsieur, and you must know he will not be denied for long.'

Sheridan nodded in agreement. He had indeed observed that the duc was not a man to have any appetite thwarted.

Her grip tightened. 'I am uneasy, sick, unhappy. You know I am entrusted with the most sacred charge. All about me I see the most dreadful snares of fraud and wickedness.' Sheridan followed her furtive, darting eyes and in the shadows, he too sensed sinister presences. It was the derangement of the times. Everywhere one might imagine agents and spies.

'You are a true friend, Monsieur Sherrie. I know that we may rely on you.'

'On my honour you may, madame.'

'Then you will call on us, my dear Sherrie.'

He escorted the party to the waiting carriage. Handing Pamela up to her seat, he was certain that she squeezed his hand.

As he made his way to the rear of The King's Theatre in search of the manager, it was all that consumed Sheridan. The sparkle of Pamela's eyes, her warm hand in his, that imperceptible pressing of his fingers. Was it all in his imagination? Surely not. And yet. He was a man past forty and she scarcely into womanhood. She was likely of royal blood, whilst he was that which had dogged him at school, 'a player's son'.

The theatre was going dark, performers, stage crew and hangers-on having mostly vacated the building in search of other entertainment. He should have picked up a lantern. If it were Drury Lane he would have been confident in the narrow network of corridors and stairs backstage, but here at The King's Theatre he fumbled for the steps, tripped and cursed the manager loudly.

He had turned in the direction he imagined the theatre office to be when in the gloom ahead he made out a figure. He must delay him.

'Sir, a moment, pray.'

The figure turned in a swirl of cloak.

'If, sir, you —'

A blow struck him hard to the side of his head and all was dark indeed.

CHAPTER TEN

Sheridan started. It was a ghastly apparition — the white face slashed by a grinning red mouth. But for the glittering eyes, large and wild in their black-browed frame, it could be the face of a painted corpse. All caught in the flickering glare of a lantern. For a moment he wondered whether he was waking or had stumbled into a nightmare.

'Mr Sheridan?'

Sheridan shuddered, the pain in his head cracking behind his eyes. 'Joe? Joey, is that you?'

'Yes, sir.'

'What the devil are you?'

'Clown.' The boy's bright eyes sparked and his lips widened to their grotesque limits.

Sheridan groaned.

'You have tumbled, sir.'

'No, by God! I have *been* tumbled! Some rum mizzler has waylaid me and I daresay emptied my pockets!'

'Let me help you up, sir.'

Sheridan felt the power in the lad's grip. He regarded him in his garish pantaloons and painted mask. At thirteen, young Joseph Grimaldi was already a veteran of the stage. An irrepressible bouncing ball of undiluted whizz, springing back from every fall and comic beating only to play again the same pranks, a veritable monkey. A part which he had famously played as a small boy in a monkey costume. At the climax of his tricks, the late Signor Grimaldi would swing the child around on the end of a chain at terrifying velocity until one evening the chain had snapped and young Joey had flown high through the air, out over the pit, over the front rows, and onwards to land in a flailing of arms and legs in the lap of a portly gentleman. How the audience roared their appreciation and laughed to see the little imp grinning foolishly up at the startled good gentleman.

'Thank you, I am a little unsteady.' Sheridan dabbed about his pockets and found with surprise and satisfaction that his purse was still in place.

Joey grinned. 'It would be rum if you were not, sir, and perhaps a little rum might do the trick.'

'Yes, perhaps a little spirit might restore my balance. The fellow seems not to have succeeded; you must have frightened him off — as you would anyone who might meet you after dark!'

With relief Sheridan located the flask which he kept in an interior pocket and unscrewed the lid.

'Not me, sir. I saw no one and you were fast out when I found you.'

Sheridan grimaced as he raised his throbbing head to imbibe the brandy. There was a mere dribble, and with annoyance he thought that it must be replenished forthwith.

'Well, we must alert Old Fletch and whoever else might be about at this hour, the watchmen, that there is a rogue afoot in the theatre.'

Sheridan groped for the walls of the corridor to steady himself and to turn himself about in the narrow space. 'Lead the way, Master Grimaldi.'

They were stopped almost immediately by the sound of a low moan from somewhere in the dark recesses behind them. They listened, attentive for a moment.

Then young Joe shrugged. 'A draught in the wings, sir?'

It came again, more faintly.

Sheridan shook his head. 'Perhaps I am not the only victim tonight. Come. Shine your light.'

They edged warily into the nether regions of the theatre.

'What is back here, Joe? I do not know The King's Theatre so well as Old Dame Drury.'

'It is the place where the chippies and painters work, sir, those that build and paint the scenery. I have often helped them to the finish.'

'I wonder you find the time, boy. Are you not scuttling back and forth to perform at The Sadler's Wells?'

'Yes, sir, I will be glad to be back at Drury Lane for the convenience.' Joey paused. 'We are ever grateful to you, Mr Sheridan. My mother and I.'

Sheridan coughed. 'Quite so. Quite so.' He was glad of the boy's appreciation, for he had indeed been generous. After the elderly Signor Grimaldi's death, the executor had absconded, leaving the family near destitute. But Joe had talent, no question of that. The public loved him and he might have a great future one day, which would be all to Sheridan's benefit.

They had come to the entrance of the workshop. A series of high windows allowed a little moonlight to complement the lantern. Around the workshop the great frames for scene-painting exhibited the day's work. There was soon to be an opera and Sheridan could make out the contours of castle walls, turrets and a stormy seascape.

The low moan came again and this directed them to the area behind a workbench. Joey held the lantern aloft to reveal a huddled form.

'Who are you, fellow? We are here to assist.' As Sheridan drew close to the shape, he perceived a wet slippery substance under foot. A dark pool spread from the figure on the ground. He hoped that it might be the spilled contents of a paint pot but with a lurch already felt this hope forlorn. The man gurgled and moaned again.

'Bring the light close, Joey.'

'Dan! It is Dan, sir.' Joey stared aghast at the man whose face was contorted in a rictus of pain.

Sheridan knelt beside the young scene painter. A hand reached out to grasp him.

'What has happened here, Dan?' Sheridan attempted to prop up the young man's head with an outstretched arm.

Dan's eyes bore into Sheridan with pleading insistence. He struggled to speak. 'Look —' His face sagged with effort.

'Be still, Dan. Do not exert yourself, pray — we will send for a surgeon straight away.' Sheridan nodded up at the boy and Joey, taking the instruction, sprang away to answer the need.

Sheridan was left in the gloam of moonlight, with only poor Dan's laboured breath and his own pounding head for company. He felt the scene painter's grip tighten again with urgency.

'You see!'

'Yes, Dan, yes.' Though of course he could not. He could scarce see anything.

'Look, ah —'

What was it the fellow wanted him to see? Sheridan darted a glance to either side of the workshop, where huge black shapes loomed impenetrable in their darkness, and he felt a stab of terror. Was their murderous assailant still at large? Lurking and hiding in the shadows, awaiting an opportunity to fulfil his deadly purpose?

'— after…'

Sheridan bent low to the young man. 'What? Where, Dan? Tell me where.'

Dan's eyes widened to their whites, and his last breath came almost as a whisper. 'You see.'

The scene painter slumped, his grip released, and although his eyes continued to stare, Sheridan knew that he was gone. A bleak silence wrapped around him. Sheridan hung his head in weary despair.

A soft thump and skittering brought Sheridan back to the present horror. He must face it now. He leapt upright and braced himself for an assault.

The cat purred and twined about his leg. 'Harlequin!' It was the tabby which had been brought from Drury Lane. An object dropped at his feet. He knew it was the gift of a mouse; Harlequin was an excellent mouser.

Then there were lights and Joey returned with Old Fletch and one of the nightwatchmen of the theatre bringing up the rear. The Runners from Bow Street and a surgeon had been called for, although too late now for anything other than the pronouncement of death.

The surgeon complained. He had been brought from his bed when there was no urgency. Daniel Webster was dead. The most cursory examination confirmed this irrefutable fact. The vicious stab to the chest had precluded any other outcome. The business might have waited until the morning. In passing, the good doctor noted the thin, flicking strokes of the blade to the man's neck, signs that he had perhaps resisted his attacker. A man of the night patrol was assigned to see the medical man safely home.

'There is still some remnant of that earlier disorder about the streets, Mr Sheridan,' Constable Nicholls explained.

'Nicholls, I am glad to have you here. What is to be done for poor Dan?'

The Runner shook his head sorrowfully. 'It seems we are to be engaged once more with murder, Mr Sheridan.'

'That we are, Constable.'

'I have ordered a search of the building in case the assassin might still be at large.'

'It is unlikely.'

Nicholls shrugged. 'Better to be certain.'

They placed the body on the workbench and Joey went to find a piece of cloth to drape over it. Sheridan looked down at the sad corpse.

Poor fellow. He felt a pang of loss. He remembered Dan as a skinny and earnest country boy, brandishing a weathered folder containing his daubs and sketches and petitioning at Drury Lane for employment. An untutored talent, but Sheridan had seen sufficient promise to give him the nod and a coin to buy a good meat pie before the boy collapsed from starvation. The set designer, Thomas Greenwood, had grudgingly taken him as an apprentice and Daniel rewarded Sheridan's faith by proving himself to be a careful and able copyist.

Ten years later and some fiendish rogue had extinguished the life from him, and for what? A few paltry coins. From what Sheridan recollected Dan had family back in Staffordshire, near to his own parliamentary seat. It was a hazard of Sheridan's double life that he was constantly petitioned and approached for employment in the theatre by his constituents. Dan, he remembered, had regularly sent monies home to his mother. She would be heartbroken. He must endeavour to do something for her and give her son a decent burial.

'Stern death cut short his being… Strange, these cuts to the neck. They look almost deliberate.'

Nicholls stopped by his side and nodded. 'It is a possibility that they were deliberate. The villain was demanding money or valuables and giving a taste of what might happen if Mr Webster did not hand them over.'

Sheridan shook his head in puzzlement. 'An odd choice of victim, a poor scene painter. There would be richer pickings amongst the gentlemen tumbling out of the theatres and taverns.'

'Is Mr Webster married, sir?'

'Not that I have ever heard — and I am sure I would have.'

'Or courting?'

'You imagine a love rival?'

'Mr Webster is a young man. The other fellow was perhaps warning him off and then in the heat of a passion dispatched his rival for good.'

Sheridan nodded along at this interesting scenario. 'Constable, do I take it that you have become prone to fanciful conjecture these days? I considered you were ever a man for facts.'

Nicholls smiled. 'I saw the value of such speculations last year, sir, in the business of your dead Harlequin. But I can assure you, Mr Sheridan, it is facts that I act upon.'

Sheridan sighed and pointed again at the stripe of cuts. 'These markings are like the scratchings of a cat playing with a mouse.'

Nicholls nodded. 'But the death blow was no play, sir.'

'And yet the assassin missed the heart.'

'My uncle that is a carcase butcher often remarks how few people know the true anatomy of a man,' Joey proffered and began to lay the drape over the body.

'Well, he is done for and it is a sorry end.'

'One amongst many, sir. There is much violence in the city of late.' The constable sighed and left them as one of his men signalled to him.

Sheridan turned to Joey. 'Do you know Dan's lodgings?'

Joey nodded. 'Near to our own in Great Wild Street, sir. An old woman that weaves baskets and has rooms.' He paused and glanced at the cloth half laid over the corpse. He frowned.

'Something is awry, Joey?'

Joey nodded slowly and picked at something from Dan's jacket collar.

Sheridan glanced at the insect which Joey had carefully extracted, holding it delicately between his fingertips.

'What is it — a fly?' Sheridan shrugged.

Joey shook his head slowly. 'Not any fly.'

'Is a fly not a fly?'

'Why no, sir, there are many thousands of species!' Joey examined his find, peering closely at the markings. 'It is a type of dragonfly... I cannot be sure, but it may be one that is commonly named as the White-faced Darter, a rare one, Mr Sheridan, and certainly not to be found anywhere hereabouts.'

'How do you know this, Joey?' Sheridan looked at the boy, bemused.

'I collect them, sir, butterflies, insects. I have a reasonable assemblage already. My own favourites include the Dartford Blue and the — would you like to see them?'

Sheridan rubbed his head. 'Perhaps not at this present, but I see there are no flies on you, Master Grimaldi.' He extracted a white linen handkerchief from within his waistcoat. 'And here, this White-faced Darter might very well have been named for you! Let me keep this most particular insect so I may examine it in daylight.'

Carefully Sheridan folded the handkerchief over until the insect was safely wrapped and returned it to an inner pocket, patting it. 'Here may be a trap, a veritable flytrap. Now, Joey, you must go home to your poor mother who will wonder at this late hour — and wipe that mask off your face, or you shall scare all who walk abroad half to death.'

Joey bid farewell with his usual broad grin and somersaulted to the door.

Constable Nicholls returned at that moment with his man.

'No sign of any stranger about the building, Mr Sheridan. I am afraid that the killer is long gone and appears to leave no trace.'

Sheridan was about to mention the fly but then thought better of it. The bump on the head had made enough of a noodle of him for one night.

'But we have found that someone may be living in the canvas store: a rudimentary bed has been constructed — and a pot is still warm.'

Sheridan shrugged. 'That might be any of the stagehands. One that a landlord has turfed out because all his rent goes on gin. Perhaps Old Fletch will know of such a fellow.'

Nicholls shook his head. 'No man, sir. There are a woman's trinkets and items of her person in this cubbyhole.'

'A woman, you think? Well, one of Mrs Petty's laundry or sewing girls then — for much the same reason.'

'But we cannot find her. That bird has flown.' Nicholls paused. 'Perhaps in fright. The store is very close by. She may have heard the fracas and been witness to these events.'

Sheridan placed a parting hand on the shrouded figure. 'This is an odd business, Constable.'

'That it is, sir.'

'What would you suggest now, Nicholls?'

'Offer a reward. Only means we have to flush the villain out. Someone may know of a cause for murder. A love rival. A debt. Some known grudge. Your "female lodger" may have useful information and be tempted to come forth.'

'Of course. We shall put up twenty — no, thirty guineas for the capture of poor Daniel's killer.'

Nicholls nodded. 'That might do it, sir.'

'Good. Good.' Sheridan blinked back the weariness tugging at his eyes. A thin dawn light was edging at the windows.

The constable bowed sharply to take his leave.

'One thing —'

Nicholls looked back, enquiring.

'You speculated on a love rival, that sort of thing... Daniel spoke before he died. He gripped at my jacket — I see there is still some stain of blood from his hand.' Sheridan flicked at the bloodstain. 'I thought the poor fellow said, "Look … you see." Couldn't quite make sense of it, except to imagine our attacker was still present, lurking in the shadows. But now, do you know, I think that he was saying, "Look after Lu-cy".'

'And who is Lucy, Mr Sheridan?'

'Well, there's a question to be answered, Constable. Who is Lucy?'

CHAPTER ELEVEN

It was already nearing midday when Sheridan set off for Brighton to answer the summons to the Marine Pavilion, enjoining his coachman to make all possible speed. In all honesty Sheridan felt little inclined to make the trip, but his presence had been requested and the Prince of Wales was not a man to be denied, however affable he might pretend to be. The call was in all likelihood to smooth the ruffled feathers of Mrs Fitzherbert if there had been a lovers' quarrel. The good lady had been some time out of sight, and Sheridan speculated on the birth of a child who would be spirited away to foster parents. What an impasse for the heir to the throne to be attached to a Catholic woman of such high morality. Sheridan almost felt sorry for him. Maria Fitzherbert would be pining and out of sorts, ever conscious that her 'marriage' to the prince could never be openly acknowledged, let alone any of their offspring declared legitimate.

On the other hand, His Royal Highness may merely want him to amuse some new guest, perhaps another fashionable émigré from the court of Versailles.

Sheridan had snatched a few hours' sleep at Nerot's Hotel, and a set of clothes had been sent by his manservant from Grosvenor Street. The morning was all business and bustle. Daniel's body had been removed to a corner of the cellars for safekeeping and out of the sight of morbid curiosity. With grim faces the carpenters set about making a coffin and his manager agreed to organise the funeral, whilst Sheridan himself undertook the sad task of writing to the scene painter's poor mother.

He assured Mrs Webster that the murdering villain would be caught and that her beloved son would be given a fitting farewell by the company who had held him in high esteem. Sheridan went on to elaborate on his own regard for Daniel and he hoped that he might call on the bereaved mother when next he was in Stafford to impart an account of the proceedings.

His labours were punctuated by a succession of interruptions. Various members of the company arrived at his door. They all expressed their horror and dismay at the shocking news of the young scene painter's murder. Mr Shaw, the one-eyed stage manager, swore vengeance. Actresses swooned, fearing for their own lives. Actors were avid to know what might motivate so brutal an outrage. Thomas Greenwood presented a watery eye and sniffed back a tear as he offered to contribute to the funeral expenses. The Wardrobe Mistress shook her head and clutched her hands to her capacious bosom.

'Such a good lad, Mr Sheridan, a kind-hearted boy. Was sweet on one of my laundry girls.' She raised an eyebrow and sneered, 'Hah, but she is putty to some devilish fly man, foolish girl!'

'Lucy?'

'Pardon, sir?'

'The laundry girl, is her name Lucy?'

'It is Hannah. I have no Lucy.'

'And Dan made no quarrel with the fly man?'

'I should think not, sir! Harry is a mean brute that sometimes fights for sport.'

Sheridan sighed. 'You know of no other girl that Dan might have cared for, Mrs Petty?'

The Wardrobe Mistress shrugged. 'How might I know where men make dalliance? Well, he will no more, poor boy.'

As she was about to depart, the good woman turned, raising a hand in recollection. 'One odd thing I do recall, sir.'

Sheridan put down his pen again.

'Some weeks back I caught young Dan coming from my costume store with a gown, rather plain and green but with a pleasant purple trim. I asked him why he had this garment. Well, he blushed, sir, and mumbled a little and confessed he was sent up by an actress of the company. When I later went to retrieve the garment, none amongst the ladies knew of the request. I know not why the lad wanted a dress, though it might have fitted him, for he was slight, but I did not think he was a molly, sir, given his fancy for Hannah. I meant to question him further, but we are ever short of time and it slipped my mind entirely until today.'

'Thank you, Mrs Petty. You are right, it is odd. But let us have no stain on Dan's good name now that he has met such a sorry end.'

'Right you are, sir, right you are. No stain there shall be!' Mrs Petty shook her fist to underline the pledge, and Sheridan felt certain that no blemish on Dan's character would remain once she had wrung it out.

Still, the affair with the gown presented a mystery. His mind took flight of fancy. Young Daniel had artistic aspirations. In his desire to be accounted a true and proper artist, he had offered his services amongst the company as a portrait painter for a modest fee. Might this Lucy have been a muse to the young scene painter? There was a thought to toy with. One of the actresses? Although no Lucy presented amongst them, the name might be of Dan's own devising for this role. He halted his conjecture. The ladies of the company would have loftier ambitions than the attentions of a scene painter.

Some pretty young woman of the neighbourhood then? A cordwainer's daughter who had caught his eye? Or, and now he nodded sagely, a lady of the street, a rose to be plucked from the filth. Any young artist that needed a model, perhaps not always robed, need look no further than the alleys beyond the stage door and into the nearby rookery of St Giles. Was that his Lucy? A muse he draped from the rich and varied store of the Wardrobe Mistress? A woman who might have become more to Daniel than a model, a woman he had begun to care for, despite her profession — and one who might even bear him a child? Was that the reason for his last desperate plea? Sheridan thumped the desk. Here was an answer. Well, if she could be found, then something might be done for her.

Sheridan was sending a boy to the printer with a draft of the reward poster when Constable Nicholls arrived. He asked permission to speak with such members of the company that might be present, the scene painters and carpenters and any backstage crew with whom Daniel might have kept counsel. Anyone who might know of any cause for the murder other than a robbery turned fatally violent. The constable also had in mind that someone might know the woman of whom the deceased had spoken with his last breath, convinced that this Lucy could hold the vital information which would assist the magistrate to make an arrest.

Sheridan eyed his young friend thoughtfully. He took stock of the quick intelligence in his glittering dark eyes and the sense of purpose in his demeanour, unusual for a member of the policing force. The Runners seldom conducted active investigations, relying on the reward to draw forth snitchers or noses; but Nicholls had proved himself an exception when he had sought to track down the assassin of an actor in the Drury Lane company the year previous.

'I do believe your interest is piqued in this tragedy, Mr Nicholls?'

The constable looked shyly askance for a moment. 'Only my natural curiosity, sir. Like you, I sense there may be unusual aspects to this killing.'

Sheridan nodded. 'But we may yet find that Dan had simply outrun his credit with some bookmaker from Marylebone Fields.'

'Whoever the villain is, we will catch him, Mr Sheridan,' Nicholls reassured.

'That is what I have promised his mother.'

Nicholls turned to leave.

'Constable, I would be grateful if you would share with me the outcome of your enquiries when I return to London.'

Nicholls paused in the doorway. 'Of course, sir.' His features remained set, but Sheridan could see a glimmer in his eye when he acquiesced.

A weak moon had risen as Sheridan's carriage kept a goodly pace along the familiar roads through Sussex with fresh horses that had been changed at his regular staging post, The Star and Garter. He had leisure at last to dwell on the present difficulty with his son, Tom. The boy was just turned seventeen years old and had been for some years schooled in Warwickshire by Dr Samuel Parr. From his own days tutored by Parr at Harrow, Sheridan had always admired the doctor's intellect and willingness to share that knowledge, making allowance for an occasional pomposity. Tom had been happy boarding in Hatton. He was a naturally lively and jovial child.

'Tom has great acuteness, excellent understanding, wit and humour, but not a particle of knowledge, my dear Richard,' Dr Parr had opined after the first term, scrutinising Sheridan with knowing candour.

Sheridan had chuckled in agreement. He saw himself in his son, recognising that he too was prey to distractions of every kind. But lately, following the death of his dear mother, Tom's waywardness and mischief had become unmanageable. Dr Parr had thrown up his arms in despair and asked that he might be removed.

So, Sheridan had brought him away and Tom had spent the summer running wild around their country retreat in Isleworth. He was impatient to shoot swallows and swim in the river and lark with the local sons of gentry, much to his father's dismay and dread.

What was to be done with Tom? Sheridan was averse to sending him away to any institution which might quash his natural exuberance and subject him to the cruelties of the bullies who would reign there. He knew he was over fond and indulgent as a father, but this was not a time to be harsh and stern. For all his show of bravado, Tom was a sensitive boy and his mother's death had touched him deeply.

It had felled both of them. The thought that Eliza no longer breathed could still catch Sheridan painfully unawares, even though her death had not been unexpected. After the birth of Mary in March she had deteriorated rapidly. Her constitution had always been delicate. He thanked God that he had been with her in her final hours.

For Tom there was also the added knowledge of his mother's transgression with Lord Edward Fitzgerald and the child which had come of it, his infant sister Mary. The conversation had been unavoidable and painful for Sheridan as he explained to his son his own feelings of remorse and the large extent to which he blamed himself for driving Eliza into the young lord's arms and the ensuing affair.

At Brooks's only the previous evening, Sheridan's ears had pricked to hear the sly innuendoes. Some fellow had smirked that Sheridan had been left to hold the baby. But Sheridan was proud to give the infant his own name. He would love and treasure Mary Sheridan every bit as fiercely and more for simply being Eliza's child, and her care was the last promise he could keep to his dying wife. Through frequent sleepless nights he had stood anxiously over the cot until the nurse would drag him away for fear of waking the infant. And when she did wake, what a wailing there would be! Sheridan had no doubts that Mary Sheridan would be as accomplished a soprano as her mother one day.

Tom seemed to understand. But did he? Tom was entranced by his sister and yet at times seemed to find her physical presence unsettling. In any case, Sheridan had agreed with Mary's guardian, Mrs Canning, that the best course would be to move her to the recently acquired house in Wanstead, close by Eliza's old friend.

But what was to be done with Tom? The boy had expressed an interest in the army. Sheridan shuddered to imagine his precious son in a field of war, dashing as he might look in a coat of red. That ambition he must forestall. Perhaps a barrister? This had been his own father's desire for him and for which profession he had trained and entered the great Gate of Power at the Middle Temple, until the world of letters had made a stronger call. Well, whatever profession chose, Tom must be educated.

It should be at home, Sheridan determined, there and then. Perhaps Tom should also move to Wanstead, where Hitty Canning might keep a motherly and watchful eye. Yes. Sheridan would have Tom close and set about finding a tutor for him. Resolved on this course, he allowed himself to nod off and enjoy the respite of a momentary slumber.

CHAPTER TWELVE

Attired in a splendid uniform of naval pretensions, the prince was engaged in his favourite entertainment, singing popular arias to his captive audience in the glittering salon. '*Io gia t'amai*,' crooned His Royal Highness in a passable tenor and with only a slight slurring of the lyrics to the assembled guests. Amongst whom Sheridan found that there were indeed new arrivals from France. An old roué, the Marquis de Thiers-Auberet and his crooked son, both painted and bewigged in outlandish fashion, together with the second wife of the marquis, a slender girl of scarcely seventeen. Skiffy Skeffington took delight in informing him, with a barely disguised stage whisper, that the son was rumoured to be half-demented with an inherited pox and would soon need a mask for his rotting nose.

As the party were moving towards a late supper in the dining room, Mrs Fitzherbert excused herself from the gathering; she was feeling indisposed. The prince seemed barely to acknowledge her, and Sheridan had time to note that she was looking a little pale and pinched. She passed him on her way out and took hold of his hand.

'Sherry, my dear friend.'

He bowed. 'Madam.'

'Tell me, how is little Mary?'

Sheridan caught the sincerity in her enquiry. Like many who were privy to the child's origins, Maria Fitzherbert had been initially censorious of Eliza's relations with Lord Edward Fitzgerald. But since Sheridan's assumption of paternity and Eliza's tragic death, she had softened in her attitude.

He could not suppress an instant glow of pride. 'She is a pretty thing and a delight to us all.'

'You will take very great care of her, will you not, poor motherless child!' Sheridan noted a catch in Maria's voice. She was grieving for some loss of her own, he felt certain.

'It is my only desire.'

'But you look tired, Sherry.'

'Ah.' He grinned playfully. 'We are entertained nightly into the very small hours by my daughter's high notes, conducted by Signor Incisor himself! There are already two prodigies that have made an appearance.'

'Two teeth already? Indeed, that is remarkable.' Mrs Fitzherbert patted his hand. 'You are a good man, Sheridan. If you were not such a...'

'A fool, madam, I own.' He smiled and bowed when he saw that she responded in kind.

The table groaned with a sumptuous array of dishes, a fish course of dories, halibuts and salmon, the plenteous shellfish that were to be had from local lobster catchers and all that was in season, platters of partridge and larks, teals, snipes and widgeon. The guests were engaged in lively conversation. Sheridan found himself absorbed in the current controversies. The young Duke of Bedford pressed him on when they might expect his return to Westminster and then wondered aloud what might happen next in France. The call was for the king, or Louis Capet as he was to be known, to be brought to trial for treason.

'It seems the French are determined to follow where we led some century and a half ago.'

'But it will be no Glorious Revolution, rather they too will have their bloody Civil War.'

'*Mon Dieu!*' the marquis exclaimed. 'It is impossible that our friends in Europe will allow these savages to touch a hair on Louis' sacred head!' He glared at the party of diners, defying any to deny such a friendship.

'Chop, chop, chop!' his son tittered and demonstrated with his fish knife the action of the new contraption named after Dr Guillotin.

The prince looked askance at the grinning zany, then turned towards Sheridan.

'Sherry, Sherry, give us your toast! For the marquis. One about the dimples!' His Royal Highness laughed in anticipation, encouraging the ageing marquis to likewise raise his glass.

Sheridan reluctantly set aside the gratifyingly succulent doe venison, cleared his throat and stood. He must be careful where he cast his eyes. They alighted first on the bewitching beauty that was Letitia Lade and he raised the toast in her direction.

'*Here's to the charmer whose dimples we prize,*' he began.

Letitia snorted. 'You whore's kitling, Sherry!'

'Prize her dimples, hey what! Almost as much as her use of the vulgar tongue!' The prince guffawed and nodded over to the marquis. 'Learnt it all from a highwayman! With whom they say she danced before he jigged his last under Tyburn Tree. Damn fine horsewoman, though. Where'd you learn that, Letty? Plenty of horseplay in the rookery, what?'

'None worth a nun's fart!'

'To the vulgar tongue of Letty Lade!' The prince quaffed his claret in one and it was promptly refilled by the servant at his shoulder.

Sheridan turned his gaze to Skiffy with his powdered wig and rouged face and raised his glass.

'Now to the maid who has none, sir.'

The prince roared his approval and Skeffington nodded, taking the jest in good part.

'And here's to the girl with a pair of blue eyes.'

Sheridan bowed tenderly towards the fair young marquise, who blushed coyly, applause rippling politely around the table before glasses were lifted again.

'Here! Here! Well said.'

In the hiatus that followed, Sheridan then placed a hand over his left eye.

'And here's to the nymph with but one, sir.'

'Hurrah!' yelled the prince.

The wine continued to flow and the generally convivial atmosphere lulled Sheridan into a false sense of security; he forgot that there might be a particular reason for his summons that evening. He was alerted to a change of tone by the raised and tetchy voice of the Prince of Wales, who had clearly drunk too much and become out of sorts. Turning to his equerry, who was sitting beside him, His Royal Highness wantonly threw the contents of his glass into George Hanger's face, without any apparent provocation. There was a moment of stunned silence around the table. Even from a prince, this was an unpardonable insult. The wine dribbled down the dandy's powdered cheek. After a moment Hanger smiled politely at the prince, picked up his own glass and threw it into the face of the fellow next to him.

'Do pass it along, I bid you.'

Sheridan laughed. Hanger was a clever fellow.

The son of the marquis, too impatient to await his turn, shrieked with glee and flicked wine at his pretty stepmother.

Lady Lade rose. 'Ladies, let us retire and leave the gentlemen to their foolery.'

The prince nodded, and the women at the table needed no further encouragement.

'You were late last night, Sherry!' the prince snapped as Sheridan entered his private rooms the following morning.

'I beg pardon, Your Royal Highness. Any excuse is but a paltry offering.'

'Damn right! You are late for everyman, Sherry, but I am not Everyman!'

'That is certainly true, sir.'

George Hanger winked at Sheridan from behind the prince and quoted the current witticism at Brooks's.

'*Of wit, of taste, of fancy, we'll debate,*
if Sheridan for once, be not too late!'

'Well, you are here now, Sherry, and you will want to have a little of that wit about you.'

The prince lowered himself onto a chaise longue, and Sheridan could not help noticing how the buttons of his waistcoat strained. The prince, still only a man of thirty, was putting on weight rather too rapidly. Not for the first time, Sheridan pitied him. Some ten years previous, he had felt drawn to the handsome young heir to the throne — his charm and enthusiasm, his willingness to embrace notions of reform, his relish of conversation and delight in the world of the arts had all been endearing. Sheridan had then felt himself in the presence of a young man whom he would be honoured to serve as future king. But after the recent Crisis of the King's Madness, where was that hope now? His Majesty had recovered his sanity and was fit as a fiddle.

The intervening years had not been kind to the Prince of Wales. His desire to serve had been constantly thwarted by his distant father. He had watched whilst younger brothers earned their spurs on faraway battlefields or sailed the seas. The prince, meanwhile, must idle at Carlton House with little channel for his churning energies other than the pursuit of pleasure, endless redecorations of his houses and a determination to disappoint his father.

'That fellow Cardonnet you have at Haymarket…'

Sheridan stiffened. This was a line of conversation he had not anticipated.

'Recommended by Dr Sibly, I thought he could help with an occasional ailment I experience.'

Sheridan had heard of Sibly's enthusiasm for the sexually therapeutic benefits of animal magnetism and supposed this might have some bearing on the prince's 'ailment'.

'Strange fellow, Cardonnet. Pretty little daughter. Félicité. Charming. She had her hands all over me with the mesmeric passes. Ticklish sensation. Very nearly had the convulsions.'

'I have heard that can be an effect, sir.'

'This fellow Cardonnet was practically sitting on my lap, staring into my eyes. Had his hands on my knees. I know it is perhaps a part of the treatment … but for a royal personage…'

Sheridan nodded in agreement at the potential for affront.

'Then the impertinent rogue put me into some sort of trance!'

'Oh.' Sheridan shifted uncomfortably.

'Seems I might have said something I maybe ought not.'

'Your Highness?'

'This Cardonnet demanded our meeting was private. Mustn't disturb the magnetism, he insisted. Damn and blast the man. Hanger here didn't even have the wit to eavesdrop at the door.'

Hanger bowed low. 'That was extremely remiss of me, sir.'

Sheridan shook his head and frowned.

'Damn it, Sherry! Well, don't you see?' The Prince of Wales stamped his foot. 'Don't you see the pickle I am in? I have said something to this charlatan, but I know not what! He had me in his spell, the villain, with his —' The prince clicked his fingers impatiently.

'Artificial somnambulism, Your Royal Highness,' Hanger offered, tending to the rose he wore in his buttonhole.

'Dr Cardonnet is attempting to blackmail Your Royal Highness?' Sheridan's mind fluttered across any number of possibilities for the prince: numerous affairs, his secret marriage to Mrs Fitzherbert, a love child, or could it be some other indiscretion?

'Would it were that simple. He is too subtle a villain. It is all intimation, Sherry. He writes me —' The prince clicked his fingers towards Major Hanger, who retrieved a letter from his inside pocket and handed it to the impatient royal. The prince scanned the page. 'How delighted he is at my patronage... And hark you this: *I am honoured, Your Royal Highness, to have been entrusted with your most intimate secrets.*' The prince slapped his knee. 'Damn it, which ones?' He read again: '*Your Royal Highness, I am most eager to be of service to you.* Service! The rogue!'

Sheridan nodded slowly. 'That is sly.'

'What does the fellow want? That is the question.'

'And I am to find out, sir?'

'You are to sort the scoundrel out once and for all!'

Sheridan felt his heart sink. 'Of course, Your Royal Highness.'

*

Sheridan took a good deep breath of sea air. Clouds scattered across the horizon, but above him the sky was a brilliant blue. He raised his face to bathe in the autumn sunlight. The sea, the sea. He might have liked to live by the sea. The constant lapping of water on the shore was soothing to his nervous disposition. He observed the local fisher folk at work, casting their nets from their hog boats, drawing their lines, and wished that he could exchange places. But it was a momentary desire. If he gazed too long at the waves, it allowed for reflection, and that was for Sheridan a melancholy prospect.

'Dick. A word, if you please.'

Hanger arrived beside him on the shingle.

Sheridan nodded. 'It is a pretty pickle.'

'More than you know. More than His Royal Highness will ever know.'

'How so?'

'This man Cardonnet... I let it be known to a friend in the government that the prince had private audience.'

'And?'

'It is believed on good authority that he may be an agent.'

'For the Jacobins?'

'For whom seems to be a matter of some doubt. For the most part the Jacobin faction are vociferous in their condemnation of mesmerism.'

Sheridan snorted. 'They view the medicinal claims as quackery, I should say, as do I.'

'Apparently it is considered an aristocratic decadence.'

Sheridan raised an eyebrow.

Hanger continued, 'And yet the Jacobins also have believers amongst them — I have heard claim recently that radicals in France are transmitting waves of animal magnetism in order to sway the English populace into revolution.'

'That would be an act I would consider hiring myself for the sheer spectacle.'

'If the Prince of Wales has been chosen as a target, it is devilish difficult to discern the reason why.'

Sheridan nodded. 'I confess Cardonnet is something of an enigma to me. I cannot readily imagine from which quarter this conspiracy may have originated.'

'Or to what end?' Hanger looked puzzled.

Sheridan inclined towards the equerry. 'To what end indeed. As we know from our experience last year, Hanger, fanatics are at both extremes. Those who would encourage revolution here in England —'

Hanger's eyes narrowed. 'And those who wish to stir up the warmongers in our government to take military action against the French.'

Sheridan sighed. 'Either way, it seems we must continue to see conspiracies all about us.'

'You may know the surgeon, John Pearson?'

Sheridan flicked a nod.

'Pearson believes this artificial somnambulism may be used to corrupt the administration of this country, throwing all into crisis. And Mr Pitt seems to take the threat seriously; he will scarcely look a fellow in the eye. Now it appears our Royal Family may likewise be targets.'

'Cardonnet's gifts are real enough, and there may be dangerous applications I can see.'

Hanger turned to face Sheridan. 'The prince may fancy this is some artful blackmail for a past sexual peccadillo but there are those, including myself, who suspect it is something altogether more sinister.'

'I fear you may be right, Major.'

'We do not know what the prince has said. We cannot simply clap Cardonnet in irons and confine him to Bedlam. Dr Cardonnet is a *cause célèbre*. He must be dealt with — but quietly, behind closed doors. You have the advantage of proximity, Sheridan.'

'And you think I may serve this cause?'

'No better man.'

Sheridan's heart sank.

CHAPTER THIRTEEN

It was Sheridan's intention to call in at the theatre on the evening of his return to London, and his mind raced with the devices he might employ to confront Dr Cardonnet. There would be funds from a government purse to lubricate the enterprise, he was assured by Major Hanger, who offered any assistance that might be necessary. But so many nights with little or no sleep had taken their toll. His head nodded onto his chest and thoughts scattered and tumbled into nonsense as he struggled against the regular motion of the carriage and its soporific effects. Sheridan was no stranger to insomnia and his hours of business had always been erratic, but he felt himself overcome by a drowning weariness, due not simply to a lack of sleep but to a more general malaise. He was tired of so much death, of so many cares, so many demands on his energies. As the carriage rattled through the suburbs south of London towards the Thames, he redirected his coachman to the house he had taken on the High Street in Wanstead.

Arriving there, Sheridan felt instantly revived and rushed straight up the stairs, nearly toppling the necessary woman and her unsavoury load. He hurriedly apologised and continued up to the landing, with the woman calling after him, 'Sir, she is with the wet nurse.'

Sheridan would not be delayed; he flung open the door and was greeted by the sight of little Mary sucking and guzzling at the plump breast of Mrs Wilkins. He smiled broadly and all cares slipped away. The infant rewarded him by pulling away from the bosom and stretching out her arms in delight. She was an extraordinarily beautiful child. Sheridan had been assured that it was not only he that thought so. From his pocket he drew forth a rattle purchased on the seafront before leaving Brighton and shook it, jangling the bells. Mary's eyes widened and her joyful laughter smote his heart. Mrs Wilkins held the child towards her doting father and he clasped her in his arms, making a dumb show of conversation with the rattle.

'I do believe I see another tooth, Mrs Wilkins!'

'Aye, sir.' The wet nurse retied the strings of her bodice. 'And I may feel it.'

'She is growing.'

Mrs Wilkins nodded. 'Six and more months, sir. She's bonny enough, small and delicate as she is.'

'My bonny girl, my bonny, bonny Mary!' Sheridan hugged the infant and she cooed with delight whilst tugging at his powdered hair.

'Richard, you will overexcite her, come away!'

Mehitabel Canning stood frowning in the doorway.

'Ah, Hitty, do you not see how glad she is to see me —'

'It is time for Mary's cot.'

Reluctantly Sheridan relinquished his daughter into her guardian's arms as Mrs Wilkins waddled past them.

'And you look in need of your sleep too, Richard. You have been in Brighton, no doubt.'

'Good Sister Christian, how you care for us all.'

Mrs Canning raised a brow at the familiar nickname and gently swayed the now drowsy child, caressing her soft down.

'And you have too many cares, Richard. There is a troubled look in your eye.'

Sheridan hesitated, but felt the need to unburden at least one of those cares to his old friend. 'There has been a murder at the theatre. A young scene painter. I was with him at the end.'

'Oh, Richard, that is a horror.'

'I cannot fathom why he was so killed. And he bade me to "*Look after Lucy*". But I do not know who this girl might be.'

'Richard, these should not be your concerns. The villain will be discovered and arrested. As to the girl, there will be others who may care for her — why must you take everything upon yourself?'

'You are right, of course, Hitty.'

Sheridan leant forward and kissed the soft head of his daughter. Mrs Canning stroked the child, murmuring a lullaby, and headed towards the cot.

Why indeed must he make all this his business, Sheridan wondered, as he headed to his rooms. In the next instant a fresh thought struck him and he itched to have a pen between his fingers.

As Sheridan entered at the stage door of The King's Theatre, Old Fletch accosted him.

'Mr Sheridan, sir … that Frenchman, Doctor Whatsit.'

'Cardonnet.'

'Him. He wants a word, sir.'

'How convenient. He's the man I want to see too. You may let him know that I am in my office.'

'And, sir —'

'Yes, my good man?'

'The young Bow Street man, he was here earlier.'

'Right, well, have word sent to him that I am returned.' Sheridan tossed a coin for the messenger.

In passing he popped his head into the wings. He could hear the musicians practising below the stage, their director furiously tapping his stick to keep the rhythm and shouting insults at the first violin above the sounds of workmen calling to each other as they replaced candles in the chandeliers. On the darkened stage young Joey was rehearsing a new comic scene, but as soon as he caught sight of Sheridan he made cartwheels across the boards to land at his feet.

'Mr Sheridan.' His eyes gleamed with excitement. 'I am certain that it is *Leucorrhinia dubia*...'

Sheridan laughed. 'Of what do you speak?'

'The dragonfly. I am sure of it. The White-faced Darter.'

'Well, that is good to know.'

'The markings on the abdomen were dark, not yellow, I think?'

'I think so.'

'Though the light was poor. That would be a male.'

'Well done, Joey.' Sheridan patted him on the back. 'It is an unusual interest you have.' He was about to turn away.

'You would not find it in London, sir.'

Sheridan paused and then spread his arms. 'There is countryside in every direction out of London, Joey. Perhaps Daniel went a-strolling and lay down wherever one might find these insects.'

Joey shook his head. 'Daniel was not one for walks abroad. Lately, he seemed forever here, even when at his leisure. And this insect is rare to its own habitat.'

Sheridan regarded the boy, his brow furrowed. 'You think this dead insect came from some distance?'

Joey nodded.

'And was perhaps passed in the scuffle with Dan's assailant?'

Joey nodded again.

'And you think this man was a countryman?'

Joey shrugged.

Sheridan pondered. 'Daniel was from Staffordshire. Your White-faced Darter — might it be found there?'

Joey's eyes lit up. 'Why yes, sir. It is mostly to be found in parts of the Midlands and in the Highlands of Scotland. They thrives best in peat bogs and must have a certain type of moss.'

'Hmm. It is something to consider. Daniel may have known his killer. Someone from his county, and from his past.'

Joey nodded enthusiastically.

Sheridan shook his head. 'And yet ... Daniel came to London when he was a boy, scarcely older than you, Joe. What grudge so strong might follow him here, some ten years later?'

Joey looked comically deflated.

'You have done well, Master Grimaldi.' He patted him again on the shoulder. 'I am stupendously impressed with your knowledge. When all this business is done, I would be delighted to examine your collection.'

Joey brightened. 'Mrs Jordan thinks it very fine.'

'Does she now? That is a high recommendation.'

A mass of new bills had been delivered to his desk. Sheridan sighed and eased into his chair, fumbling for the flask in his inner pocket. Before he could fully extract it, a sharp rap came at the door. He sighed more deeply and let the flask slip back into its snug.

'Enter.'

Dr Cardonnet flung open the door and advanced into the room.

'Ah, Doctor. Do seat yourself.'

Cardonnet cast an eye about, but no surface presented that was not loaded with play scripts and papers. After a moment, in which Sheridan felt sure that the Doctor expected him to scurry to make room, Cardonnet approached a nearby chair and swept the paperwork to the floor. He then pulled the seat disconcertingly close to Sheridan so that he faced him eye to eye.

Sheridan's instinct was to shrink back from this invasion, but he held steadfast.

'Dr Cardonnet, you wished to speak with me?'

'Listen to me, Monsieur Sheridan... Listen to me...'

'I assure you, sir, you have my full attention.'

The man's eyes were fixed deep into his own. 'You are feeling drowsy, I think?'

'No more than usual.' Sheridan's eyes fluttered.

'You wish to sleep...'

Sheridan suddenly felt extraordinarily tired.

'You wish very much to sleep...'

Sheridan's eyelids drooped.

'You are seeing clouds, many clouds...'

Yes, he could see clouds. Big fluffy clouds.

'And there are numbers within?' Was Cardonnet blowing softly into his face?

'Thirty-six...' The cloud melted away.

Cardonnet blew again.

'Twenty-two...' Whoosh; away went the cloud.

Cardonnet blew. Sheridan fully closed his eyes, his lids as heavy as lead.

'Fift... Fif...' Clouds surrounded him, he was diving into them.

Cardonnet was speaking, but he could not make out the words. It felt as though he were drifting through a thick fog, all sound muffled and indistinct, his movements petrified. Could he move at all? It mattered not. The sensations were so very pleasant and soothing.

The doctor was saying something. It was important. He grasped that much. Something about ... a tiger?

From somewhere far away he could hear a knocking and someone called out his name. He could not answer.

And then there was a clicking sound. His eyes blinked open and Dr Cardonnet smiled at him, which Sheridan found rather alarming.

A loud knock came on his door.

'This person sounds urgent,' Dr Cardonnet prompted.

Sheridan blinked again and called out, 'Come in.'

He noticed that Cardonnet was now sitting at some distance from him. But he was certain that only moments before the doctor had been nearly nose to nose with him. He shook his head, trying to catch at memories which were already incoherent whispers.

Constable Nicholls appeared in the doorway.

'Well, our business has been satisfactorily concluded, Mr Sheridan. I thank you,' Dr Cardonnet rose to his feet.

'It has?' Sheridan frowned.

Cardonnet bowed stiffly. He turned to the constable. 'You are from Bow Street I see, *mon homme*. Are we to hope that you have now caught this murderous villain?'

Nicholls' eyes narrowed as he held Cardonnet's gaze. 'Not yet, monsieur, *mais j'espère à bientôt.*'

Mrs Rummage was not a woman to mince her words. Sheridan and Constable Nicholls had no sooner been admitted to her parlour than she laid bare her grievances. Daniel Webster still owed rent on his lodging and who would pay for it? And if she must scour her memory for information about the young man, then who might reimburse her for her time? She was a hard-working, respectable woman. All this she had already conveyed to Constable Nicholls on his first visit.

'Never marry a basket weaver, sir. It is a wretched trade, and my son has long gone to the army rather than follow his father, God rest the old fool.'

Sheridan nodded to all of this whilst from the corner of his eye he caught sight of Nicholls rolling his eyes.

'And they do say there is a reward for information.'

Sheridan took the cue and drew forth his purse. He placed a guinea on the table. Mrs Rummage's lips remained pursed until it had been joined by a fellow. He observed her throughout the transaction. A mean, crotchety woman with knotted hands, calloused and hardened from her years spent bending and weaving the reeds from which she made her baskets. She clawed at the coins and deposited them in an inner fold of her gown.

'Good Mrs Rummage, you have told Constable Nicholls here that you have information which may be of interest to us.'

'Happen as may be.'

'We are all ears, madam.'

Mrs Rummage sniffed. 'I comes in from market, couple of weeks back, and hears voices coming from Mr Webster's room upstairs. And one a female voice, Mr Sheridan! Well, I am a respectable woman, I'll have you know, and it is well known hereabouts I am a Christian woman and I keep a good, honest house for single gentlemen. My gentlemen know they may have no female company here. It is a rule and condition of residence, sir.'

'And what did you?'

'Straightaway I knocked upon his door to have words.' She sniffed again. 'I could hear a scuffling and scrape. I knocked again and called out until Mr Webster opens to me. Well, he presents himself all innocent, but I'll have none of that, I tell him. I am not born behind the cartwheel. There is a woman within and I will not budge until she is out, I says!' Mrs Rummage straightened herself on her dignity.

'And did she? Come out?'

'Indeed, she did, the little madam.'

'Lucy?'

Mrs Rummage's eyes narrowed. 'You have her very name, sir.' She tapped on the table where the coins had been deposited. 'She is of interest to you, Mr Sheridan?'

Sheridan forced a smile and placed another guinea in front of the landlady. 'Did Daniel have an explanation for her presence?'

'That he did, sir, a tall tale. "Mrs Rummage," he says to me, "this is my young sister, Lucy." Well —!'

'Sister?'

'And ain't you heard that one before!' Mrs Rummage snatched up her coin and shook it under Sheridan's nose. 'If I had a penny for every *sister* that's come calling on my gentlemen, well, I wouldn't be weaving baskets no more, that's for certain. But this is a respectable house and we will have no *sisters* here! And that's what I said to Mr Webster. I looked about that room and I could tell at once that the girl was already settled there. He'd snuck her in, God only knows when, the blaggard! Well, I'll have none of that! I said he could sling his hook and all, though the boy had never been any trouble before in the seven years of tenancy. Well, he set up such a caterwauling about how his sister was in need of his protection and had no one else to go to. How she was a good girl that had been sorely abused and now must seek refuge and help from her only brother. A sorry tale from first to last.'

Nicholls frowned. 'A distressing tale —'

'Oh yes, quite a performance, Constable! I do not forget Mr Webster works in the theatricals.'

Nicholls shook his head with frustration.

'When was this?' Sheridan enquired mildly.

'Some three weeks past.'

'Do you know where the girl went?'

Mrs Rummage shrugged. 'How should I have a care? Back to her rookery, I shouldn't wonder, little trollop. I felt sorry then for young Dan, he looked so forlorn, and I says he might stay on in the room but no more *sisters*, if you please!'

'Well, this may explain the stowaway at the theatre, Mr Sheridan,' the constable offered.

Sheridan nodded. 'Yes, but where is she now?'

'Another thing — I don't like to gossip, not in my nature, but the girl was with child, though she tried to hide it.'

Sheridan and Nicholls looked at each other with a start. This would be a pressing reason the scene painter would want his sister to be cared for.

A noise in the room above brought a sudden scowl to Mrs Rummage's features.

'And who is that? That is Dan's room.'

At once Nicholls flew from the parlour. Sheridan caught at his wits and spun around to follow him, clattering up the rickety stair.

He entered to find Nicholls already half out of the open window and yelling, 'Stop! Thief! Stop!' before he too dropped into the common yard in pursuit.

Sheridan rushed to the window in time to see the constable stumble forward and clutch at his ankle, which he had clearly caught on the edge of a mangle.

'Blast! God's teeth!' Nicholls writhed in pain.

The cloaked intruder sprinted into a dark passage without a backward glance.

Mrs Rummage appeared at Sheridan's back. 'Has he caught the villain?'

'I fear not.'

The landlady looked around the room and Sheridan followed her gaze. There were papers and sketches strewn all over the floor.

She trembled. 'This is ill, sir, very ill! Am I to fear for my life? Will I too be murdered by this villain?'

Sheridan knew not how to answer. He felt certain that this was no simple act of burglary. There above the small fireplace rested a gilt-framed portrait, an object to catch the eye of any ordinary thief. A woman and her young daughter with a strong family likeness to Daniel; his mother and young sister, he would hazard. No, the intruder had been looking for something amongst Dan's possessions that was of a more particular value. Had he found what he had come in search of?

'Mrs Rummage, I will send someone to pack up Mr Webster's belongings forthwith. You need concern yourself no further.'

He picked up the portrait and showed it to the landlady. 'Is this the "sister"?'

Mrs Rummage raised her spectacles and peered narrowly at the portrait. 'Well, she is but a child there, eleven or twelve, I would say … but a fair likeness, I'll admit.'

Sheridan nodded as he gazed at the dark-haired girl. 'So, here you are at last, Lucy.'

CHAPTER FOURTEEN

As the parson intoned the brief funeral service, Sheridan's mind was elsewhere. His thoughts raced to the note which he had received that morning from Madame de Genlis. It informed him that there had been an emissary from the Duc d'Orléans. There was to be no further delay. Sheridan's heart sank. Pamela returning to France so soon? Before he had had opportunity to lay bare his ardent feelings for her? To wish that she might hold him in some like regard and might even consider his suit for marriage? Madame de Genlis hoped that they could expect a visit from their dear Monsieur Sheridan before departure. The girls were insistent and near to tears. Well, he must drop everything. He must not lose this last opportunity.

It was all a madness, of course. But what was life but one mad rush to the grave? Today was witness to how fleeting one's sojourn might be. A man must seize the moment. Sheridan would have to act quickly. A wild and daring plan of sorts was already formulating in his mind and he could think of little else. He was grateful that his set designer, Thomas Greenwood, had offered to read the eulogy for Daniel Webster. His own mind was in too great a turmoil.

The funereal gathering processed behind the coffin to the freshly dug grave at Bunhill Fields. It was an ancient burial ground that had once been 'Bone Hill' and he shivered to think of a thousand years of dead souls writhing beneath his feet. It would soon be Halloween and this would not be a place to visit then. The whole cemetery was shrouded in a swirling fog and the darkness of evening drawing close. What a dismal end to a shortened life, Sheridan reflected. As Daniel's coffin was lowered into the ground, he cast his eyes about amongst the company clustered at the graveside. He was searching, he knew, for some connection to this sad ending. Was the murderer himself amongst their party? Come to witness the finality of his deed?

There were faces less familiar than others, but most he recognised from the theatre. Thomas Greenwood, as Daniel's mentor and master, took a central place amongst the mourners, along with his scene painters. Young Joey was looking solemn and thoughtful for once, and standing beside him was the towering figure of Black Sam, who had been the Grimaldis' footman during their more prosperous days. Mrs Petty, the Wardrobe Mistress, clucked and patted the shoulder of a young girl whose cheeks were raw with tears. The laundress Hannah, it appeared, had some feeling for poor Daniel after all.

And then hovering at a short distance under a tree Sheridan spied a figure, hooded and cloaked. He strained to make out her features. She was pale and young, but that was as much as he could ascertain. Could this be Lucy? Had she ventured out to witness her brother's final departure from this world? To bid her own farewell?

The girl caught the intensity of his gaze and shifted uncertainly. Then, decisively, she moved away. Sheridan felt his heart race. He edged from the graveside party and discreetly slipped onto the path. The leaves of autumn were beginning to fall and cover the ground. Soggy underfoot, they dampened sound. He strained to hear the light footsteps scurrying ahead. Quickening his pace, he continued his pursuit. Through a swirl of fog, he caught sight of the young woman's retreating figure. He was at a trot, she weaving in and out of his vision.

'Lucy!' he called out. She seemed to pause for a moment and then hurried on with even greater haste. Now he must give chase. Sheridan ran, cutting through the gravestones, leaping over a low tomb. He glanced in passing at the freshly engraved name of William Blackburn, an architect his own age he had known briefly. But he must not be distracted! He caught a glimpse of the girl again.

'Lucy! Stop, I pray!'

She disappeared behind a large monument. Sheridan hurried on, half stumbling over an ancient fallen headstone. He reached the tomb. The girl was not to be seen. She had disappeared into the enveloping grey. He ventured a little further but met a crossroads in the path. All was silent. Unnaturally so. He could hear nothing.

'Damn and blast!' Sheridan slapped his thigh in frustration, furious that he had missed this opportunity to contact at last the object of Daniel's final request. Reluctantly he turned about and began to head back.

A skittering of loose gravel brought his attention to the monument. With a determined speed and lightness of foot, he skirted the edge of the mossy stone and found himself looming over the girl's cowering figure.

'Sir, why do you chase me?'

The terrified young woman quivered and looked pleadingly into his eyes. Her hood slipped back a little. She was fair; a blonde curl dropped forward. This was not Daniel's sister. Not the subject of the mother and daughter portrait.

'I beg pardon, madam.'

She looked ready to take flight again.

'I did not mean to frighten you,' he reassured. 'I thought … I thought you were Lucy. Lucy Webster. Sister to our deceased friend.' He nodded back in the direction of the funeral, although nothing was to be seen in the all-consuming spume of fog. 'I took it that you had come to pay your final respects to the dead.'

The girl's lips quivered. 'Daniel was a kind, good soul.'

'You knew him then?'

The girl nodded. She looked up and the hood slipped further away from her face, revealing the rosy lustre to her pale cheeks.

'You were his muse.' Sheridan smiled kindly as he recognised in full the features which Daniel had sketched over and over in one of his notebooks.

'You are Mr Sheridan?'

'Yes, I am he.'

'Daniel spoke of you often, sir. He said that you were unlike other men.'

'And what did he mean by that?'

The young girl blushed. 'I think he thought you almost a god.'

Sheridan stifled a laugh. 'I can assure you, madam, I am every inch human. And frail,' he added humbly.

'It was your talents, sir, which impressed on him as far above the ordinary. Poor Daniel. He would say, "If I had only one small part of that gift, I might make you proud to know me, Tilly." He would sit and draw me for hours, but he was never happy with the result.'

'I have seen those drawings, and he need not have feared for his own talents. In you he had truly found his subject.'

'I would like to have one as a keepsake.'

'You shall. And I shall have it framed for you.'

A longer pause ensued and Sheridan sensed that the girl grappled with her thoughts.

'Lucy is in such a state as I cannot manage,' she whispered at last.

Sheridan was all attention now.

'Weeping day and night for Daniel and for herself. She is very much afraid. I know not what to do, sir.'

'Let me help. Allow me to assist.'

'She will see no one, speak to no one. She tells me there is no one that she can trust. There is no one to believe her, sir.'

'Believe what, Tilly?'

The girl shook her head. 'Lucy will not tell. Only that there is a great secret and there are those who would want her dead.' Tilly looked anxiously about into the enveloping gloom. 'She must protect the baby.'

They heard a footfall in the muffling fog. Tilly started and backed away.

'I want to help,' Sheridan hissed urgently. 'I made a promise to Daniel.'

The girl nodded. 'I will speak to her.' She slipped from sight.

The footsteps had stopped somewhere close. Sheridan felt a lurch at his breast. He knew that he was overfanciful, but the unsavoury whiff of death, of malevolence and evil intent, pervaded the damp air of the cemetery. He must regain the company.

Sheridan groped his way through the swirling fog, hoping that he moved in the right direction. He felt a sharp stab of relief when he espied the headstone of William Blackburn. He paused a moment. The footsteps neared ominously on the path. Why did he feel such dread? It was ridiculous, he thought. Who would want to harm him here? And was he not a man who had fought two duels? He straightened and stepped forward with greater purpose — only to find that the earth disappeared beneath his feet and with a shriek he was tumbling headlong into a pit of moist soil.

He realised in an instant that it was a grave, freshly dug. Cursing his misfortune, Sheridan spat the mud from his mouth and scrambled to his knees.

'Hail, sir! Are you hurt?'

The man who looked down over the edge of the grave had a fair, open face which then creased in shock.

'Why, is it Mr Sheridan?'

It was a face which Sheridan recognised but which he could not quite place for the moment. A fellow near to his own age. He frowned and the man took the cue.

'Samuel, sir — you were with us at Sandbourne this last summer.'

Sheridan staggered to his feet. 'You are Lord Cannock's man?'

Samuel nodded. 'That's right, sir.' He leaned down into the grave to clasp the arm which Sheridan then raised.

'Beg pardon, I recognise you now of course, Mr Hanley.'

'I would not blame you, sir. There was much tragedy and drama on your last visit. We are not yet recovered ourselves from those events.'

Sheridan shuddered at the mention of that other murder.

Hanley's grip was strong and despite the slippery conditions Sheridan was soon on level ground again.

'Thank you, Samuel.'

Sheridan was glad that he had worn a thick cloak in anticipation of the miserable weather and sensible boots which he now kicked against a nearby tomb to scrape off the mud.

'How come you here at Bunhill Fields?'

'Why, I have come to pay my respects to Daniel, sir.'

'You knew Daniel Webster?'

'His late father was coachman at Sandbourne.'

'To Lord Cannock?'

'Yes, sir,' Samuel continued. 'Daniel started as a groom in the stables when he was twelve years old, as his father had desired, but the lad always harboured other notions, fancied himself an artist, and then, when Mr Webster died, I suppose Dan took his chance to quit that life.'

'I see. I did not know of the Sandbourne connection.'

Samuel shrugged. 'His mother had hoped that he would follow in his father's footsteps. That she might rely on him. He was her eldest son. She was left a widow with three younger children besides. Her two other boys then died when they were scarce knee-high. Daniel may have felt the weight of Mrs Webster's disapproval, for he never returned to the estate.'

'But you kept in contact.'

'No, sir.'

'Oh, but —?'

'I heard that he had come to London. Then when I saw the reward poster this morning, I realised that the murdered man was the Daniel Webster I had known when he was a boy. I made enquiries of the funeral and so I am here, a little late, I fear.'

'That is a kindness.'

'Do they have the villain who has done this yet?'

Sheridan shook his head.

'He will be apprehended, I am certain, sir.' Samuel nodded forcefully.

They reached Daniel's grave. The funeral gathering had departed and a couple of gravediggers were leaning on their spades, contemplating the work before them.

Samuel bowed his head and recited a prayer under his breath. Then he stooped and picked up a clod of earth, which he threw down onto the wooden coffin below.

'Farewell, Daniel. Rest in peace.'

One of the gravediggers leant forward. 'He'll not rest until him that murdered him is hanging from the tree at Newgate.'

Sheridan gave the men a coin apiece. 'Let him not be disturbed by other villains that might rob the remains.' He turned to Samuel. 'You must join us at The Blue Anchor. There is a keg set aside.'

'That is generous of you, sir.'

'We drink that we might forget our own misfortunes. And once the niceties have been observed, then the landlord will provide other entertainment for those inclined. This is a place that is famous for its rat-baiting pit.'

Samuel shrugged. 'It is not a sport to my taste.'

'Nor mine.' Sheridan regarded Samuel keenly. 'You must know of Daniel's sister then?'

'Little Lucy?'

'It appears she had come to London to seek her brother's protection, and I am tasked by his dying wish to look after her. Would you know the cause of her distress or where we might find her?'

Samuel rubbed his jaw. 'You must know the cause, sir.'

'How so?'

Samuel stared at Sheridan. 'Why, sir, she is the maid that disappeared from Sandbourne — after the earl's cousin was found poisoned.'

Sheridan stopped dead as the events of late August charged back into his mind.

'Lucy was then maid to Lady Cannock, if you recall, sir.'

'Yes, I do, I do — and she had taken flight of a sudden, if I remember?'

Samuel nodded. 'Suspicions were briefly cast upon her — but none could fathom a reason why she would want to murder Mr Stretton. It was thought she had eloped, her mother being of a strict Methodist persuasion.' Samuel paused. 'If Lucy turned to Daniel in distress, then I may suppose that she has been abandoned by that lover.'

'Yes, that might all make sense…'

Samuel nodded. 'But she has disappeared again?'

'Unfortunately.'

'Some, amongst the household, would still point the finger in Lucy Webster's direction for the murder of Mr Stretton. And, of course, there are those who proclaim the innocence of Sir Humphrey's servant, Emmanuel.'

Sheridan nodded slowly. 'Lady Cannock is convinced of it. He awaits trial at the Lent Assizes, I believe.'

Hanley nodded. 'Since Lucy's sudden disappearance there has been no communication from her, which is strange — and points to something ill.'

Sheridan's mind was reeling. Lucy connected to the death of Edward Stretton? And now, her own brother laid in the earth by some villain's hand. What might this all signify?

CHAPTER FIFTEEN

Sheridan's dishevelled appearance occasioned some merriment amongst the assembled company at The Blue Anchor when it was learnt that he had taken 'a grave step' himself. The ensuing laughter lightened the sombre atmosphere. Glasses were raised and with them spirits too. Thomas Greenwood was praised again for his fine eulogy and led the company in another toast.

'To the capture of the rogue who has done for poor Daniel!'

Sheridan excused himself to clean up as best he could with a washbasin provided by the landlord in a private room. With some reluctance he declined the favours of the lively girl who brought the hot water and towel, tempted though he was. Sheridan returned to the funeral meal.

He sat down next to Samuel and thanked him again for his timely appearance at the cemetery. He then enquired whether the Cannocks were still at their residence in London. Hanley informed him that the earl and countess intended to stay at least another week whilst their portraits were completed by a Mr Hoppner.

'Ah, Hoppner, a fine portrait artist. He once rendered me not unfavourably.' Sheridan decided that he would call on the couple soon. It was a visit that was overdue.

When he deemed it no longer impolite to the proprieties of the occasion, Sheridan rushed from the tavern and found his carriage. These were strange developments and he needed time to think. Where might he go? Tom was still at the country villa in Isleworth and Mary under Mrs Canning's charge in Wanstead. He had another house closer by, in Grosvenor Street. It had been abandoned for some time. Sheridan had not faced it since Eliza's death, preferring to stay at Nerot's Hotel when in town. But no one would come looking for him at Grosvenor Street.

His servant was surprised by his sudden unannounced arrival in muddied cloak and boots. Haste was made to light fires and the man's wife set about preparing a cold supper which Sheridan would take in his chambers.

'And a bottle of brandy,' Sheridan reminded.

'Yes, sir.'

At last he was at the desk in his bedchamber. Here he might organise his thoughts, for they were in some disarray. He must think back to the sequence of events at the end of the summer, two months previous. Sheridan recalled the first instance when he had heard the name Lucy Webster on that dreadful day. And the speculation which had ensued about the missing lady's maid. At the time he had not made the connection with Daniel. Although now, as he tapped his fingers on the table, he did fancy he had overheard one of the footmen exclaiming that Lucy always had ideas above her station, boasting of a brother who was a phiz-monger in London.

Was it possible that there was some connection between these two murders — the one in Staffordshire and the other in his theatre, here in London? On the surface there did not appear to be any connection. The servant, Emmanuel, had been arrested for the death of Stretton — the young man had not disguised his hatred; it was there for all to see in the grotesque facsimile with the nails hammered in, one at the neck. Things did not look well for Emmanuel at the next Assizes. This second murder at the theatre had been committed by a man unknown, the cloaked assailant who had knocked Sheridan to the ground. No connection, that was obvious. Only the name of Lucy Webster. Which gnawed at him as something odd.

There was a puzzle as to why Daniel had been murdered. It appeared that nothing had been stolen from him. No unpaid debts had come to light. No known grudges were held against him. Constable Nicholls had questioned all who might know Daniel's business. The mystery of his violent end all came back to those final words, '*Look after Lucy*'. Was there more in the desperate urgency of his expression than simple brotherly concern for a sister who had been seduced by an unknown swain and left expectant with child? Sheridan nodded to himself. There had been terror in his eyes. Which is why he had at first assumed that Daniel was trying to warn him of their murderous assailant. *Look ... you see*!

Yes, he did see now. The injunction to look after Lucy was driven by a real fear for her safety. Daniel had put himself in harm's way in order to protect her. He had stowed her away in the theatre, kept her close and guarded for weeks. He had sacrificed his own life to allow her the opportunity to escape the man who meant harm. The girl at the cemetery, Tilly, she knew that much. What had she said of Lucy? *She is very much afraid.* And there was more. Sheridan strained to remember her precise words. *Lucy will not tell. Only that there is a great secret and there are those who would want her dead.*

What might that secret be? She had come from Sandbourne. She had taken flight when Edward Stretton had been murdered at the end of August. During Sir Anthony's interrogation there had been speculation that Lucy was seeing some lover, a local swain. With whom it was now clear, from Mrs Rummage's observation, she had been got with child. Knowing there should be no seal of approval from her Methodist mother, Lucy had eloped. Then she had been abandoned by this blaggard of a lover, who had perhaps used her cruelly, and sought refuge with her brother. Her flight from Sandbourne could be a mere coincidence of timing. But Sheridan had formulated his own theory regarding coincidences. All very well on the stage, but in real life as rare as hen's teeth.

Now he began to toy with the notion of *connection*, and that led him inexorably to the notion that it was Edward Stretton who was the lover. Yes. He was convinced of it. If this lover were Stretton, then it would tally with the tutor Mr Cray's hints that Edward had seduced one of the maids. Stretton would be the father of Lucy's unborn child.

The next factor to consider was her sense of danger, *those who would want her dead...* Lucy Webster had flown in terror to her brother Daniel and begged his assistance, and he had kept her hidden. Who did she fear? Had Daniel sought help against this threat? He did not appear to have confided in anyone at the theatre. There was something else that Tilly had said: *There is no one that she can trust. There is no one to believe her.* Brother and sister had felt that there was no one to whom they could safely turn. Damn the fellow — Sheridan thumped his desk. If only Dan had come to see him, had trusted him.

All seemed to lead back to Sandbourne. Lucy had taken flight when she had received news of Edward's death — did she know who the assassin was? Was that her dread? Were those who might want her dead the same who had done for Stretton? Had Edward known this *great secret*? Was that why he had been killed?

The fire was burning low in the grate. Sheridan watched the flames spark and leap as he added more fuel. Papers lay scattered across his table, along with the debris of his supper. Notes and lists of queries to be answered. He shivered, whether from the frost without, spreading across the window, or the memory of that look of horror on the face of the earl when they had seen that Stretton was murdered, he knew not. He must gather his thoughts. So much had happened in the wake of that dreadful discovery. He must try to order and remember the particular details. He poured a generous measure of brandy, reflecting on the tongues of fire in its amber nectar as he swilled the glass.

Then another disturbing thought assailed him: what if Lucy Webster herself were the killer of Edward Stretton? She had left the house early enough on that fatal day. She had access to the key and the laboratory. Lucy was pretty but also described as clever and ambitious. She may have naturally acquired a knowledge of plants and poisons and the workings of the syringe. She may have lured Stretton to the meeting at the temple.

Yes, of course! Sheridan struck his head. The third note. The note which had been delivered when they were at billiards and which Edward had assumed was from Lieutenant Harding and then stuffed into his pocket. The third note, which Edward had perused later and found not to be from Harding, for that one had already been delivered to Dodson, but from one who held promises of a change to his fortunes. Information sufficient to alter his mood from one of dark dejection to one of hopeful anticipation.

He and Cannock had forgotten to mention the note delivered to the billiard room in all the distressing business of that following day. Who had the missive been from? Well, it was an easy matter for Lucy to leave the note on a salver in the vestibule. She could both read and write, Lady Cannock herself had seen to that.

Sheridan paced the room. If this scenario were correct, what might be Lucy Webster's motive? The girl would have had to make careful plans and preparations for an assassination. Acquiring the syringe and the poison, writing the lure, committing the deed itself. And she had done all of this — why? Because she had realised at last that Stretton had seduced and betrayed her. Lucy had learned of Stretton's false promises to Miss Harding and then, most crucially, of his rumoured betrothal to the heiress in Shrewsbury. It had been the talk of the servants' kitchen that evening when Lieutenant Harding had arrived in pursuit of Stretton to throw down his challenge and demand satisfaction for the insult to his sister. Lucy had realised her position. Would have known that she was expectant with child. That should be a further encouragement to her to confront Stretton on that morning in the temple. She then murdered him in a passionate rage. And destroyed the incriminating note which was still about his person.

Then Lucy had made her way to London. A fugitive in fear for her own life should she be caught. Sheridan nodded to himself. Was that her secret and her dread? The great secret she had hinted at to Tilly — that she had committed foul murder? Did Lucy sense the hangman's knot? Was she consumed with despair for the future of her unborn child?

Sheridan stopped. But why then had Daniel been killed? Lucy may have slain Stretton, but she had not done for her own brother. No. He had tried to protect her to the last. Sheridan rubbed at his eyes. Maybe there was no connection after all between the two deaths. Except that, according to Tilly's account, Lucy spoke of those who *would want her dead*. Who would want her dead — and why? Vengeance? Lucy had loved and murdered someone above her station in life. But who would avenge Edward Stretton's death by seeking hers in this way? None that Sheridan could think of. He felt himself clutching at straws. Perhaps there was some other reason she might be in danger; the secret was not that she was an assassin, but something else.

Sheridan poured out a last balloon of brandy and wondered whether he should call for more. The streets outside were silent now. His man would have retired. The hour must be late. He would not disturb the servants. A warming pan had been placed between his sheets. The bed would be comfortable, welcoming. He might slip into it and with luck slide into the blessed oblivion of sleep, were he not so troubled.

The fire was almost out. He picked up a shawl from the back of an armchair and wrapped it around himself. It was one which had belonged to Eliza. When he had last visited Grosvenor Street, he had extracted it from a box of her shawls and buried his face in its cloth. Between his wracking sobs, he had taken in deep breaths of her scent. The servants had been ordered not to return it to its storage without instruction, and so it had been lying where he had left it last. There was still some trace of that scent, he thought.

At times his life seemed one long series of unfulfilled good intentions, albeit his achievements were weighty and he had entrée into worlds his father could not have dreamt of for him. But few of his real ambitions had been truly realised. He knew that he could blaze like a firework. But also, he was just as unreliable. As likely to fizzle out as a damp squib. His head felt fuzzy. He had drunk too much. Of late he had downed far greater quantities than was good for his constitution. Grief, naturally. But more. A looming sense of his own inadequacy. What must he do? What must he do about this business? Or the prince's business? Or his duties at Westminster? Or his debts over the new theatre at Drury Lane? Or Tom? Or

Pamela? Or any of it? His mind fizzed and gurgled. He must not pick up some cause only to drop it down again. This matter of Daniel Webster. Sheridan felt the pressing demand of the dying man's last words. *Look after Lucy*. It all added up to one thing for certain. He must concentrate his thoughts. He must find her. And then he might find sleep.

CHAPTER SIXTEEN

At the theatre, late the following morning, Sheridan asked for any messages or enquiries that might have come for him. Nothing of note, he quickly assessed. Another creditor or two. Or three. Nothing from the girl at the cemetery. Of course, it was too soon to expect anything from Tilly. Their meeting had only been the previous afternoon, although it already felt an age. The theatre was quiet. No doubt the eulogies to Daniel had continued long into the evening and few would have stirred from drunken slumber to greet the morning. His own head thrummed with the excesses of his sleepless night. He sent out for a pie and a jug of small beer with which to alleviate those symptoms.

A crate had, however, appeared in his temporary office. He removed the lid. It contained the sum total of Daniel Webster's belongings, retrieved from his lodgings at Mrs Rummage's house. Sheridan sifted through. He did not know what he looked for. The clothes and boots might all be distributed amongst the scene painters. He would ask Thomas Greenwood to arrange this. There were a few books concerned with art and drawing. One had been a gift from Greenwood. A watch and chain, the gilt-framed portrait and some coins which he would put aside for Daniel's mother. There were paints and pens and sketchbooks. As he flicked through one of them, an idea occurred and he set it aside to act upon shortly. At the bottom of the crate lay a bundle of letters tied with string.

They came from Sandbourne and spanned ten years, written in an awkward hand which improved only slightly from age eleven to twenty-one. They were from Lucy to her brother.

Sheridan riffled through them. For the most part they were concerned with family events.

Their mother's distress and anger at Daniel's departure. Pleas from Lucy for him to return home. Her own delight that he had found work to his liking. The beginning of her employment as a maid at Sandbourne. Her mother's attachment to the Methodists and the sermons which Lucy must endure when she visited on her mornings off. She wrote that she was thankful that she lived up at the big house, where she shared an attic room with a girl he might remember from the village.

Another letter mentioned the earl's cousin. He had come from the Indies and there was general fascination with the young servant he had with him. Sheridan scanned through other letters, which spoke of the sad deaths of first one of the younger Webster brothers from a fever and then the other.

There was an account of the great festivity at Sandbourne with the unexpected marriage of the earl. Then fulsome words in praise of the new mistress and her kindness — Lady Cannock even visited their mother and offered comfort. And then, much to Sheridan's amusement, he found mention of himself.

Mr Sheridan is a very entertaining gentleman and we have not heard so much laughter for an age. I have only seen him from the end of the corridor but Hephzibah and I are agreed that he is very handsome. How I want to tell him I am your sister, Dan'l! And that you have written often about him and all that happens at Drury Lane. Oh but I long to visit London. How I should like to see you and all those wondrous sights!

Then there was the general joy at the arrival of the new baby.

His name is most unusual but it begins with an S and he is very plump, has hair that is almost red and Her Ladyship swears he was born laughing, not crying! He is a jolly little fellow for certain.

Lucy wrote much about the running of the household, gossip about servants who would clearly have been familiar to Daniel, and expressed her determination to learn to be a lady's maid. She was most attentive to all that was done by Miss Dickens. At night she practised hairstyling on poor Hephzibah, who would rather have been below stairs, canoodling with the footman in the scullery.

At seventeen Lucy wrote that she was beginning to receive attentions from Mr Hanley. Sheridan's interest was piqued.

His father has died and Mr Hanley is to take his place by the lord's side. They are together constantly, for as you may recall Samuel assists His Lordship in the laboratory. It is most strange; I have often overheard them when I come to clean or on some errand, and they speak more like brothers than master and servant. The laboratory is the very devil to dust and clean, all those bottles! Samuel is very kind to me and I am very fond of him, but I do not consider marriage, though he persists and speaks of the advantage of his position. He is much too old, some twenty years above me!

Sheridan sighed; she was young, of course, with romantic notions and perhaps at seventeen unlikely to recognise what a sensible match these overtures might represent.

Then there was news that the earl's cousin, Mr Edward Stretton, was to live in a house close by. He had lost his interests in the Indies. The word amongst the servants was of a failed venture and gambling debts. Lucy was glad for his visits. Sandbourne had few guests and was dreadfully quiet and dull.

There was much tittle-tattle, and then it was Miss Dickens who was to be married. To Mr Cox, a curate in a parish near Stone. Lucy could scarce believe her good fortune; it had been agreed that she would be the new lady's maid and Miss Dickens was to instruct her in all that was necessary before she departed. Lucy was straightaway to be fitted with new dresses and would have Miss Dickens' lovely little room, which looked out over the woods. Sheridan smiled to think of such simple pleasures.

And then there were pleasures of a more sophisticated nature. The longed-for trip to London — Lucy brimmed full of the delights. Her joy at seeing her brother again, albeit briefly. What pride she felt to see his work in the scenery on the stage at Drury Lane, even from the height of the Gods. Her admiration for Mrs Siddons, the tears shed at her performance, and her enthusiasm for Mr Kemble who commanded all on the stage. The streets of London, the grand houses and the noise and the traffic, it was all a wonder to Lucy, and she wished that they might have stayed longer but Lord and Lady Cannock had little taste for London.

And then there was an update which, reading between the lines, seemed to Sheridan of no surprise whatsoever.

Well, I have a suitor. I may not say. But we are so very much in love. It is a SECRET for the moment. I dare tell no one, not even you.

She hoped to see Daniel again later in the year.

His Lordship and Her Ladyship are to have their portraits painted in the autumn and will stay at their house in London for a hole month!

In April:

I feel sure you will not censor me, dearest Dan'l. Mother is become so Methodist I do not know who to confide in. We are married! He is so considerate to me and I am sure that all will be well when eventually we can make public our marriage.

Here the letters stopped. Married? There had been a marriage? Sheridan sighed deeply. What a foolish, naïve girl. She had spent most of her life on a country estate, and that with few visitors. It was clear that she had placed her trust in this suitor. Edward Stretton, he would hazard on his life. And if this was Stretton's handiwork, he could only believe the 'marriage' had been some subterfuge to ensnare Lucy into his seduction. And now she was bearing his child. Believing herself to be his widow and the child legitimate.

He paused to re-evaluate. He held the letter. He reread it. Lucy had clearly believed herself to be married to this lover, a marriage which had been kept secret. He did not imagine Stretton to be a man of honour. But what if it were a legitimate marriage? Legitimate and yet not quite so. He called to mind another marriage of questionable legitimacy. There was no doubt that Mrs Fitzherbert considered herself to be the legitimate spouse of the Prince of Wales and only remained silent on the marriage for his sake. She knew how much he longed for the crown; it was the very substance of his existence. But His Royal Highness — how did he view the legality of their wedding? Well, if it came to the crux, he might make a hasty retreat behind the Royal Marriages Act. Edward Stretton's plan may simply have been to deny his marriage at a later date. He had perhaps bribed someone to perform a ceremony. Who would believe a lady's maid without some irrefutable proof?

Sheridan's mind reeled.

Here might be a motive for Lucy. Another scenario leapt to Sheridan's mind. On the evening of the dinner, at some point Lucy had pressed Edward for a private word. She had confronted him with the rumours of his engagement to the heiress. How could this be, when he was already married? He had laughed in her face. She had perhaps reminded him that she was with child, hoping to sway him. He had challenged her to prove her claim. Lucy had cruelly discovered that her marriage was a sham, that she was going to be abandoned by Edward and left to shame and ruin with a bastard child. That very evening she plotted her revenge.

Sheridan then allowed himself to contemplate another scenario. If the marriage was legitimate and could be proven, then what did it mean for Lucy and her child? Some inheritance due to Stretton? He had nothing by all and every account, quite the reverse; he had only debts. Debts to Acton Greaves. That snake had been there, in the vicinity of Sandbourne. What had Greaves meant when he claimed that the business was not over? Sheridan's mind was all a-jumble.

If Lucy gave birth to a legitimate boy, then, should anything untoward happen to Sempronius, this child might be an heir to title and wealth — although Sempronius seemed a very healthy boy. But what if there was some question mark over his legitimacy? Could that be possible? The Cannocks seemed a most devoted couple and the earl doted on his son. If he claimed paternity, how might it ever be proven that Sempronius was not the earl's own flesh and blood? The world was complicated, Sheridan knew all too well. He need only look at little Mary. And then by that to know that even a good woman like his wife Eliza might stray within marriage. Something, nevertheless, had convinced Stretton that his fortunes might be turning. It must be to do with the estate of Sandbourne.

It all came back to one thing. Sheridan must find Lucy! He pocketed the final letter and retrieved one of the sketchbooks. He must go to Bow Street. He must speak with Nicholls.

The constable was abroad on police business. Sheridan was about to quit the magistrates in search of a nearby coffee house when Officer Biddulph emerged from an inner sanctum.

'Ah, Mr Sheridan, sir. May I be of assistance?'

'I came only to enquire after Constable Nicholls and whether there is any progress in the matter of my scene painter.'

'There are indeed developments of sorts.'

Sheridan was alert. 'Yes?'

Biddulph guffawed. 'Oh, the usual numbers have come forth to try their luck for the reward. Thirty guineas has brought out all the squealers of the borough. That is the problem, sir, with any significant amount. They all slither out from their holes and rookeries. The regular snitches, that is — or them that have their own grudge and will dob someone in for a crime they may not have committed. Many an innocent may have hung on that fatal tree from time to time, but they are all guilty of something, Mr Sheridan, and may as well hang for one crime as another.'

Sheridan's face fell. 'No information of any import then, Biddulph?'

'We have this morning arrested a man that has been suggested and have him in custody.'

'Does he confess?'

'You may hear a wailing, sir.'

Amongst the general hubbub Sheridan could now discern a high-pitched howl.

'That is his wife, who swears he was in his bed.'

Sheridan frowned. 'You have reason not to believe her?'

'It is her regular alibi. But as the fellow works at night it counts for little.'

'Who is this fellow?'

'One that we know for a snatch-purse about the theatres, but that sometimes runs with the cut-throats of Covent Garden.'

'And your informant can place him at The King's Theatre?'

Biddulph spread his hands and shrugged. 'It is all justice in the end, sir. But you know that; I think you have sat on the magistrates' bench at some time in the past.'

'I would like to see the right man hang for Daniel Webster's murder.'

'We do what we can, Mr Sheridan, with our limited means.' Biddulph inclined his head. 'But here is our suspect being brought up before Sir Sampson.'

Sheridan turned to see a man in shackles being led up from the cell below and into the corridor that connected to the court. The wailing woman clutched at him as he passed her. Sheridan started. He recognised the fellow.

'You might like to observe proceedings, given your interest, sir.'

'I would. If you'll excuse me, Biddulph.'

It was the pockmarked assailant who had accosted him the week before amidst the trouble outside the shop of Monsieur De Lubac. On the very night that Daniel had been murdered. Could this really be the assassin?

CHAPTER SEVENTEEN

The magistrate, Sir Sampson Wright, squinted and looked down his nose towards the man brought before him. He glanced through the papers set before him by the clerk.

'Isaac Joseph Fethard?'

The guard knocked the cap off Fethard's head and thrust it into his shackled hands.

'Yer Honour.' The man shuffled.

'An informant has given sworn testimony that you went to The King's Theatre with villainous intent and slipped past the watch to gain access to the parts behind the stage. This on the night of the murder of Daniel Webster. Have you anything to say for yourself?'

'It is all a lie, sir. I was in my bed. My good wife —'

'Yes, yes. We all know her trustworthiness, do we not?'

A Runner sniggered.

'You had some thought, no doubt, to steal and plunder. Perhaps you thought that you might find the night's profits? And Mr Webster caught you about this act and paid for it with a blade thrust viciously into his chest!'

'No. On my life, sir, on my life!' Isaac Fethard had gone pale, the marks of the pox standing out all the more clearly. He thrust his chin forward as he addressed Sir Sampson. 'And who is this man that claims that I was there, when I was all along with Ned Cribbins?'

'Ah-ha — not abed with your wife then?'

Isaac's eyes widened at this snare. He hesitated. 'I am distressed, sir, and confused — as is she.' He nodded towards the woman at the rear, who was now smothering her sobs in her shawl. 'This was a Friday? I recall now, and Ned will tell you. Ned will tell you!'

'And where might this Ned be found?'

'He can be sent for, sir,' Isaac Fethard pleaded.

'I am here.' A voice came from the rear of the spectators.

A young weasel-faced man stepped forward from the dark corner where he had been lurking. Sheridan knew him at once. This was the blaggard who had attacked him outside the watchmaker's shop.

'That is most convenient for you, Mr Fethard. Am I to suspect some collusion and conspiracy with Mr Cribbins?' The magistrate turned to the new witness. 'Step forward then and say your name and what you know.'

'Edward Cribbins, your honour. Friday last I was drinking at The Duke's Arms with Isaac — Mr Fethard. I had won a wager, and there are others that can speak for that.'

'Until what hour?'

Ned shrugged. 'I dunno. I do not have a timepiece, sir.'

There were titters amongst those gathered. Ned looked about to enjoy this bit of fun. His eyes widened when they locked on Sheridan, who was standing near the rail.

'You stayed in the tavern all night? This murder happened after the theatre was emptied.'

Ned's face was pinched and angry. He pulled at his filthy cravat.

Sheridan continued to stare. Did Ned Cribbins feel the hangman's noose already?

'You stayed at The Duke's Arms all night, Mr Cribbins?' Sir Sampson pressed.

'We may have ventured forth to try another place I know.' Ned looked shifty.

'Ventured forth?'

Sheridan stepped forward and bowed to the magistrate. 'Sir Sampson —'

'Ah, Mr Sheridan.' The magistrate raised an eyebrow.

'You must know my interest in this case. Daniel Webster was in my employ. He was a scene painter and I was with him at the end.'

'Mr Sheridan. We are honoured by your presence.'

'It seems I have another interest here now, if you will let me speak.' Sheridan bowed politely.

The magistrate nodded. 'You are welcome, sir.'

Sheridan looked across at Isaac Fethard, whose eyes darted towards Ned with renewed concern. But there was no Ned. Ned had slipped away.

Stepping outside, Sheridan paused to determine which way to turn. He had a ravening hunger now and needed to sit down at a good eating house before he set off on the journey ahead. He needed to find a quiet corner and think through what had passed. The letters this morning. And now the arrest of Isaac Fethard. The wretch would be transferred to the prison at Newgate with an added charge of affray but no conclusion to the case for murder, which would be heard in the next sessions at the Old Bailey. He wished that he could accept that Fethard was guilty and lay the matter to rest. Likewise, he desired that the mounting doubts he now harboured over Emmanuel's guilt would melt away. But in neither prospect of conviction was he at peace.

'Mr Sheridan, I believe you have been asking for me.'

It was Nicholls. Well, this was fortunate.

'Yes, Constable. I wanted to ask for your assistance with some new information that I have. But it may be neither here nor there to you, for I have now learned a man has been detained for Mr Webster's murder.'

Nicholls smiled thinly. 'Fethard. He is a villain, sure, but of the petty sort, not one to fight or flash a knife unless from behind another's back.'

'You fancy he is a scapegoat?'

'It is probable. He is easily expendable. Mr Biddulph is satisfied. The magistrate is satisfied. The judge at the Old Bailey will no doubt be satisfied; the matter is resolved, and the Runners may move on to other business.'

'But you are not satisfied, Constable.'

'I am never satisfied, sir. This is a city brimming with filth and corruption, with canting crews and prostitutes and misery of every kind.' Nicholls' eyes narrowed. 'You mention some new information, sir?'

'Ah, yes.' Sheridan held out the sketchbook. 'At the funeral yesterday, I spoke with a young woman. She knows where Daniel's sister Lucy is hiding but will not say. I am told that she is very much afraid. I do not know if they will come forth.'

'You think she may identify the killer of her brother, sir?'

'Perhaps. But it is Daniel's injunction to look after her which most presses on me.' Sheridan opened the book. 'Here. The girl's name is Tilly. It is a strong likeness. As you can see from the number of these sketches, Daniel was most eager to catch that likeness.'

'You think I might know the places to find her?'

'Mr Nicholls, may I place their safety in your hands?'

The constable nodded slowly. 'I shall make enquiry.'

Sheridan handed over the notebook of sketches. 'Thank you, I am grateful.'

'Mr Sheridan!'

Samuel Hanley approached hurriedly and bowed curtly to both Sheridan and Nicholls.

'Constable, I am glad to have found you.'

'Samuel, what brings you here to Bow Street?' asked Sheridan.

'I am sent by His Lordship. I informed him of Daniel's brutal end and he is most distressed to hear of it. The earl knew Daniel's father well.'

Sheridan nodded. 'I recall. You said the late Mr Webster was the earl's coachman.'

'And my lord remembers Daniel as a young lad in the stable. He wishes for more information and to know if there is anything he might do. That is why I am here.'

'They have a man below who has been arrested for it,' the constable offered.

Samuel eyes widened and he almost smiled. 'That is good news! Good news, sirs.' He turned to Sheridan. 'The earl will be most gratified to hear this. Do they have the cause from him? It was robbery? So most of your company were agreed last night at The Blue Anchor.'

Nicholls intervened. 'That is not fathomed yet, Mr...?'

'Hanley. Samuel Hanley.' Samuel bowed again to the constable.

'Or if they have the right fellow,' Sheridan added.

'There is some doubt?'

At that moment two officers of the Runners were escorting a woman into the building. Wild of hair and reeking of cheap gin, she flailed about in their arms, protesting at their treatment. One such movement caught Nicholls' arm and the book of sketches fell open on the cobbles.

The constable retrieved it swiftly. 'Have a care!' he shouted after his fellow officers and reordered the loose sheaves.

One slipped out. A portrait of Tilly. Hanley stooped to pick it up and then held it out for Nicholls.

'I think you may have sketches there — by Daniel's hand?'

When Nicholls did not answer, Samuel smiled again. 'He was ever drawing on whatever scrap he could find. There is one portrait of myself I still keep. I thought it very skilled for a boy of thirteen. He had captured my likeness to the life.'

'He had a natural talent,' Sheridan agreed.

'Perhaps there is someone as yet unknown amongst these sketches who might know something of the cause for his violent end?' Samuel turned to Nicholls. 'Is that what you conjecture, Constable?'

Nicholls snapped the book shut. 'I simply act, Mr Hanley. It is not for the police to conjecture.'

'Well, I am glad to have met you, gentlemen, and will convey all to my master. If there is anything that the earl can do to be of service, he will wish to do so. I hope this fellow you have arrested shall confess, for all our sakes. Good day, gentlemen.'

They watched the manservant hurry away.

'Do you tell me all that you suspect, Mr Sheridan?'

Sheridan shook his head. 'My mind is too much befuddled. I am relying on you, Mr Nicholls, for plain, simple facts. Here I must leave matters. I have another most pressing engagement which requires my attention. I bid you *adieu*.'

CHAPTER EIGHTEEN

The fogs and rain had cleared and it was a beautiful afternoon that heralded Sheridan's arrival in Bury St Edmunds. An avenue of trees had turned to vivid oranges, reds and yellows in a fiery display of all that was best in autumn. They were complimented by the crisp blue of the sky overhead with scarcely a cloud to be seen on the horizon. Sheridan took it all to be a good omen for his three-day visit. He had left the cares and troubles of London behind and stayed overnight near Newmarket, where he had slept like a log in the homely tavern. He was refreshed and his mood had become lighter and more cheerful the further away the road took him; at the end of the journey, there would be Pamela. His darling girl.

It was a year almost to the day since he had first met her, at a gathering at the house of the notorious radical John Stone. Stone had since gone to Paris, whether to contribute directly to the Revolution there or to escape an increasingly repressive government in England was matter for speculation. Sheridan was beginning to consider the latter. Mr Pitt had shown himself to be relentless in the pursuance and persecution of anyone who espoused radical ideas. Sheridan knew that his own position was at times precarious and he must increasingly walk a tightrope. It would be William Pitt's greatest pleasure to see one of the most frequent thorns in his side at Westminster arrested for treason.

He had been struck immediately by Pamela's likeness to Eliza. Generally, it was commented upon as most striking. Sheridan had been reminded of what a great beauty Elizabeth Linley had been in her youth. Eliza's features had been captured forever by Gainsborough in the portrait with her beloved sister Mary, when they had both been at the height of their celebrity. Pamela's likeness had even struck Eliza herself. Indeed, she had apparently suggested to Lord Edward that when she should die, as she knew was imminent, he should marry Pamela Syms. Well, it would not be Fitzgerald that would marry Pamela, it would be Sheridan himself. The Irish lord, it appeared, had been disinclined to even make her acquaintance. More fool he. Pamela was an exceptional young woman in every way.

She was intelligent and infinitely playful. That was a notable difference between the two women. Where Eliza was shy and retiring and must be cajoled into performance, while Pamela was vibrant, with a love of theatrical expression which was exemplified in her 'Attitudes'. It set Sheridan's pulse racing to conjure the liveliness of her features. There was no coyness in her. She was a modern woman, all fresh and open and eager to rush into the world. Here was a woman who would restore his own flagging optimism. With Pamela by his side, what might he not achieve? And were her reputed father, the Duc d'Orléans — or Philippe Égalité as he now insisted — to become the stabilising force in France, might not Sheridan then be the man to bridge amity and peace between the two great nations? He felt heady with the exalted prospects before him.

As Sheridan descended from his carriage at the house which had been rented in the town, he longed to rush to Pamela's side, but first he must pay court to Madame de Genlis. He would need her blessing for any proposal of marriage and, besides, there was another business she might help him with. He was ushered into the salon and could see immediately that

His hostess was in an agitated state. Tea was sent for and then she launched into her travails.

'Monsieur Sherrie, how grateful I am that you have come to see us, but I believe we are now beyond assistance. The duc's emissary is here with us and I must give answer tomorrow. If we do not all agree to return to Paris at once, he is instructed to take my dear Adéle with him.'

'Madame —'

She tutted. 'Come, we are dear friends now. You must call me Stéphanie.'

'If you will allow for Richard, madame.'

'Richard, the heart of the lion.'

'There were less celebrated Richards.'

'Ah yes, the crooked one that is most villainous in Shakespeare.'

'I think I may settle for the dolt in the middle, Richard the Second.'

'Richard, you are not the fool. It is the duc, I fear, who is losing his wits. He thinks it is enough to call himself Philippe Égalité. He is so caught in the middle between one estate of government and another he does not see that there are those who want to be rid of all vestiges of the *ncient regime*.' Madame's face creased in distress. '*Mon cher* Richard, events are moving far more swiftly than Philippe or you can imagine. This declaration of a *republique*, it must be taken seriously. You see what is happening to poor Louis? See how they make him jump through hoops? Now he is to be addressed simply as Monsieur Louis Capet; he is a prisoner, not a king!'

'But Philippe Égalité is held in high esteem in Paris; he would not let any harm come to his cousin.'

Madame de Genlis shook her head vehemently. 'The duc does not see he is not in control. They will not defer to him.

He plays a dangerous game and he puts us all in danger. Mademoiselle Adéle. Pamela. Myself. Of course, we all agree with the ideals of the Revolution, but now it is forged in blood and fire, and if one stands too close you will be burned. On all sides France is threatened with war, is under attack. And the duc wants us to go back to Paris! What am I to do? Who am I to trust? You, Richard, must advise me.'

Sheridan shook his head. Here was a strange predicament. However much he might long to shout, *Stay! You must on no account return to Paris. Pamela must remain here!* He knew it would be unwise. Égalité feared that his daughter, Adélaïde, a Princess of the Blood, would be listed as an émigré and this would not be politic for him in his position. Mademoiselle would be brought back to him with or without the support of Madame de Genlis. And if she did continue to resist his call for their return, then what might her future be? Or Pamela's future? That was not to be countenanced.

Madame de Genlis was an authoress with a vivid imagination. She saw conspiracies and dangers in every quarter. He must calm her nerves. The dangers in Paris were not nearly so great as she allowed herself to believe. They would be under the protection of Philippe Égalité; they would be feted and lauded in Paris. No. The Duc d'Orléans was not a man to be thwarted, as Sheridan knew only too well. In that moment he determined that he would visit the French capital himself in the New Year, if that should be the only way to press his courtship of Pamela. So determined, Sheridan set about the task of allaying madame's fears.

He deployed all his soothing charm, flattering her importance to the cultural life of Paris, which she was denying the poor Parisians by her long absence, emphasising her role as confidante and council to the duc himself. Madame de Genlis' anxieties were at last assuaged.

She patted his hand. '*Cher* Richard, you are right. I will return to Paris, but only if you will keep this solemn promise to follow us.' The playful twinkle had returned to her eyes.

'I will be delighted, Stéphanie, to attend you in Paris,' he reassured, 'and to enjoy in your company the many delights of that most famous city.'

'*Trés bien*. Let it be so. I knew I might count on your good advice. I will inform the emissary and arrangements will be made to leave for Paris next week. But for now, we must talk of our own entertainments!'

'Madame —' He corrected himself with a little nod. 'Stéphanie. One question, if I may?'

Madame de Genlis smiled indulgently.

'You came recently to The King's Theatre and, as you know, we have presently a follower of Monsieur Mesmer who has arrived from your country.'

'Dr Cardonnet.'

'Precisely. I wonder, do you know anything of his history? Of his patrons? His Revolutionary sympathies, perhaps?'

'I know little of him. In Paris the followers of Mesmer have been discredited, you know. Many view them as charlatans. Mere tricksters.'

'The Jacobins, I daresay?'

'Yes, for certain. Perhaps that is why Dr Cardonnet has moved to London; he fears the censure of Monsieur Robespierre. But myself I feel there is merit in the practices. Why do you ask of him?'

'You have spoken often of spies and agents, Stéphanie. It is a hazard of our times. I believe that Dr Cardonnet may be working in someone's interests. I am sure of it. Do not ask me how I know this but I am confident of my informant, only the question of who this sponsor might be has not yet been answered.'

'Do you think this Dr Cardonnet means to harm me or my charges?'

Sheridan took little pleasure in playing with Madame de Genlis' multitude of fears, but he determined that this was for a good cause on several accounts.

'I have no reason to believe that you are the object of his interest, Stéphanie, but there are others of my close acquaintance who may have good reason to be concerned.' He played his trump card. 'The Prince of Wales…'

The good lady's eyes widened. 'What is it you suspect?'

'I rather think that Dr Cardonnet may be in the pay of an émigré faction. Those who want to restore the *ncient regime* and to which end would provoke Britain to declare war.'

'*Mon Dieu!*'

'Exactly.'

'War is a catastrophe.'

'My thoughts entirely. Everything must be done to prevent it. Madame, you have your friends in Paris, many friends and supporters who I am sure keep you well abreast of events in that city — might they discover something more about Dr Cardonnet?'

Madame de Genlis nodded, emboldened to this mission. 'It is accomplished.'

'Good.' Sheridan clapped his hands. 'And now what entertainments have the girls devised for our diversion?'

'Oh, Richard, but we have longed for your plays and your charades!'

*

The following days were amongst the most carefree and pleasing that Sheridan had enjoyed since his wife's decline. Although he felt himself to be a wolf amongst a flock of highly desirable sheep, he kept rein on his burgeoning passions, snapped shut his jaws, and behaved with the utmost propriety. Aside from the pleasant walks in nearby woods and the merry rounds of cards or charades in the evening, Pamela and Mademoiselle Adéle had drawn him into a frenzy of preparation for a drama to be based on the fashionable story, *The Abduction from the Seraglio*, a light romance with elements of comedy set in a Pasha's harem.

It would allow for garish and elaborate costumes evoking the world of the Ottoman, romantic set pieces and comic interludes. It was a piece all charged with lust and sexual fervour, and that suited Sheridan's ambitions very well, he considered. Pamela was in a feverish ecstasy of production. Parts were assigned. As a Bourbon princess of the house of Orléans, the fifteen-year-old Adéle would naturally take centre stage as the heroine Constanza. One of the young Beauclerk boys, who was also visiting in the area, was to be her lover Belmonte, a Spanish Grandee, come to rescue Constanza from enslavement. The Pasha Saleem was to be played by Captain Charles Fitzroy, presently equerry to the younger brother of the Prince of Wales, the Duke of York. Fitzroy was also one of the local Members of Parliament, an institution in which he had never spoken in all of his five years. Pamela would be the feisty maid Blondel and that left the roles of her suitor, fellow captive Pedrillo, and the lecherous but doltish overseer Osmin.

Sheridan knew immediately that he must claim the part of the villain, Osmin. It was not the romantic figure in which he might have wished to be cast opposite Pamela, but Osmin was the part best calculated to create the greatest impression and entertainment. It was a role which called for an actor's skills, one which might steal the show and with it a lady's heart. Sheridan was prepared to take the gamble.

Madame de Genlis, infected by the enthusiasm of her young household, had offered her own services as the musical accompaniment. This was greeted by her charges with exclamations of delight, for she was a harpist of great renown.

They were to perform to the assembled guests on the evening before Sheridan's departure. Over the following days he sat alongside Pamela as they adapted and co-wrote the play's script. The two of them giggled like errant schoolchildren as they worked in each risqué innuendo or thinly veiled jest and jibe at the expense of the local gentry and dignitaries who would attend the entertainment. Every so often Mademoiselle Adéle would enter with some new swatch of cloth. Swirling material around them, she would discuss which might be turbans and which the baggy pantaloons in the Turkish style. Sheridan was immediately inspired to set about inserting an elaborate wordplay on *pantaloon*, giving the lines to Pamela's character and with Osmin as the butt of the joke, an ageing buffoon of *commedia dell'arte* fame.

Together with the Comtesse de Genlis he had organised the moving of furniture in the large reception room and a rudimentary theatre set had been designed using yet more swathes of cloth as drapes and curtains. Pamela exclaimed in delight and marshalled the newly arrived actors into their rehearsal. Sheridan playfully cuffed young Freddie Beauclerk and then turned to welcome Captain Fitzroy, whose company he had kept many times at Carlton House. For all that Fitzroy favoured Pitt in most politics, Sheridan had found that they could agree wholeheartedly on Catholic emancipation and abolitionism. He was a decent sort and a good soldier, by all accounts. Fitzroy had brought along a fellow officer from the Scots Guards to play the part of Pedrillo.

Captain Stewart was tall and well figured, with dark curls framing his even, chiselled features. He was damnably dashing in the uniform of the Guards, and to crown it all he bestowed the most charming of smiles on the company. Sheridan saw at once that Mademoiselle Adéle was in a girlish swoon and he looked swiftly and anxiously to see if a similar effect had been wrought on Pamela. She was transfixed. At the prospect of a rival for his affections, Sheridan's hackles rose. He pursed his lips; he must go on the offensive.

The evening's entertainment was to be the household's last major social event before their departure for France. A farewell to Bury St Edmunds and the notables of the district. It was a simple tale, calculated to amuse.

The applause lingered long in Sheridan's ears. The evening was a triumph. There had been sighs. There had been pathos. And best of all, there had been laughter. All the little in-jokes at the expense of various guests had been taken in good part and added to the general hilarity.

He had milked the role of Osmin for all it was worth. From his grotesque makeup with the addition of swirling mustachios to his padded costume and voluminous pantaloons, he had looked every inch the outlandish buffoon. He had allowed Pamela's character to run rings around Osmin and every joke had elicited great peals of laughter, very gratifying to her. The two heroes he also allowed their moments of comic ascendency as they befuddled the pompous and lascivious overseer. He counted his performance in the famous drinking scene charting Osmin's increasing intoxication as one of his finest.

But the high point of the evening had been his own little improvisation when, in the final capture of Belmonte and Pedrillo, he had succeeded in luring Pedrillo in between two flowing drapes of a diaphanous cloth and then trussed him up like a cooked goose, to great roars of laughter. Stewart's bewilderment and fury at finding himself in this unrehearsed entanglement only added to the overall comic effect.

Holding hands, the lovers stepped forward to take their curtain call, with himself and Fitzroy standing to one side and joining in the applause. Adéle and Beauclerk looked youthful and flushed, Pamela was striking poses, and Stewart graciously allowed her centre stage and then in a chivalrous gesture bowed and kissed the soft white hand which he held in his own. The audience roared their approval.

Captain Fitzroy in his turn received partisan cheers from his constituency supporters and merry catcalls from his political opponents.

Sheridan at last stepped forward to take his bow. What a cheering and stamping of feet then. He smiled his gratitude and held a hand out towards Pamela, urging her to join him. He then extolled her talents as the author of the piece, allowing little credit for himself. Pamela fairly glowed with pleasure and the audience rose to their feet as one. As Sheridan joined in with the thunderous applause, he glanced sideways at Stewart. The shadow of the dashing captain's brief allure for Pamela had all but disappeared in the brilliant sunlight of this, their joint success.

The evening was altogether a splendid achievement. Sheridan felt emboldened in his courtship. And if all went as he had planned, he would see Pamela again much sooner than she might anticipate.

CHAPTER NINETEEN

The house was at the edge of a newly fashionable area in Mayfair, one of a terrace of large, comfortable houses which had sprung up in the decades following the great fire of the century before. The first Earl Cannock had been quick to seize the opportunity to acquire a residence in the locale — a foothold near the city, a chance to establish his family name. But by all accounts, the present earl was seldom in residence and Sheridan could recall no society gatherings or parties assembled there. The Cannocks were in London because John Hoppner had been commissioned to paint their portraits, both separately and then more informally *en famille* with young Sempronius.

Sheridan was shown into a small reception room by the same footman who had brought the note to Edward in the billiard room at Sandbourne.

The man bowed. 'I will inform His Lordship of your arrival, sir.'

'Good fellow, one moment.'

'Sir?' The young man bowed again.

'You may think this slightly odd. I know some time has passed. But the Justice, Sir Anthony Peake, is keen that there should be no loose ends in the matter of Mr Edward Stretton. On the evening before his unfortunate death, you came to the billiard room with a note for him. Tell me, do you recall from whom the message had been sent?'

The footman paused In remembrance. 'Why no, sir. I found the note left on a salver in the entrance hall. I merely took the opportunity to deliver it.'

'No matter. Thank you.'

'Sir.' The young man bowed again and retreated.

Sheridan sat. No nearer to an answer then. He drummed his fingers on the arm of the chair. Yet the possibilities narrowed. Lucy Webster could not be discounted as the authoress. No callers had been mentioned, so it was probable that the note was from someone within the household. His instincts told him that this note, its contents and its author were the key to what had transpired the following morning in the temple.

He smiled ruefully. All his musings were taking him further and further away from the general and public consensus that the servant Emmanuel had committed the fatal act as part of some ritual of African witchcraft. His motives had seemed plain. His grudge against Stretton ran deep. He had been yanked from the bosom of his mother as a boy in Barbados, and given as so much chattel to Edward, who had himself exchanged him in payment of a debt to Sir Humphrey.

But there were those who had never accepted Emmanuel's guilt as proven. Lady Cannock had appealed to him on Emmanuel's behalf and he had ignored her pleas, dismissed her conviction of Emmanuel's innocence. He must make amends, it seemed. It occurred to him that if there were some connection between the assassination of Edward Stretton and the murder of Daniel Webster, then Emmanuel could not have committed the second crime whilst locked up in the gaol at Stafford.

Again, he had the sensation that some thread connected him to Lady Cannock, that when Ann tugged at his conscience, it would always snag. He had caught the look in her eye on that summer visit. Lady Cannock had expectations of him which he felt compelled to rise and meet or else suffer her disappointment.

As if to underline his very thoughts, Lady Cannock entered at that moment, her hand extended to greet him.

'Richard. What a pleasant surprise!'

'Lady Cannock.' He bowed and took her firm hand.

'We had not thought to see you in London. We know how very busy you are between the politics of theatre and the theatre of politics.'

Sheridan smiled. 'Well put indeed. But I am never so engaged that I should not make time to see my good friends.'

'That, I trust, we are.'

Lady Cannock sat as tea for four was brought in. She had brief words with the servant then turned again to Sheridan. 'John will join us in a moment. He is as usual ensconced in the library with Dr Burton, who presently stays with us in London. His Lordship and the good doctor have been abroad in the city, acquainting themselves with the new men of medicine and various innovations.'

'Would that include animal magnetism? I recall you both attended one of Dr Cardonnet's demonstrations at The King's Theatre.'

An image came into his mind of the Cannocks sitting in the box across from the Duchess of St Albans. The shadowed figure in their company, he now felt certain, was Dr Burton. It struck him momentarily that the elderly medic was a ubiquitous presence. A grey figure. Easily overlooked. But he would put this thought to one side for now.

Lady Cannock looked at him wryly.

'You were not persuaded of the efficacy of his contraptions, Lady Cannock?'

'I found that Dr Cardonnet exhibited rather too much of the circus for my taste, Richard.'

The earl and Dr Burton entered at this point and Sheridan rose for the exchange of polite greetings.

'I think you were discussing Dr Cardonnet when we joined you? An interesting evening.'

'That it was, my lord,' Sheridan responded pointedly, an evening that had seen foul murder committed. His eye passed swiftly over the elderly physician to see if he would flinch at this other insinuation.

Cannock nodded toward his wife. 'Ann thinks it all hokum.'

'But you do not, sir?'

'The showmanship naturally detracts from any serious scientific speculation.'

Dr Burton grunted. 'That cauldron contraption, the baquet with its various pipes, a piece of frippery channelling nothing but hot air!'

'Nevertheless,' His Lordship continued, 'the Mesmerist ideas of animal magnetism may have some substance. Whilst in London I have been introduced to an old colleague of Dr Burton who has an extensive library of books on oriental practices. I have found in them most fascinating reading. They speak of Chakras and Chi, lines of energy which travel through the body and Ih by the use of touch or the insertion of pins may be influenced to act against any unhealthy blockage. The Mesmeric passes may have unwittingly aped the very same principles.'

'I would like to see how he would mend a broken thigh bone!' Dr Burton snorted.

The earl smiled with indulgence at his older friend. 'Dr Burton, as you may surmise, is less convinced by these ideas. He is a man who likes to work with flesh, blood and bones, and has little time for talk of unseen energies.'

'My husband found Dr Cardonnet's use of artificial somnambulism equally fascinating. I wonder if he wishes to cast me into some trance that will bend me to his will,' said Lady Cannock with a laugh.

'It is I who is ever under your spell, my dear,' the earl interjected gallantly. 'But yes, I am intrigued by the powers of suggestion wrought on the human mind whilst in this demi-sleep. There are many and various medical ends to which the technique might be applied. I confess I wish to learn more and have written to Dr Cardonnet requesting a meeting to discuss these matters further.' His Lordship sighed. 'He has yet to respond.'

'Dr Cardonnet is an enigma to me, I will admit, sir, but if there is any way in which I can assist to make an introduction...' Sheridan sipped his tea, doubting that he would ever acquire a taste for Lapsang Souchong.

Dr Burton grunted again.

Cannock's face fell into one of solicitude. 'We were saddened to hear of the fatal assault on your scene painter, Daniel Webster, once of our own employ at Sandbourne. I strain to remember him, he was but a boy then, but I must thank you for your consideration, Sheridan. His mother is a good Christian woman and I was exceeding fond of his father, our coachman for many years. You have our condolences.'

'Thank you, sir. Daniel was well loved in our Drury Lane company.'

Dr Burton stirred his tea. 'They have the villain, Hanley tells us.'

Sheridan hesitated before looking squarely at the doctor. 'They have a villain but not the right one, I fear.' The doctor's eyes flicked up and Sheridan saw a flash of unease.

'They say Justice is blind,' said Lady Cannock. 'Yes, she is. Blind to true innocence!'

'You speak of the servant Emmanuel?'

Ann turned swiftly to Sheridan, her eyes fierce and probing. 'I have come to share your conviction, Lady Cannock,' Sheridan continued. 'I do not believe that Emmanuel was responsible for your cousin's death.'

Cannock leant forward in his chair. 'And is there something specific that brings you to this conviction? Something we may use in his defence?'

'Nothing which may be of practical assistance, my lord, only that there are other suspects in this business who have not been pursued.'

Cannock nodded. 'I have learnt that the man who held the main part of Edward's debts is a most unsavoury gentleman with undoubted criminal connections. You warned me, Sheridan, that this Mr Greaves was not a man to be trifled with and it seems that he had come to Stafford to call in those debts. It pains me to think that the refusal of my cousin's pleas may have precipitated his fatal end. Whilst going through Edward's affairs I have found many violently threatening letters.'

'That does not surprise me, sir.'

'Sir Anthony has been informed. It is a connection which should not be dismissed. And now it seems that an associate of Mr Greaves, a local to our area, has since been arrested for a brutal assault. We hoped this fellow, Swain, who will likely hang in any case, might be persuaded to confess to killing Edward on Mr Greaves' behalf.' The earl sighed. 'It is a hope forlorn thus far.'

'But hope we must,' Lady Cannock urged. 'We have until the Lent Assizes. That is one blessing. Although the days and months in prison must be a torture to Emmanuel, that the murder took place so soon after the Summer Assizes is in our favour. There is time. Time to plead on his part, or he will surely hang at Sandyford.' She shivered.

Sheridan felt that he must offer his opinion. 'Mr Greaves will not so easily be brought to book, I fear. I do not doubt that he would have sought his revenge on Edward, but murder? He should rather want to have the debts paid. And the use of poison and this syringe do not speak of his likely method. These are not the tools of the typical criminal, for all he is a clever sort, and certainly not the likes of this fellow Swain, who I had the misfortune to meet at The Stafford Arms. Other avenues of suspicion must be explored if Emmanuel is to be freed.'

The earl nodded slowly. 'You are correct in all likelihood. We clutch at straws, do we not?'

The silence of despair descended upon the room. Sheridan shifted uncomfortably.

'Sheridan, you must forgive us. We are poor company.'

'At the best of times, I should think.' Lady Cannock attempted a teasing smile. 'We are simple souls and have not the sharp wit of your usual acquaintance.'

'One can have too much of sharpness; it has a cutting edge, and don't doubt I have as many scars as my fellow wits. I take great pleasure in your more soothing charms, Lady Cannock, and only wish that you were not so troubled as at present.'

'Well, we must go to The King's Theatre again and seek a lighter mood.'

'There is to be a very comical pantomime shortly and you must be my guests.'

'You are most gracious.'

Sheridan stood to take his leave.

Dr Burton rose. 'And we must make haste, my lord, if we are to keep our engagement with Dr Pierce.'

'Ah, yes. The venerable Dr Pierce.' Cannock chuckled and turned to Sheridan. 'He is a complete man of science whose work on the disorders of the blood is far more to Dr Burton's taste than the mesmeric passes of our Dr Cardonnet.' Cannock bowed. 'We hope to see you again soon, Mr Sheridan. You are always most welcome here.'

Sheridan was about to move towards the door when Lady Cannock rose and laid a restraining hand on his arm.

'Stay, Richard, I would have a word with you.'

The earl bowed again and ushered Dr Burton away.

'Please do sit.'

He did as he was bidden and watched, bemused, as Lady Ann began to pace the room, clearly agitated.

'Is there something I might do for you, Lady Cannock?'

'I have not known who to turn to.'

Sheridan looked quizzical.

'This is not a matter for my husband. He is too honourable.'

'And I am not, of course.'

She stopped before him. 'Oh, Richard. You have honour, I know it. But yes, you are a scoundrel too.'

'That is beyond contesting, I admit.'

'And that might suit this business — you understand the necessity for discretion. I can trust you?'

There was a plea in her voice which cut Sheridan to the quick. He rose and took her hand.

'On my honour. That may be slightly tarnished, but is no mean thing.'

She hesitated a moment and then patted the hand which held hers. 'When Edward Stretton was laid out by our housekeeper, Mrs Hanley, a note was discovered in an inner pocket.

Realising its significance, she brought it straightaway to me. We have not always been of one mind, good Mrs Hanley and I. She was wet nurse and nursemaid to Cannock and is like a lioness in her protection. She will let no one harm the earl. I had sight of those claws extended when first I came to Sandbourne as its mistress. And on another occasion too. But thus far she has not scratched. She knows, you see, that my loyalty to Cannock is every jot as fierce as her own.'

'I do not doubt that. The note — you say it is significant?'

Sheridan felt his heart race. Surely here was the third note at last. The one which might reveal all.

Lady Cannock retrieved a folded paper from her purse, the seal broken. She took a deep breath and handed it to Sheridan.

I have discovered a great secret about my lord which will be our FORTUNE! Sandbourne will be ours by RIGHT. Meet me tomorrow at six at the usual.

Sheridan considered the scribbled note. The awkward hand was familiar.

'This is Lucy Webster's handwriting, is it not?'

Lady Cannock started in surprise. 'You recognise the hand? How so?'

'A number of her letters were amongst her brother's possessions.'

'I see. Yes, it is Lucy's hand.'

'You suspect that the "usual" was the temple and it was a venue for their trysts?'

'Sadly, yes. Foolish girl.'

'This might be seen as evidence that your maid Lucy had arranged to meet with Edward Stretton on the very morning of his death.'

'It would seem so.'

'And this might suggest that it was Lucy Webster who dispensed the fatal poison?'

'That is what I fear.'

'Why do you show this to me now, Lady Ann? Why have you not brought it earlier to your husband? To the Justice, Sir Anthony? This might serve to release Emmanuel immediately.'

Lady Cannock shook her head, wringing her hands. 'I have not known what to do, Richard.'

'This note? What does it mean? This great secret which the girl alludes to —'

'The note was a lure.' Ann stopped in front of him and shrugged in an offhand manner. 'There is no secret.'

Sheridan eyed her keenly. 'That is wicked.'

'Lucy must have known something of the straits that Edward was in and that any talk of fortune would bring him out.' Lady Cannock's sharp, intelligent eyes caught Sheridan in their full beam. 'Lucy had heard all of the distressing business with Lieutenant Harding the evening before. She could be under no illusions then — whatever Edward had been promising her. Here was Harding claiming that Edward had abused and jilted his sister in favour of another woman. A Miss Wentworth, as it happens, who lives near to Shrewsbury. In her fury Lucy hatched the plan to exact her revenge.'

'An elaborate one, for a servant?'

'She would know about the instruments in the laboratory; she had often been in there through most of her service. She would have overheard or understood what some of these potions might do. And for a young woman against a well-built man, here was a weapon that might be swift and sure if delivered with surprise.'

'That is a most plausible and convincing portrait, Lady Cannock. Again, why have you not sought to divulge this information?'

Lady Cannock squeezed her hands. 'I do not condone what Lucy may have done, but she has my sympathies. You know I have some knowledge of medical matters.'

Sheridan nodded. 'An interest you share with His Lordship.'

'I believe that Lucy was, is, expectant with child.'

'I see.' Sheridan pursed his lips. 'Stretton's child?'

'I am sure of it. I was on the point of speaking with her. I wanted to help. A girl in her condition. The disgrace. Can you imagine what happens to such girls? Our society is none too kind. Her mother is a very religious woman, a Methodist; Lucy would not have gone to her. Perhaps she had been gulled into believing that Edward would do the honourable thing and marry her. Then this latest information about his true character may have induced a kind of wild and furious madness in her. So, you see, Richard, I have felt unable to place her on the scaffold.'

Sheridan hesitated. He wondered if he should reveal that Lucy already considered herself married to Stretton. What a flimsy contract that clearly was in retrospect. A charade. The girl had been duped. He could well believe that madness might ensue.

'And yet I know you would not see Emmanuel on the scaffold in her place.'

'Oh, how I have endeavoured to find any other means to point to his innocence! He must be suffering dreadfully.' Her distress was writ large across her expressive features.

'He is a young man —' Sheridan sought to soothe.

'I had hoped that Cannock or you, Richard, might find some way. Cannock knows nothing of Lucy. I would not place him in that position. He is minded that justice will be done. John has such faith.'

'Which you do not.'

Lady Cannock's hand went to her brow. 'If I must — then must I expose Lucy?'

'It's a devil of a choice, Lady Ann. It would be prudent to wait. As you say, there may be other ways to cast sufficient doubt on Emmanuel's guilt, enough to save him. And Lucy is not found.'

Lady Cannock nodded. 'I do not know if that is good or ill. I have prayed that she has fled abroad, perhaps taken ship to the Americas. There she might make a new life for herself and her unborn child. If I could only know for sure that she is beyond the reach of Sir Anthony, of the law, then I would not hesitate to expose her murderous deed.'

Sheridan felt himself in a quandary. Lucy Webster was not safely abroad, wearing respectable widow's weeds in Boston or New York where she might find gainful employ. She was here in London, hidden and afraid in some dark corner. Should he inform Lady Cannock? If Tilly were to make contact, they might find her. Damn the girl — there had been no word and a full week since the encounter at Bunhill Fields. Constable Nicholls had yet to track her down.

Tilly might be anywhere. Nicholls had centred on St Giles but even so, it was like looking for a needle in a haystack and ill advised to call attention to the search, never mind venture into that notorious rookery as an officer of the law. But if they were to locate the two young women then, perhaps with funds from Lady Cannock, Lucy Webster might well be smuggled onto a ship and delivered from present danger. With the discovery of this note written in her hand, Sheridan's mission had become more urgent than ever.

'And here is mystery and horror again. I did not know of her brother until Samuel came to us with news that he had been violently murdered at The King's Theatre. On the very evening of our attendance.' Lady Cannock shuddered. 'He believes that Lucy would have come to London and would have thrown herself on her brother Daniel for assistance. When I heard that he too has been murdered, I did not know what to think! Only that poor Lucy must be deep in distress. And this matter touches you again, my dear Richard. You found poor Edward and I believe you were with this young scene painter when he breathed his last. That is why I turn to you. You must promise to advise me. You are a man who knows the world.'

'All too well.'

CHAPTER TWENTY

Sheridan was spending the evening at the club. George Hanger had arranged to meet him in the Subscription Room. There was little either could report on Dr Cardonnet. Sheridan assured the equerry that he had plans afoot but they would take a little time to rganize and rehearse. He did not tell him about the disconcerting encounter with the mesmerist in his office. Whether something had occurred or not he was uncertain himself, so why trouble the major? Had he been subjected to artificial somnambulism? He was no longer sure. He had not slept the night previous, and perhaps he merely nodded off momentarily whilst Cardonnet discussed some aspect of his act, or 'demonstration', as he preferred it to be known. Only that one word — tiger — continued to nag at him. What the devil did that mean? Dr Cardonnet had perhaps said something else entirely in his heavy French accent. 'You are *tired*, Monsieur Sheridan.' The ears could play tricks on one. 'Look, ahh, you see.' Or 'Look after Lucy.' Well, there was a Lucy after all. But no tiger.

Major Hanger's informants, it transpired, had followed Cardonnet from one fashionable salon to another. Clearly the mesmerist's clientele was growing, but he seemed to favour no particular political colour. The government's spy, Mrs Elliot, reporting from Paris, believed that the doctor had close connections to both Monsieurs Danton and Desmoulins of the Jacobins, but on the other hand he was vociferously despised by Monsieur Robespierre and his cronies.

'One other nugget of note...' Hanger leant in closely. 'Cardonnet was earlier a protégé of the Marquis de Thiers-Auberet.'

Sheridan raised an eyebrow.

'Yes. That has been something of interest.' Hanger poured another glass of port. 'It seems that Dr Cardonnet grew up on one of the marquis' estates and, being an exceptionally bright boy, was sent for medical training. Apparently, the marquis had hopes that young Cardonnet might use his talents in the treatment and cure of the pox, particularly after his son and heir's condition became apparent. Cardonnet has specialised in sexual therapies but at some stage became a devotee of Joseph Mesmer. That was not quite the object of the marquis' investment and the rumours are that they had a falling out. Without stipend Cardonnet has been forced to live on his own wits, and being a widower with a young daughter, he appears to have opted for the exhibitionist career we now behold.'

'Together with the rather lucrative spoils of blackmail, Major?'

Hanger snorted. 'True — our little problem may be no more than that after all, and we have been chasing our tails all along.' He grinned and, clicking his fingers, signalled for another bottle of port.

The two men enjoyed a half hour of court tittle-tattle before Hanger was tempted away to a gaming table. Sheridan could not keep still and roamed from room to room, presenting a cheerful aspect but avoiding conversation where he could. Now that his meeting with Major Hanger was concluded, his mind was free to envisage the live drama which even now he hoped might be drawing to that satisfactory finale which he had so carefully devised and scripted.

It was an elaborate ruse. He had been inspired by Mr Goldsmith's drama *She Stoops to Conquer*, the trick played on Mrs Hardcastle, a comedic tour de force which always brought the house down in gales of laughter. Sheridan had never been averse to re-using or appropriating a plot or two. The illustrious Mr Shakespeare had done so often enough, so why not he? Bribing the footman and the post boys hired for the journey had been an easy matter, but there was no predicting how the French lackey might react or indeed for that matter the Comtesse de Genlis herself. Sheridan was as much on tenterhooks as he might be were this the first night of any of his stage productions, with the critics ranged in the stalls like so many vultures ready to pounce on any loose morsel in the plot.

It was a desperate throw of the dice, but a calculated one. After Pamela's exuberant parting kisses to his cheek, the tears of farewell and her protestations of affection, he had felt there could be no further delay in the pursuit of his tender ambitions.

When the servant entered the Card Room and looked about with frantic searching eyes, Sheridan was already moving towards him.

'Sir! Mr Sheridan!' The man bowed. 'You are called away post-haste to your house in Grosvenor Street.'

'What matter is this?'

'The messenger did not say. Only that you are to come at once without delay.'

'You had better fetch my coat and stick then.'

'They await you at the door, sir.'

As he made his way from Brooks's Club, Sheridan could not refrain from grinning from ear to ear. He would have to compose his features soon enough, and restrain the skip in his step which hastened him towards his town house.

*

They had been in the gravest danger.

'*Mon Dieu*, Sherrie!'

Madam de Genlis trembled. They had set out that morning to complete the final stages of the journey which would take them to the coast and the ship which would return them to France, having hired a footman and post boys for the expedition. All her fears had been made actual and horrific on the perilous crossing through Kent towards Dover.

As Sheridan listened with avid concern, sincerity and attention, it became evident that the fervid fancy of the countess had peopled the *antres vast and deserts idle*, as she described them, with *innumerable poniards* aimed at the existence of her illustrious protégé, Mademoiselle Adéle, Princess of the Blood.

Madame de Genlis had not been disappointed of her romantic terrors. The party's French lackey began to think that they were not on the right road, a suspicion which he communicated to his mistress. She at once called a halt to the progress and demanded that the post boys be questioned. On being examined they shifted about nervously, their increasingly evasive answers arousing yet more suspicions.

'Oh, Sherrie! You cannot imagine this! But what can we do? *Mon Dieu*! We must go onwards.' Stéphanie paused to catch her breath, the memories of the ordeal still fresh and alive within her. Pamela took her mother's hand and stroked it, calming those nerves. She then turned her liquid eyes on Sheridan and took up the tale.

'And so, you see, dear Sherrie, we carried on and the carriages were travelling ever faster and we could scarce recognise any sign of where we were. When we could see a signpost for some town or village, we may as well have been in

Holland as Kent, for we had no notion of the country we were passing through. So, we must stop again and ask these post boys *where the devil are we?*'

'Again, their answer is laconic!' Madame de Genlis cut in. 'And they are off again and when we call to stop, they ignore us and I begin to be afraid. Very afraid. Here is some conspiracy! And we are to be abducted by these villains.'

The lady shuddered and Pamela placed a consoling hand on her shoulder. 'At last, of course, they must come to a stop and then we had the simple truth of it,' Pamela continued. 'They had lost their way and were afraid to admit it, but assured us that they had now seen the road to Dartford, which was not far, and we would rest at that staging post.'

'Only it was all lies! Lies to confuse and confound us! Another hour we are travelling, and then I am insisting when we are come to a village that we must inquire of a local gentleman. I am adamant. And, Monsieur Sherrie, what is our horror when we discover that we are twenty-two miles from this Dartford!'

Stéphanie clutched at her breast. 'Well, it is enough, I say! And from this kind gentleman we have directions that will bring us back forthwith to London, which is only some little distance!' She heaved a great sigh. 'So we are here. A mercy! That we have survived such a conspiracy, such cruel machinations! Oh, my poor dear girls!'

Sheridan jumped up and slammed his fist into his palm. 'I shall have words with these rogues and we shall get to the bottom of it all, you mark my words!'

'Yes. Yes, Sherrie. But for now, we are safe. We are with our dear friend.'

'Indeed, madame. And my carriage will take you all to my villa at Isleworth, where you will be comfortable and may rest and stay for as long as you like to recover from such terrors.'

'Monsieur Sherrie, you are our saviour! Is he not?'

Madam de Genlis looked to the two girls and all three cast their grateful and adoring eyes towards him.

CHAPTER TWENTY-ONE

Henry Holland was showing Sheridan the plans for the new Theatre Royal at Drury Lane. It would be one of the largest theatres in the whole of Europe, seating up to four thousand with a full house. There were three tiers of boxes flanking the stage and two shilling galleries above that. A stage that would be forty-two feet wide with a drop of well over thirty feet from the flies above. On the street it would take an entire block. A single-storey Ionic colonnade surrounded the building, allowing for shops and taverns, and there were four storeys of Portland stone.

Its scale staggered him. This was his to be his palace. His estate. The well spring of all his ambition. He had no vast tracts of acreage in the countryside providing the wealth which came with land. He had no fortune from cotton, tobacco or sugar built on the backs of slaves in the Indies and Americas. He had made himself a Gentleman with his wits. And seizing a moment of opportunity he had begged, borrowed and nigh on stolen to take a small share in the old theatre on Drury Lane and then by enterprise and persuasion he had risen to be master of this domain.

The theatre had opened those precious doors to Westminster, to Carlton House, to Sandbourne. He, Richard Brinsley Sheridan, the unpromising third son of a Dublin player and elocutionist, had risen to be a man of influence amongst the highest in the land. And yet, as he gazed at the extravagant designs put before him, he felt that old familiar sensation — that he teetered over a breathtaking abyss. How easily all might be lost. The bills would soon mount and he must drum up more sponsorship. He seemed always to be scurrying hither and thither, scrabbling for monies.

Henry Holland discussed some minor adjustments which needed to be approved as the work on the foundations was already underway. The architect continued to talk through the details of materials, the delays in securing one and the rising costs of another. He spoke of the talents of one stonemason over a rival. He pointed to a feature here and another there. Sheridan tried hard to listen and nodded frequently, encouraging Holland's enthusiasm, but on that morning his heart and mind kept tugging him back to Isleworth. It was still a matter of fresh wonder to him that all his little schemes born of the moment in Bury St Edmunds had borne such fruit. What delights now lay in store.

Despite her complaints at the short notice, his housekeeper, Mrs Tucker, arranged that the cook work miracles with the breakfast table to cater for the extra guests. There were muffins and pastries, cheeses, chutneys and assorted cold meats, and the ladies seemed to have regained a hearty appetite now that the fears of the night had begun to fade. He had entered the dining room that morning to find the little party ensconced with his son Tom. The boy was brimming over with the excitement of all these unexpected visitors and agog to hear of their adventure, his eyes gleaming with each twist and turn of the tale.

'You were fortunate not to be set upon by highwaymen — I hear there are many fierce cut-throats in that direction!'

Mademoiselle Adéle gasped, wide-eyed. '*Mon Dieu!*'

'Oh, but please do not be alarmed any further. You are in no danger now, mademoiselle. Pa and I will make sure of that!'

Tom leapt up and, grabbing the poker at the hearth, he assumed a fighting stance. 'I have been taking lessons in readiness for the Guards — and Pa, you know, was taught by the famed Mr Angelo himself and has fought and won two duels!'

Pamela turned a teasing smile on Sheridan. 'Monsieur, you fill me with marvel. I always thought it was the pen that is your only sword, words that are your greatest weapons. We did not know that we are in the company of a renowned duellist.'

'You fought for your wife's honour, dear Sherrie. I remember the stories now.' Madame de Genlis made a florid gesture. '*Très romantique*!'

'Have at you, Captain Mathews!' Tom made a play with the poker, stabbing and slashing at the air. 'Take that and that and that, you rogue!'

Mademoiselle Adéle giggled with delight and Tom, no doubt to impress her, leapt onto a chair in pursuit of the imaginary villain, stabbing him to the quick. He then turned and bowed to the young royal, leapt down, and dropped to his knee.

'It would be the deepest honour if you would allow me to be your champion, princess.'

The duc's daughter rose and tapped him with her breakfast knife.

'Arise, *mon* chevalier!'

Sheridan viewed the flirtation and banter between the two young persons with paternal indulgence. There would be a welcome return of laughter and play in the household following the months of bereavement. It would be good for his son to be in the company of these playful, intelligent and accomplished women. Tom missed the feminine influence. He had been left too long to his own devices.

'You fought a military man — how brave you are, *mon cher* Sherrie!' Pamela struck a pose that might have been warlike Athena in full armour.

'Poor Captain Mathews was not quite a military man. His sharpness was all at whist, and I made a poor showing, dear girl. I make no claims for my skills as a swordsman.'

'But you were the victor, not once but twice!'

'That may be a point of debate, for there were any number of broken swords. Still, Mathews was forced to retract his slurs.'

'And you were wounded! It comes to me now. Near fatally!' Madame de Genlis clasped a hand to her breast. 'Oh, dearest Sherrie — such a loss would have been tragedy indeed. The world without *The Rivals*!'

'Some say the play might not have been created without the inspiration of my youthful adventures — there is truth in that.'

Pamela had risen from the table and approached him. 'You were wounded? You bear the scars?'

'None that may be seen, my lady.'

A smile twitched at her lips as though she longed to say, *not yet*!

Sheridan bowed. 'I am afraid that I must leave your pleasant company and away to the tedium of business. I will return as soon as I am able but, in the meantime, you must all make yourselves comfortable in our humble home and take rest. I have written to the duc to tell him what has transpired and to assure him that you are in safe hands.'

Yes, they were safe within the keep of his castle. Well, a villa in Isleworth. Madame de Genlis embraced him as their truest friend, their saviour. Soon, very soon, she might embrace him as her son-in-law.

'And here I thought we might embellish the design a little further. Also, I have toyed with a vaulted blue sky overhead. What think you, Dick?'

There was a rap at the door.

'Come in.'

Sheridan was still engrossed in the drawing of the auditorium which Holland had laid before him when Joey appeared at his side. He leant forward with a gleam in his eye.

'Is it the new theatre, Mr Sheridan?'

'Yes, Joey, and Mr Holland here will build for us the most magnificent in all of London. No — in all of Europe.'

'Trapdoors, sir.' Joey looked at the architect. 'Can there be plenty of trapdoors and the machinery under the stage? We can't have enough trapdoors, can we, Mr Sheridan?'

'Not with all your tomfoolery, Joe. Trapdoors there shall be and wings capacious, enough for all our flights of fancy!'

'Oh, sir. I had almost forgotten my mission. Old Fletch has received this from a boy at the stage door. There seemed some urgency.'

Sheridan broke the seal of the note. His stomach lurched. This familiar hand again.

Sir

I rite in haste.

If you would meet with Matilda at Mrs Salmons this aftern at four of the clock, she will bring you to that place where I am to be found. Please may you take disguise as one of a very Ordinary sort. There are those who watch.

Yur servant

Lucy Webster

'I take from the look on your face this is important business, Dick?' Holland nodded towards the note as he began rolling up his plans. 'Mine is done for now, so I will leave you to yours.'

Sheridan nodded. 'Thank you, Henry. I will think on the ceiling. If you will excuse me.'

'Of course.'

Joey was also about to leave when Sheridan stopped him with a hand.

'Joey, I will require your services.'

Joey brightened. 'Yes, sir!'

Sheridan and Joey riffled through a rack of clothing as Mrs Petty made complaint about a pair of buff gloves which had not been returned to the wardrobe on the previous evening.

'And I know that young actor will say he has forgotten in his distractions, but he will have worn them tidily enough out of the building and fancied himself very fine, I am sure, on his wanderings. If they are returned without a stain or a tear, I will eat my bonnet!'

'You must fine the rascal, Mrs Petty. If he will not pay, send him to me and I shall thrash him for his insolence.'

'And so he should be. I try to keep all in orderliness, Mr Sheridan. And you know it is a business with so many as we have in the company! Here I am with half a dozen dressers already wanting to take to their beds with their coughing and sniffling. And might not I like to keep abed!' She sniffed loudly. 'But I must soldier forth and keep all afloat!'

Sheridan drew out a pair of green breeches. They were worn and patched but might still pass for the Sunday best of a careful workman.

'You are the very paragon, Mrs Petty, of selfless industry.'

A dun waistcoat followed.

'These might do very well for Mick Cassady, itinerant cobbler.'

'And these for his son, John Joe.' Joey grinned as he held up a checked jacket with matching trousers.

'A trifle loud, but we'll leave it as in his character. And your name can stay at Joey, in case I should forget my lines.'

'Right you are, Pa!' Joey grinned.

Mrs Petty observed the duo with a measure of curiosity.

'This is some new play you are to participate in, Mr Sheridan? I did not think you to tread the boards?'

'It is a private entertainment, Mrs Petty.'

'Well, I must about my business. Only be sure and tell Betsy what you have taken so we may look for the return.'

'And should there be any delay I shall fine and thrash myself most soundly, on my honour.'

'Oh, Mr Sheridan, you are a one!'

Mrs Petty waddled off to her inner sanctum.

Sheridan completed his costume with a tatty red wig and an old tricorn, whilst Joey set about with a little paint to ruddy his features.

'I see you have our John Joe as a drinking man.'

'Are not all Irishmen?'

Sheridan hesitated. 'They have much need to drown their sorrows.'

'And here's me thinking it's just a taste for taverns and porter.'

'They are also of a sociable disposition.'

They had made their way to Fleet Street and now stood in front of Mrs Salmon's Waxworks. A billboard hinted at the pleasures to be experienced within. A scene of Charles I upon the scaffold. Another of the tragic British Queen Boadicea and her traduced daughters. A figure of Old Mother Shipton, 'The Famous English Prophetess', which had been mechanised, an idea which thrilled young Joey. The exhibition also advertised a number of exotic tableaux, the women of Cannae offering their children to the bull-headed god Moloch and an Ottoman Seraglio. This last brought a smile to Sheridan's face. There would be none so fair in this harem as his darling girl Pamela had been but lately in their own Turkish entertainment.

Sheridan consulted his watch. They had made haste but with sundry preparations were still some half hour beyond the appointed time for rendezvous.

'Come, let us partake wit'out delay, me ladeen!'

Sheridan had been refining his Irish accent en route and felt certain he could bluff any native of The Pale. Joey was to keep dumb.

The interior led them through dimly lit rooms, which created their atmosphere by an artful use of carefully positioned footlights, lanterns and candles throwing eerie shadows on the various painted backdrops to the scenes that they beheld. The low level of lighting contrasted with the radiance of the theatre, where all was light and on display. In Mrs Salmon's famous waxworks one might strain to see an exhibit. This was not a little to do with their age, Sheridan suspected. Costumes no longer pristine, wigs in need of replacement, some no doubt already home to any number of creatures. And the models themselves a little grubby in their waxen attitudes.

The attraction was passably popular nevertheless, and Sheridan and Joey had to elbow their way to a better view in each room. Alongside the Londoners and country visitors he made out a number of foreign tongues. German, Dutch, Spanish and French were spoken in nearly every room. With a start Sheridan recognised the Marquis de Thiers-Auberet and his young wife, with the foolish son in tow. The marquis was tittering at the shabbiness of the exhibition, which he loudly compared unfavourably with one in Paris, by a certain Dr Curtius. His son leant across the ropes to ogle at King Charles on the point of execution.

'*Mon père*, it is most charmingly gruesome!' he squealed.

Sheridan gave them a wide berth. He did not wish to risk discovery, however remote the possibility.

He had decided to sweep through as swiftly as he could, being fearful that Tilly might already be on the verge of quitting the establishment if she had not already done so. In the final room he looked about closely in the gloom, but could not see her amongst the figures gathered there.

'I tink we've missed our little flower,' he whispered to Joey. 'We'll back a ways, just to be sure.'

Joey nodded. 'I am sure she is still here, Pa.'

'Come on wit ye.' Sheridan nudged the boy back towards the previous tableaux.

They perused the harem again. A sorry lot, in Sheridan's opinion, and no more exotic than the fruit sellers down Shaftesbury Avenue. They continued moving against the crowd, occasioning tuts of displeasure as they made a path, their eyes scanning every nook and cranny until they had returned to the scene of sacrifice — the plump, dough-faced babies being offered by their terrified mothers to the forbidding and monstrous god of ancient times.

And then he saw her hidden in the shadows, a shawl over her head, covering her blonde tresses. She was pressed against the rear wall, watching those who were entering the room. She must not have recognised him on the first occasion. He approached her from the opposite direction, sidelong like a crab, trying not to draw attention to the encounter.

'Tilly…' he whispered through the side of his mouth.

The girl leapt away and yelped from the sudden fright.

So much for discretion.

'Is this man troubling you, lassie?'

A broad Scot stepped forward and squared up to Sheridan with a glare.

'Not at all. Not at all.' Sheridan put up his hands to placate the red-haired giant. 'Sure, isn't she the daughter of me mate that works at Bunhill Fields, is all,' he offered cheerily in explanation, putting an emphasis on their last grim place of meeting as he caught the young girl's eye.

Tilly gathered her shawl about her and nodded. 'Oh yes, isn't it —?'

'Mr Cassady — that's right, Miss, with me ladeen here, young Joe.'

'Good day, Miss Tilly,' Joey offered brightly.

The bearded Scot continued to glower. 'Well, if he gives you any bother, lassie, you come to Tam.'

'Thank you, Mr Tam. I am very much obliged to you, but I am quite all right with Mr Cassady.'

Sheridan beamed; here was the way to Lucy at last.

CHAPTER TWENTY-TWO

They had come to the southern edge of that warren of narrow streets and passages which were an infamous rookery — a rats' nest of the destitute and desperate. It was said that every kind of villainy was to be found within its teeming tenements and that the constables scarce troubled the populace for fear of their own lives.

Sheridan laid a hand on Joey's shoulder. 'Not so quick, boy. This is not a place for you.'

Joey looked to Sheridan. 'But I am Mr Cassady's son, am I not, sir?'

'And a fine son you are. But here your old Pater must leave you.'

Joey's face fell. 'But sir —'

'Your father is right.' Tilly bestowed her kind smile on Joey. ''Tis for the best.'

Reluctantly the boy stepped back. 'It was a pleasure to make your acquaintance, Miss Tilly.'

'And mine yours, Joey. You have ever been my favourite clown.'

'You know me?'

She nodded. 'Your disguise is excellent but, in these circumstances, I would know so famous a face anywhere. We are always in stitches up in the gallery when you are on the stage.'

Joey brightened, his dark eyes sparkling. 'You must be my guest next time you come to us. The pantomime this year will be most entertaining. Is that not right, Mr Sh— I mean, Pa?'

'Indeed.' Sheridan lowered his voice. 'Tilly shall be our special guest and sit by the wings, as close as she likes.' More loudly he commanded in his brogue, 'Now, away wit' you, boy. Your Pater has business.'

He caught Tilly by the elbow and guided her away.

'That was a clever foil, Mr Cassady. To bring your "son" to Mrs Salmon's.'

'You feel you are watched, Tilly?' Sheridan looked about discreetly.

'We fear so.' Tilly took his proffered arm.

A wintery dusk was fast descending and there was a throng of people at this hour making their way back to their mean shelters. Among them were Irish labourers, filthy with the muck and dust of building sites, or whatever loads they had been carting on the wharves. There were also sellers of pies that might contain anything but good meat, crippled beggars, some with the tatter of an old uniform still, and men that looked shifty as pickpockets or mean as cut-throats. Women slunk along the edges, heads down and wrapped in their meagre shawls, some staggering in the daze of gin, others casting eyes and jibes with flagrant innuendo. Ragamuffin children ran in and out about their legs.

A group of pitiful blackbirds, half starved, were gathered on a corner by a pawnbroker's shop sharing a clay pipe between them. Above his head a woman stretched out of a window to retrieve the washing that was strung up between the buildings. Eyes seemed to be upon them from every direction. Sheridan stuffed his free hand into a pocket to be sure no other hand wandered to the purse he held there.

Tilly leant in close. 'Only yesterday someone was at the door making enquiry after me. Lucy was persuaded then that we must seek your help before it is too late.'

Sheridan felt a tingle at the back of his neck. He was certain they were being followed. Tilly hurried him through a labyrinth of dark narrow passages and shortcuts, dodging and stepping over the stinking gutters. Clearly, she wanted to lose any that might be following, but he also suspected that she did not want him to know the way. He may as well be blindfolded as chart a map of this route as evening descended.

They had cut through a ginnel that opened into a small courtyard before proceeding on into the pitch beyond when a rough-looking man stopped their progress.

'In a hurry, are we?' the tall, thin man sneered, revealing his mossy teeth.

'Let us pass, if you please,' Tilly demanded firmly.

'If you please!' another man mimicked.

Over his shoulder Sheridan could see a smaller ruffian had stepped out behind them and within his fist he carried a stick or something akin to a shillelagh. Their way was barred both forward and rear.

'What's this, me boyos?' Sheridan proffered a friendly grin.

The tall man chuckled. 'Irish, heh? Straight off the boat?'

All at once Tilly sprang ahead and pushed her way past the taller man. He staggered, but regained his footing and looked ready to run after her before he then thought better of it. Instead he turned and eyed Sheridan coldly.

'Looks like your lady friend has flown. Pity.'

From the belt at his back he drew out a thin blade.

'Come on then — let us have your shilling.'

'It is the toll!' the other guffawed.

The two ruffians began to circle him in the small, dank yard, herding him inward and away from the exits. An old crone cackled on her step, delighting in the unexpected show.

The taller man lurched forward, making a feint with his blade, whilst the other waved his club.

'I have none on me!' Sheridan protested.

'Sure, pull the other one.' The man stuck a leg out and shook it. 'It's got bells on! And how would you pay for that pretty bird's favours if you did not have a shiny coin or two? She's a swan, is she not?'

'Aye — she's no old crone like that one.' The smaller man jerked his head towards the toothless woman clutching her gin to her bosom. 'You could have her for half a pint of ale!' He laughed cruelly. 'Any way you like.'

Sheridan whirled about, trying to keep both men in view. He knew by the look on their mean faces that he should be lucky to escape unscathed. He might well throw a coin to the wretches, but it would not be enough. He had heard that men could be stripped of the clothes on their back in St Giles and left for dead.

'Good lady, will you not call into your house for help? I am attacked.'

The old crone cackled all the louder until she coughed and spluttered into her jug. No one looked out from the broken windows stuffed with rags and paper.

This was not good. He could not slip by them. He would have to face the attack head-on. He was thankful now for the vicious-looking dagger which he had picked up in the prop room before setting out. He unsheathed the weapon and jabbed it about.

'Stand back and let me pass!' he demanded.

Both men paused and looked at one another. Then the taller one sneered. 'There are two of us and only one of you. And we are half your age, I'll hazard. How do you rate your chances? Are you a betting man?'

Sheridan didn't rate his chances. What a fool he had been. To think he could venture into this cesspit alone. He should have contacted Constable Nicholls. Instead, he had been swept along by the urgency of the message and his own ridiculous curiosity. Foolish. Altogether foolish. And for what? To meet with a murderess. Perhaps there had been a mad passion in Lucy's actions that might be pardoned, but they had also been cold and cruelly calculating. He felt the sweat bead at his brow. So, this was to be his inglorious end.

At that moment a checkered ball of energy somersaulted into their midst.

'Joey! No! No!'

Joey tumbled into the path of the smaller villain, who, taken by surprise, yelped and lashed out with his club. The boy sidestepped daintily and with each subsequent swing from the lethal weapon Joey ducked and swerved, avoiding the blows and bouncing up again with a taunting leer.

Well, there was nothing for it. He must use his own weapon. 'Once more unto the breach, dear friend!' Sheridan surged forward, dodged the thrusting blade of the taller brute and, coming from underneath, he rammed his dagger into the stomach of the attacker and withdrew. The man staggered from the force of the blow, clutching his wound, his eyes wide with sudden fear.

Sheridan gulped. A fatal stab, surely. He had killed the man. In self-defence, of course. He was no assassin. But a harbinger of grim death, nevertheless. And what would be the consequence, for a gentleman and a Member of Parliament? How to explain his presence here and in this peculiar disguise? The man's gaze dropped to the blade in Sheridan's hand and his frown deepened into bewilderment. Sheridan gazed down, puzzled too.

Even in the gloom he could see that the blade had not a spot of blood on it.

The villain removed the hand that clasped his injury. His open palm showed no stain of bloodshed.

Sheridan paled. He touched the tip of his dagger and pressed. He watched with sick comprehension as the vicious-looking blade retracted to the hilt.

'Is this a dagger I see before me?' he murmured.

The cut-throat roared. He had Sheridan now and flashed his own deadly weapon with gleeful intent.

'Hand over or I'll slit you ear to ear, you big lummocks!'

'Not today, laddie!'

Tam appeared behind the villain and coshed him smartly over the head. The man's eyes rolled back as he fell limp to the ground, his blade clattering into the dirt.

Joey whooped and the other ne'er-do-well took one look at the Celtic giant before legging it back up the passage.

Sheridan gasped as though winded. 'Thank you, Mr Tam.' He took in another deep breath. 'We owe you our lives, I think, and are in your debt.'

Sheridan found that he was trembling as he returned the false dagger to its sheath.

The big Scot shook his head. 'Consider it gratis on this occasion.'

'We must find our young Miss — I fear for her too.'

'Aye "Mr Cassady", you'll be wanting to keep your engagement.'

Sheridan looked with confusion at the smirking giant.

Tam shook his head. 'You do not think the wee lassie was abroad to meet the likes of you without my protection?'

Realisation dawned on Sheridan. Tam had been Tilly's guardian throughout.

'We are not far.' Tam nodded into the dark passageway. 'Follow me.'

As he cast one last backward glance, Sheridan could see that the old crone had retrieved the blade and was ferreting in the pockets of the unconscious cut-throat for whatever else she might find.

Tam skirted from one alley to another until they arrived at a door with a large brass knocker in the shape of a swan's head. Tam rapped, two short, three long knocks.

Presently a spyhole opened and the door was unbolted.

Joey sprang forward.

The Scot clamped a hand on his shoulder.

'Not so fast, wee laddie. This is no place for you. Not yet anyhow.'

'Mr Tam, can you see my boy safely from this rookery?'

'Aye. It is time he was away home tae his mammie for his supper.'

Sheridan nodded, took a deep breath, and entered the house. 'Now is the moment for truth; that mistress will not be kept waiting.'

CHAPTER TWENTY-THREE

The narrow entrance gave way to a dim and gloomy vestibule lit by a couple of spluttering candles on opposite walls. A hunched manservant in faded livery led the way and bade him wait in an upholstered chair whose sagging seat spoke of better days.

'Mistress'll be here. I do not know you, do I?' he wheezed. 'You are not a regular. Did you give a name?'

'No, sir.'

'Only I am getting a little deaf. No matter,' he wheezed again. 'It is all the same.'

A large gentleman entered from the innards of the house, sweating and red of face. He pulled a handkerchief from his sleeve and mopped his brow. A man of office or business from the cut of his cloth.

'You done, Mr D? Shall I call the chairmen?'

'If you would be so good, Job.'

The man retrieved a coin from his pocket and handed it into the servant's open palm. Job left them, wheezing and muttering to himself.

The gentleman poured himself a glass of port from a decanter on a small table, which Sheridan had failed to notice.

'Can I offer you a libation, sir?'

'That'd be very welcome indeed, so it would, sir.'

'You're an Irishman?'

'Dublin, sir.'

'Fair city, so I hear.'

It was not the finest quality of port, but Sheridan took comfort from the first sip. His jangled nerves were soothed as the alcohol flowed through his veins.

The large man lowered himself into another chair.

'Have you had the pleasure of Sukie?'

Sheridan shook his head.

'She is a handful and no mistake! I'll have no other now. But I have always had a taste for a buxom wench. Polly then?'

Again, Sheridan shook his head.

'She is very pliable, if a little simple. I want for a bit of conversation. I know not all men do, but…' Mr D downed his glass and held it out with a smile towards Sheridan, who, taking the hint, rose and replenished their glasses.

'Mr C.'

Standing in the doorway was a sharp-featured woman of middle age and at her shoulder a young tough with the same jutting chin and deep-set eyes as his parent.

It took Sheridan a moment to realise that he was of course Mr C. For Cassady.

'We have been expecting you.'

Lucy was in an eyrie at the very top, to which he had to ascend by a ladder. One small window allowed in a little light from the waning moon, which had risen in the evening sky. A low cot had been shoved into the eaves, a lantern beside. By its paltry light, Sheridan could see immediately that the girl did not look well. There were dark circles under her eyes. Yet one could still trace the natural and striking beauty which had captivated the men around her, Samuel Hanley, Mr Cray the tutor and, unfortunately for her sake, drawn the attentions of a man like Edward Stretton. Looking at her slight form, it was difficult for Sheridan to imagine that here lay the one who had murdered a large and powerful man.

Tilly sat at the edge of the bed and stroked her hand, offering comfort. 'Lucy…'

'Mr Sheridan?' Lucy queried.

He pulled off the tricorn and the matted red wig to reveal himself and moved a little closer, his head scraping the slant of the roof.

'It is I, despite appearances, madam.'

'I scarce believe that you are here, good sir.'

'I made a promise to your brother Daniel. With his final words he bade me to look after you.'

'Daniel always said you were a good man, Mr Sheridan. Daniel. My poor Dan.' She gulped back a sob.

'You were there that night, I think? Were you not, Lucy?'

She nodded. Her face creased with trembling horror.

'Daniel had hidden you in one of the canvas stores?'

Again, she nodded.

'Did you see anything of what passed?'

She hesitated, as though to collect herself, and clutched at Tilly's hand more tightly.

'There was a noise. A shout. I knew at once that it was Daniel's voice. At first I thought it was simply some business or play between the painters. I strained to listen. Daniel had prepared me with a word of warning. He said if anyone should venture into the store, which was unlikely as it was in his care, but if there should be any danger of discovery then he would shout "Oddsboggart!", an oath common to our dialect.'

'And you heard him cry this oath?'

Lucy nodded. 'I was to slip from that place of hiding and when the danger was done, he would meet me as we had arranged. Oh, how cruel that it should have been that night he should be struck down! Daniel had found another place for us both to stay on the morrow.'

'He had asked for my assistance,' Tilly interjected. 'Tam's daughter is married to a coal heaver, and they have a room that had become vacant. He is an Irishman like yourself, sir, and —' she paused before continuing — 'would keep her safe.'

Sheridan turned to Lucy again. 'You did not see Daniel's attacker then?'

Lucy shook her head and a tear slipped down her cheek.

Sheridan gathered his thoughts. Did this mean that Daniel's assassin had come looking for Lucy? And that Daniel had warned her with the agreed signal of the approaching danger? He must then have kept the fellow at bay at the cost of his own life. But perhaps Sheridan allowed his imagination too much rein; he could not discount that the attacker had been a random thief and Daniel merely warning Lucy of a more general danger. Nothing in Lucy's account truly supported the notion that the attack held any connection to events at Sandbourne.

'They have caught the villain now. That is one comfort to us, Mr Sheridan.' Tilly brushed the tears from Lucy's cheek.

Sheridan was about to offer his own doubts on this but then thought better of it. If the two young women's grief was assuaged by the arrest of Isaac Fethard then so be it, for now.

'You have been in hiding, Lucy?'

The girl looked suddenly fearful.

'You made haste from Sandbourne and came to your brother for assistance.'

'I did not know where else to turn.'

'You fear the gallows, do you not?'

Tilly looked up. 'What mean you, sir?'

'I will do all I can to save you, Lucy.'

'What does this mean?' Tilly continued.

Sheridan leant in confidentially towards Lucy. 'You were grievously wronged by a man who did not deserve your affections. Your actions were driven in those moments by a madness which stemmed from your betrayal and the ruin which you faced. There are few who would or even could speak well of Edward Stretton but many, including Lady Cannock and myself, who would speak on your behalf and would be listened to.'

'Lady Cannock?'

'She has the note written in your hand.'

'The note?' Lucy looked fraught.

'Mrs Hanley found it in Stretton's waistcoat pocket when she was laying out the … corpse. Lady Cannock has not yet disclosed it — for your sake. She would help you and hopes that you might quit the country. But we know what you have done.'

'And what is that, sir?' Lucy tried to sit up. 'That you speak of gallows!' She fell back, exhausted by the effort.

'Lady Cannock —'

'It is the servant that has been arrested. Daniel read of it.'

'That is true. But would you see Emmanuel hang?'

'I do not know who should hang for my dear Edward!' Lucy struggled to catch her breath. 'But I fear there are those who may want me dead too!'

Sheridan frowned with confusion. Perhaps the girl had truly lost her wits and might best be brought to end her days in Bedlam.

'But the note, Lucy. Given to Edward in the evening. You lured him to the temple.'

'The temple…?'

'You wrote to Edward of your secret.'

Lucy's eyes blazed of a sudden. 'Yes. The secret. I urged him to reveal our marriage. There could be no further delay for the sake of my honour, for I was growing big with child — he must talk to Lord Cannock at once.'

Sheridan frowned. This was not the note which Lady Cannock had shown to him — one which told of a fortune and Sandbourne. There had been no mention of their wedding. Sheridan's mind swam... The remains of a burnt note. Not *Harding* but 'wedding'? Could it be? But then, who might have written the note found on Edward's body? No. It was in Lucy's hand; he had recognised it immediately. The girl was playing some trick with him. Or else her mind was a tattered thing.

Lucy continued, 'I visited with my mother. She is a most religious woman, a Methodist. And I knew from the way that she looked at me and sly suggestions that she suspected...' She clutched at her belly with a feverish look in h

er eye.

'As did Her Ladyship,' Sheridan offered. 'That is why she desires to help you, Lucy, despite all.'

'Mother talked of disgrace, that she might lose another child to dishonour and ungodliness. She is wont to talk in this way. I longed to tell her of the marriage. That far from disgracing our family, I should raise it up!'

Sheridan sighed. Poor deluded girl.

'And now all is lost.' Lucy's eyes widened. 'What must I do? My child. That is all my concern.'

'No hurt will happen while you are with child,' Sheridan offered gently.

'And then Hephzibah... When I returned to Sandbourne, she spoke of a great horror. That Edward had been found most terribly murdered in the woods and they feared the assassin was still amongst them. I could scarce think. Murder!

My only thought was that I must keep my child safe, and we must get to London and Daniel would help us. Daniel. Poor Dan!' Tears welled again and Lucy threw her head into the pillow, burying her sobs.

Tilly glared at Sheridan. 'See, sir, how she is much distressed. You talk of gallows and murder. She is frightened. Her husband done to death before he could reveal their marriage. And who is to believe Lucy now? A poor servant girl?' There was a fire in Tilly's eyes that spoke of something personal. 'So was I brought into the world on such a promise of marriage.'

It seemed clear to Sheridan that Lucy had expunged her murderous deeds from her mind, those terrible events of August, and filled that place with dreads of another order.

'Tilly, I see that Lucy is not well. You must know that it is my only wish to help her. For the sake of her brother. For all the wrongs that have been done to her. Lady Cannock has suggested … there may be funds made available … if Lucy were to take ship. Boston or New York. There she might live as a widow, perhaps under some other name. I do not think the arm of the law will extend so far. Then she may nurture a future for her child if not herself.'

'Her child that might be an heir to this estate?' Tilly's eyes narrowed.

'The earl has a son.'

'That may not be his own,' she retorted.

Sheridan stiffened. 'Is this what Lucy claims? That is an unwise and unwarranted assertion.'

So, as he had once speculated, Lucy had ambitions for her child that went far beyond any foolish serving girl's dreams. As far as the inheritance of Sandbourne itself. Had these fancies been conveyed to Edward Stretton? Had Edward felt emboldened to face his debts to Acton Greaves and to delay their meeting at The Stafford Arms whilst he gathered the details of that revelation from Lucy at the temple? But then, she had murdered him. It had all been a ploy, a lure as Lady Cannock asserted. Only now, Lucy, in her madness, believed the fancies to be true. Her murderous action had unhinged her mind. Poor, pitiful girl.

'She thought that she could trust you, sir.'

'Indeed, she may.'

'I think not.'

Tilly looked behind him.

Only then was Sheridan aware of the man looming at his back. He had moved with remarkable stealth for one so large.

'Aye, lass.'

And then the cosh descended with all its lethal force.

CHAPTER TWENTY-FOUR

Sheridan awoke to find himself in the mud and puddle of a trench. His head throbbed from the blow he had received. For a moment he wondered if he had again found himself upended in an open grave. There had been rain in the night, his coat and breeches were sodden, and a chill ran through his bones. Above him a thin light cut through the early morning haze. He glanced about. Too large a trench for a grave. What then? Where was he? He felt for the spot where he had been hit. The skin was not broken but very tender and raised in a lump. To hand he saw the bedraggled red wig and battered tricorn which had been thrown down beside him. Mrs Petty would not be best pleased. He would need to fine and thrash himself.

He knew that he ought to raise himself to his feet. Find some way out of this hole. Discover where he was. Seek the warmth of a good fire. Make his way home to safety and to family. Above all, put the events of the previous day well and truly behind him. He had tried to help Lucy. He had kept his word to Daniel Webster. There was nothing more to be done. He was finished with the business. There would be no further disguises and crooks in dark alleys. He would quash all thoughts of murders and conspiracies.

He groaned. The prince. Cardonnet. That was a conspiracy he had neglected for too long and the Prince of Wales was not a patient man. He had dissembled to George Hanger when he had said that the matter was in hand. Truth be told he had given it little or no thought but rather hoped that inspiration would descend on gossamer wings trailing clouds of genius, much as it had when he was a young man and in the fullness of his career as the leading playwright of the age. But no narrative had emerged as yet. Only half-baked notions unworthy of consideration.

Sheridan felt overcome by ennui. Simpler to stay where he was. Watching the light edge into the day. Following the flight of a bird across the narrow band of sky within his view. A swallow? No. They had all flown south. Ah well. Such were the thoughts which drifted across his mind when of a sudden two faces peered down into the trench. One of them he recognised.

'Henry, how good to see you.' Sheridan smiled up at his architect in a disarmingly foolish way.

Henry Holland and his workmen had extracted Sheridan from the foundations of the new Theatre Royal on Drury Lane, together with the wig and the tricorn. He considered it rather thoughtful of Tam to have dumped him where he would be certain to be found by friends. He did not disabuse Holland of his sly assumptions that there had been some drunken escapade. Sheridan's reputation held good for that. His carriage had been called for and then delivered him to the villa in Isleworth. He was now in bed under a veritable mountain of blankets with his temperature running high and feverish.

Angels visited him, ministering to his needs. One he thought might be his darling Pamela, another Madame de Genlis. For certain it was Mrs Tucker who bolstered him with pillows and forced him to swallow a little chicken broth with strong admonitions as he tried to resist. And Tom, bouncing down onto the bed and making some joke. Even Sister Christian had called, bringing sweetmeats, though she would not come close for fear of catching something that might be harmful to baby Mary. And in between he had slept, it appeared, because the days seemed to tumble one into the other.

And then there came a morning when he was brought downstairs and made comfortable by a good fire.

'What day is it, Soanes?' he asked the footman who was appropriately placing the footstool at his feet.

'Friday, sir.'

'And what day was I brought to bed?'

'Tuesday, sir.'

'That is one more day than I thought.'

Tom ambled in.

A bell tinkled distantly.

The footman bowed and retreated.

'I am not at home!' Sheridan shouted after him, then coughed and sniffled with a strangled moan.

Tom bent down and kissed his father's cheek.

He gently pushed him away. 'You are not afeared to catch this fever?'

'You were found drenched in a ditch, Father —'

Sheridan started. 'Who knows this?'

'Don't worry, Pater. Not our elegant houseguests!'

'How do I look?'

'A little paler now. But that would not be difficult. Your face had been ruddied with actor's paint. I think you were at play, were you not?'

Sheridan regarded his son — his quick, intelligent eyes, the same dark hazel as his own, the liveliness of manner and endearingly open features. His precious boy.

'Tom. Promise me...'

'What, Pa?'

'That you will not be a buffoon like your father but take after your good mother.'

Tom grinned. 'I think it is too late for that, Pa. I am seventeen.'

'You have sprouted too fast.'

'And continue to do so, which is why I rise —' he puffed himself up to his full height — 'to my duty and must escort and entertain the ladies. This morning it is fine enough that we may walk into the High Street and look at hats! Hats with exotic plumage. Hats with bows of every size. Hats with their own gardens — carrots and celery, I do believe, are the height of fashion! And then we may have tea and cakes. *Au revoir, mon père!*' He took his father's head between his hands and kissed him on both cheeks. 'That is the French way!'

Sheridan shook his head with fond exasperation.

As Tom bounced from the room, Soanes reappeared through the door. He carried a small bottle and glass on a salver with a note.

'A tonic from Dr Burton, sir, and a note from Lord Cannock.'

'How very kind.'

'And, sir, the earl's manservant, a Mr Hanley, requests that he might speak with you.'

Sheridan hesitated.

'Mr Hanley says it is on a matter of urgent interest to you.'

'Oh, very well. Show Mr Hanley in.'

The sandy-haired factotum entered clutching his hat and bowed low to Sheridan. 'Thank you for seeing me, sir.'

Sheridan nodded. 'You must convey my gratitude to Dr Burton and His Lordship for sending the tonic. Most considerate. I shall write, of course.' Sheridan shivered and swallowed hard. He felt a sniff and a blow coming on. 'Beg pardon.'

He patted around his pockets in search of a handkerchief until finally he found one in his waistcoat. He drew the cloth out and began to unfold it before it dawned on him what he held.

This was the handkerchief in which he had wrapped the insect that Joey had found caught in the jacket of Daniel Webster. The specimen was laid out in the middle of the white linen. He strained to recall the name.

Samuel leant over with a bemused smile. 'Is that a White-faced Darter? I do believe it is, sir.'

Sheridan glanced up, startled.

'Somewhat desiccated, by the looks of it. They have been known to live into October if the weather has been unseasonably fine, but that specimen, I would hazard, has been dead for some time.'

'Yes.' Sheridan paused. 'I have a young performer who has a particular interest in insects, Joseph Grimaldi —'

'The clown.' Samuel chuckled as though at some recollected act. 'He is most amusing, Mr Sheridan.'

'We found it at the theatre.'

Samuel shook his head. 'That is strange, most strange.'

'Joey thought so too. But you are familiar with these…'

'Dragonflies. Yes.' Samuel's eyes brightened. 'It was one of the pleasures of my boyhood. The old earl would take Lord Cannock and myself for great walks upon the estate at Sandbourne and we would learn — but you do not want to hear of my childhood, Mr Sheridan.'

'On the contrary, Mr Hanley. It is most enlightening. And these dragonflies are to be found on the estate?'

'Yes, sir. There is a habitat that is favourable.'

'That is interesting. Young Joey is a collector and has quite an assemblage of butterflies and the like.'

'The White-faced Darter is a rare addition.'

'I gather so.'

'They are beautiful creatures, dragonflies.'

'Well, I had better keep it safe!' Sheridan wrapped the insect up again, sniffing all the while.

Samuel extracted a handkerchief from his own pocket and presented it to Sheridan. 'It is quite clean, sir.'

'Much obliged, Mr Hanley.'

'Samuel, if you please.'

'There is some matter of urgency?'

'Yes. Of course. I do not mean to take your time. It may not be my place to inform you, sir, but I know your interest from all that passed this August last.'

Sheridan's eyes narrowed as he blew loudly into the handkerchief. Damn it, could he never get away from the murder of Edward Stretton?

'As the Member for Parliament, you may know already that Stafford gaol is to be shut down eventually.'

'I did hear some such. The buildings are very old and decrepit and will be replaced, I understand.'

'That is so. As a consequence, they begin to move some of the prisoners. The servant, Emmanuel, has been transferred to Newgate.'

'I see.' Sheridan's interest was piqued despite his determination not to be drawn into this matter again.

'My Lord and Lady Cannock fear for him.'

'I am sure Emmanuel can be made comfortable at Newgate. Lord and Lady Cannock will see that he is housed in the new State area.'

'They hear that now he is in London the trial may be brought forward.'

'Ah. That would be of grave concern to them.'

'Yes, sir. They are both entirely convinced of his innocence, you see.'

'And they would welcome my support, naturally. Thank you, Samuel, for informing me.'

Samuel did not move as Sheridan expected at this polite dismissal but shuffled awkwardly.

'Pardon, Mr Sheridan. I must make a confession.'

'I am not a priest, Samuel,' Sheridan quipped lightly. He must not encourage this confidence.

'No, sir,' Samuel continued nevertheless. 'I am not one to eavesdrop. It is a common but disagreeable practice amongst servants.'

'That it is, for they may hear what their masters call them behind their backs!'

Samuel smiled briefly but would not be distracted from his course. 'It was only that I caught the name of Lucy Webster.'

'Lucy?'

'Sister to your deceased scene painter.'

'Yes, I know of whom you speak.'

Samuel continued, 'Lady Cannock was informing His Lordship of a letter that had been found on Mr Stretton's person.'

'A note in Lucy's hand.'

Samuel started. 'You know of this note, sir?'

Sheridan shook his head. He had said too much already. 'Please continue.'

'This message might suggest that it was Lucy and not Emmanuel who lured Mr Stretton to Her Ladyship's temple, and that it was she who dealt the fatal stab. Her flight, her disappearance, with no word since to her mother or any other servant at Sandbourne … it all looks very ill for Lucy. Her Ladyship is certain that Lucy is with child. And she suspects Mr Stretton was the father, his betrayal giving reason for Lucy's actions.'

Sheridan feigned amazement.

'My Lord Cannock insists that he will go straightaway to the Justice, Sir Anthony. It being clear now that someone else committed the murder, he said that Emmanuel should be released at once.'

'That should be the right thing to do.'

'But Lady Cannock is naturally distressed. Her Ladyship is … was very fond of Lucy, who you may remember, sir, was her lady's maid.'

'As were you, Samuel — fond, I mean.'

Samuel flushed. For a man about his own age, Sheridan suspected that Samuel had had surprisingly few romantic liaisons.

'I have Lucy's letters to her brother. They were amongst Daniel's possessions. There was no intent on my part to pry into the personal, Mr Hanley. I merely wanted some indication as to how I might find her. She wrote of your attentions.'

Samuel stepped forward with a sudden vehemence in his expression. 'Would that she had accepted my proposal, Mr Sheridan, then perhaps…'

'This whole sad business might never have been.'

'I wish with all my heart that it were so.' There was a catch in his voice and Sheridan wondered if Samuel might give way to tears.

He considered the manservant kindly. Lucy had made no promises to Mr Hanley, but the man had clearly a depth of feeling for her and had perhaps held on to his hopes and dreams only to see them evaporate. A betrayal of sorts.

'How is it you imagine that I may assist?'

'Pardon, sir, I intrude on your time.' He hurried on. 'At the cemetery you said that Daniel had asked you to look after his sister and that you were searching for her. I wondered, if I may be so bold, whether or not you had found her? That is my hope. She is in London, perhaps?'

Sheridan hesitated. He did not really want to be embroiled any further but then, seeing the fellow's hangdog expression, relented. 'I have seen her, Samuel.'

Samuel's eyes widened and he spoke almost in a whisper. 'Did she speak of ... did she... Where might I find her? I long to help her. I would not see the poor girl hang!'

'I could not tell you where Lucy is. I might as well have been blindfolded when I was taken to her. She is in a house deep in the rookery of St Giles. There is a girl that Daniel had befriended who looks after her.'

Samuel nodded. 'I see.'

'I am afraid Lucy has become quite mad with grief for what she has done, and for her brother too.'

'St Giles ... one might as well look for a needle —'

'Yes. She is not in good health, but I think she is well cared for and has her protectors.' Sheridan unconsciously felt for the bump on his head, which had almost disappeared.

'Who can protect her from the Justice? A servant girl! There is always someone who may snitch for the reward.'

'If it comes to that pass, then her marriage to Edward Stretton and the child may yet save her from the scaffold.'

'Marriage?' Samuel looked stunned.

Sheridan had said far more than he had meant, but it was too late to retract that which had been spoken carelessly and without thought. 'I believe some ceremony took place. At least, that is what Lucy believes, and that her child will be a cousin to Lord Cannock.'

'Does His Lordship know of this?'

Sheridan shook his head. 'I have spoken out of turn. Please do not repeat what I have said. It may be no matter; she does not look strong and, as I say, her wits…'

Samuel wrung his hands. 'My poor, foolish Lucy.'

Sheridan nodded slowly, and this time his dismissal was clear.

Later, Sheridan sniffed at the bottle of tonic and backed away with revulsion. Afflicted as his sense of smell was, this was a bitter medicine.

CHAPTER TWENTY-FIVE

Sheridan had scarce moved from this position by the fireside all day, but had nursed himself with port and brandy and occasionally opened the backlog of correspondence which had been delivered to him but which held too many notes from creditors to sustain interest.

As Madame de Genlis entered she smiled broadly, gesturing that he stay seated.

'My dear Sherrie! Richard. It is so good to see that you are risen from your bed. How we have prayed! My dearest Pamela is quite beside herself with anxiety for your recovery. She has beseeched every saint we could recall.'

'That is consoling, Stéphanie.'

'There is colour in your cheeks. And —' she nodded to the plate of crumbs by his side — 'you have restored your appetite, *non?*'

'For the pleasure of your company, Stéphanie.'

Madame de Genlis sat in the chair opposite. 'Oh, but your son is a very charming boy! How he has amused us.' She leant forward confidentially. 'He has quite taken our minds from those recent dangers and we have scarcely thought of the threats we must face from all those who are not in accord with Philippe Égalité. The duc, of course, has written again. I have told him we will return to Paris as soon as we have fully recovered from our ordeal. Our protégé Mademoiselle Adéle, in particular — it has been so distressing for my young charge. But how Tom makes her smile and laugh so gaily — it is a tonic to her and for us all.'

Sheridan picked up the bottle from Dr Burton. 'Tonic, heh? Sweeter than the one I am instructed to take by Lord Cannock. It is concocted by his physician and a very nasty potion it is too!'

Madame de Genlis wagged a finger as at a naughty schoolboy. 'It is good, I see, in its effect.'

'Well, it has forced me to eat, madame, just to dispel the odious taste!'

'Now, Monsieur Sherrie, I have received some information for you.'

Sheridan sat up. 'Regarding Dr Cardonnet?'

'Ah, *oui*!' The countess straightened the folds of her dress. 'My informant writes that before they both left Paris, Dr Cardonnet has been calling on the Marquis de Thiers-Auberet, a most detestable man.'

'I see. They have reconciled then?'

She shrugged. 'It would appear so. I do not know their connection.'

'The marquis sponsored his medical education, but they fell out when the doctor became a follower of Monsieur Mesmer.'

'*Alors*. The difference, it is reconciled. Only recently a friend here in London informs me that the marquis brought Dr Cardonnet to the Duke of York.'

'The king's second son?' said Sheridan in surprise.

'They attended at the duke's new home — of course you know his equerry, Captain Fitzroy, very well I think, after your wonderful comedy in Bury St Edmunds. I believe the other officer —'

'Captain Stewart,' Sheridan supplied.

'Stewart.' Madame nodded. 'The handsome one. He was also of the party.'

'The doctor is very fashionable in the salons —'

'*Non. Non*, Sherrie — this was not a salon. It is a group of gentlemen that are meeting.'

'To what end?'

Madame de Genlis spread her hands. 'My informant does not know. But not to play cards! I think they must discuss the situation in our Republic of France. The marquis is a leading émigré and the duke is a military man. Such men want war, I think.'

'But why would they include Cardonnet in their party?'

'I do not know.' Madame de Genlis clapped her hands. 'Tonight, we will play cards. I think you are not well enough yet for charades. Adéle is the very devil at whist!'

They played for pin money. Quite sufficient enough, Sheridan thought, as he saw the silver mounting on the table. Mademoiselle Adéle was indeed a whizz and gathered all their coins into her purse until on the final hand Tom triumphed. Sheridan suspected that his royal guest had manoeuvred the outcome just so — she had an affectionate glint in her eye as young Tom scooped up all his winnings and boasted of the treats which he would buy for everyone. Sheridan himself had not played well, for he was too distracted, but as a recovering invalid he could blame his shortcomings on a general fugginess of the brain.

His mind was now consumed with thoughts of Cardonnet. Even the earl's note, whilst giving him directions on how to take the tonic, had mentioned the mesmerist. It seemed that an appointment had been made with the Frenchman, and Cannock thanked Sheridan for any intercession which may have facilitated this meeting. Well, he had not interceded — he had quite forgotten the promise. And what influence would he have with the man anyway, when he was consorting with princes?

What was Dr Cardonnet up to? A visit with the Duke of York — what might that mean? Of all the siblings, York was closest to the Prince of Wales. Did His Royal Highness know of Cardonnet's visit with his younger brother? He would ask Hanger. Sheridan felt convinced that Dr Cardonnet was being used in some way to further the war interest, to push England, through the Duke of York, into declaring war on the French Revolutionaries. That seemed the most likely scenario. Now, more importantly than ever, with Pamela Syms about to return to Paris, how might he foil those plans?

In the days which followed Sheridan revived and found his energies much restored. Madame de Genlis teased that it was no doubt due to the noxious Dr Burton's Tonic, which she made sure he continued to imbibe as prescribed. There were plays and games all weekend and various callers anxious for an opportunity to meet with his illustrious houseguests. Although quite as many of the stuffier denizens of Isleworth would avoid any and all such association with so radical and scandalous a woman as Madame de Genlis.

Tom confessed to him that when they ventured forth, he had to steer the French party away from any encounters where they might be snubbed, and this was no mean task.

'Today on the High Street it was a perfect hopscotch from one pavement to another, Pa, and I had to stand in front of the countess so that she would not see the evil looks cast on her by Mr and Mrs Forsyth!'

But there were enough like-minded or curious neighbours to make for an almost continuous round of entertainment and invitations given and received. Sheridan noted with pleasure how Pamela in particular charmed and delighted all who made her acquaintance.

Reluctantly he determined that it was time to return to business at the theatre and his affairs, but before doing so, there was one matter which called to him with increasing urgency. For all his outward confidence he fluttered with nerves as he approached Pamela after breakfast.

'Won't you come into the garden? I would like my roses to see you.' He bowed with exaggerated formality.

Pamela's laughter tinkled pleasingly. 'And I would very much like to make their acquaintance!'

He proffered his arm and they walked out onto the garden path. It brought them to a quiet sheltered nook, which was indeed still showing a profusion of pink climbing roses.

'You see we still have an abundance even at this time of the year, and I think it is your presence which causes my roses to blush and linger.'

'And you, Monsieur Sheridan? Does my continued presence please you?'

He caught her hand, which clasped his own, warm and tender.

'I am a rose by any other name and that name being Sheridan, though not so fair, would blush and linger all the day.'

She turned to him with a glint in her eye. 'You know, I have wondered if our little sojourn here was not orchestrated…?'

'That would have been a most elaborate undertaking, Miss Syms.'

'Yes. It would need someone very capable to concoct the precise scenario. And a little cruel —' she examined him closely — 'to place Maman in such a state of terror.'

'There is only one possible justification for such a dastardly ruse.'

'And that is?'

'In all the best comedies it would herald a proposal of marriage.'

He stared deep into her eyes. They were hazel, not unlike his own colouring, but one was slightly darker than the other. This lack of symmetry he found appealing, a flaw which somehow made Pamela more vulnerable and only added to her allure.

'And you are not a writer of tragedies, my dear Sheridan.'

He shook his head. 'In my plays the answer is always "yes" and the lovers are always forgiven.'

She cast her eyes heavenward and fondled one of the roses coyly. 'But naturally our adventures on the highways of Kent were no play but only all that they seemed.'

He smiled. 'Pamela, I would be most honoured if you would accept my hand.'

She paused.

He held his breath, marvelling at her beauty, the fresh bloom of her cheek, wanting desperately to hold her in his arms. She could not refuse him, surely? Were there other suitors? There must be. She was the most perfect blossom, at eighteen flowering in all her glory. Was she already secretly betrothed? He felt himself tortured by apprehension. How should he read this long silence? If she refused him, he would behave as though it were all some ridiculous jest all along.

'I would like very much to take your hand, *cheri*.'

'To be my wife?' He had to be sure. There must be no pleasant ambiguity.

'To be your wife.' She laughed, a high fluted sound. 'Mrs Sheridan. I shall like that name very well.'

'I hope one day there may be a more fitting title before it.'

'Lady Pamela Sheridan?' She struck a pose, her eyes glistening. 'Yes. That would be delightful!'

Had he ever felt a moment of such exquisite joy? If he had, he could not recall it. He grasped her hand tighter and held it to his lips.

'My dear, I will follow you to France once parliament is in recess, and then we may declare our betrothal and marry in Paris.'

'Of course.'

He was about to draw her into his arms for a more fulsome embrace when she held a hand out before her. 'You will need to seek the approval of Maman and the duc.'

'Naturally.'

Pamela smiled sweetly. 'For now, it is our secret, *cheri*.'

He kissed her hand passionately.

'How shall I contain myself?' Laughter played about her lips and she leant forward to kiss him heartily on the cheek.

Oh, how he longed to clasp her in his arms! His blood was risen to the boil. But she was young and tender still, and he must wait until all was settled.

'Monsieur Sherrie! *Ma cher* Pamela!' Madame de Genlis appeared on the path behind and called for them again.

Sheridan stepped out from the nook, waved and bowed towards his future mother-in-law, before turning back to his beloved.

'Unfortunately, I am called away by very particular business.' His eyes locked with Pamela's. 'But I leave my character behind me.'

CHAPTER TWENTY-SIX

He stayed two nights in town in order to be nearer to the Haymarket and his affairs. On the second evening Constable Nicholls called on him and was shown into the front reception room.

'Sir, beg pardon for seeking you at your home but I did not wish our conversations to be overheard.'

'Please be seated, Constable. Can I offer you refreshment?'

'No, sir, I am on duty.'

'That does not stop your fellows, I can assure you.'

Sheridan poured himself a glass of claret and sat. 'I have not seen you for some time, Mr Nicholls.'

'I heard you were taken ill, sir.'

'And heard much else besides, I am sure. Old Sherry found drunk again in a ditch — is that what they were writing in the Grub Street press?'

Nicholls was silent.

'As it transpires, I was very sober. Some *friends* in St Giles *dropped* me home to old Drury Lane; but you see there are only the foundations of my theatre there at present, so the drop was deeper than expected.'

Nicholls looked up. 'The girl, Tilly?'

'And her Scottish giant.'

Nicholls inclined his head with interest. 'So, sir, you were brought to see Lucy Webster?'

'Yes, Constable. I received a note of invitation. With hindsight — which is a wonderful teacher, don't you agree? — I wish that I had notified you of the rendezvous. But it was all in a flurry of haste.' Sheridan sighed. 'And you will no doubt want me to tell you where she is for your own interview — but I do not know. It was a veritable labyrinthine journey to the house of ill repute where she is kept, and unlike Theseus I failed to lay a trail of thread, though much good it would have done me.'

'The House of the Swan.'

'The House of the Swan? What a delicious name for so tawdry a place. Come to think of it, a ruffian who waylaid us did speak of Tilly as a "swan". I thought nothing of it at the time, being solely focused on the blade he was waving in front of my throat.'

'It took me a while, sir, but from the drawing that you gave to me and using my contacts amongst the Huguenot community in St Giles, I have managed to locate Tilly. The House of the Swan is her aunt's establishment. A Mrs Bloomer. Tilly was orphaned as a young girl and thrown upon her mercy. To her credit, it does not appear that this madam has used her ill. Not yet. She employs her as a seamstress to her smuts. I cannot think Mrs Bloomer was best pleased when Tilly brought a pregnant girl into the Swan's nest.'

From the large pocket of his coat the constable drew forth a handbill and unscrolled it before Sheridan.

'Nor when she saw this.'

Reward
100 Guineas
Lucy Webster
20 years
Lady's Maid
wanted for the heinous murder
of Mr Edw.d Stretton Esq.

'I see. Lord Cannock has wasted no time.' Sheridan drained the claret. 'You have her in custody?'

Nicholls rolled up the bill and returned it to his pocket. 'No, sir.'

Sheridan's eyes narrowed. 'Why do you hesitate, Constable?'

'I do not, sir. The bird has flown and Tilly with her. Mrs Bloomer and her household will say nothing.'

Sheridan digested this information whilst he poured another generous glass for himself.

'I would ask you, Mr Sheridan, to relay to me the conversation which you had with Lucy Webster.'

'You think her guilty of this crime of murder?'

'It hardly matters what I think, sir. I know nothing of the events in Staffordshire. I only know that it is my duty to bring Lucy Webster safely before the law, where she may answer her accusers.' Nicholls paused before continuing. 'Perhaps you ask the question of yourself, sir? Have you formed an opinion?'

'You are right. I do ask myself whether or not she is guilty. Everything now points in that direction and yet…'

'You find it is unsatisfactory, this conclusion, sir?'

'I feel that there is something I am missing, despite the note that has been produced by Lady Cannock.'

Nicholls leant forward. 'You have the sense that people you might be inclined to trust — young Mr Webster, even the girl Tilly — they were not frightened of Lucy as one might be of a murderess, but instead they were frightened *for* her? You wonder still who killed Daniel? You are not convinced that it was Isaac Fethard who stabbed your scene painter and then attacked you in the theatre as he fled. You wonder who searched Daniel's lodgings, and for what?' The constable's eyes narrowed. 'You feel that there is some connection to Mr Stretton's assassination?'

'Yes, damn it! Nicholls, you have the nub of it. I have tried to believe that the girl is fallen into a murderous madness, but only because…'

'Because?'

'I am afraid to think otherwise.'

Nicholls nodded sagely. 'You fear to know the truth behind these dreadful deeds.'

Sheridan sighed and recounted to the constable the particulars of his conversation in the attic room of Mrs Bloomer's establishment. He included his notion that Lucy would now be brought to the home of the Irish coal heaver who was married to Tam's daughter, though he doubted she had been really well enough to be moved.

Nicholls thanked him. 'That may be anywhere along the river, and every other coal heaver is an Irishman these days — and a Whiteboy too, I'll hazard. Not a man with whom to cross swords.'

Sheridan nodded. Many of those infamous Irish rebels in their white smocks who had wrought havoc with the landowners in the country of his birth had escaped the law and were now in hiding amongst the throngs of men working the Thames docks.

'I shall do the best I can, Mr Sheridan, with our limited resources. It may be safer for Lucy were the Runners to find her rather than those others you are afraid to name.'

'I fear for her, and she is not in good health.'

'There is one last thing.' Nicholls rose to depart. 'Isaac Fethard has been found guilty today of the murder of Daniel Webster and of the disturbance and affray outside the shop of Monsieur De Lubac. He has been sentenced to be hanged at Newgate when next there is a hanging.'

'Which will be?'

'The end of next week.'

After a morning spent negotiating the business of the next production, Sheridan took himself away from the theatre in search of one of his most favourite lunchtime repasts: a good veal pie with a rich gravy and a mountain of crushed potato, downed with a pitcher of humming bub. He was consuming the meal with gusto and enjoying the delights of his own company in Mr Bellamy's pie shop when a well-dressed gentleman wiped the chair opposite with his handkerchief and sat down to face him.

Sheridan's fork paused in mid-air as he looked up to see who had so joined him without invitation.

'Dr Cardonnet.'

'You 'ave found me out, Monsieur Sheridan.'

The fork remained hovering in mid-air as he tried to work out which piece of information the Frenchman was alluding to. 'How so?'

'The excellent veal pies of Monsieur Bellamy! I too have succumbed. The English food, it is most terrible in almost every respect, but there is some virtue in the pies.'

'They are indeed virtuous pies.'

The morsel at last reached its destination and Sheridan savoured the hard pastry of the pie crust with the soft meat and succulent juices.

Cardonnet drummed his fingers on the table and continued to eye Sheridan, who, shifting uncomfortably in his seat at this intense perusal of his eating habits, felt obliged to continue in a conversational manner.

'We shall be saddened by your imminent departure, Dr Cardonnet. You have held our audiences entranced.'

The mesmerist gave a shrug, as though it were a little matter to fill a theatre.

'You have acquired premises on the Strand, I gather?' Sheridan continued.

'They are suitable for my present needs.'

'And royal patronage, so I understand.'

Cardonnet raised an eyebrow sardonically.

'You are quite the celebrity, Dr Cardonnet.'

'I am a doctor, Monsieur Sheridan, a man of science. There are too few, alas, who recognise the serious nature of my impulse.'

'Your motive, yes.'

'One gentleman, nevertheless, has such a perspicacity. I believe you are acquainted with Lord Cannock.'

'Indeed, a fine mind.'

'He speaks most highly of you…' Dr Cardonnet offered this aside as something perplexing.

'The earl wished very much to meet with you, Doctor. He asked if I could… Well, clearly there was no need for my intercession. You have met.'

'A most fortuitous encounter. The earl is a person who appreciates, how can I say, the limitless boundaries of the scientific mind. One that should not be curtailed by religion or society or even —' he paused for effect — 'morality.'

Cardonnet's own veal pie was delivered at that moment and he emitted a deep sigh of satisfaction.

'The earl has a very powerful interest in my ideas and is very knowledgeable, really most erudite.'

Sheridan nodded in agreement. 'His library is splendid and rather exceptional in that it is one of the few I know where the books are actually read.'

'His Lordship understands what might be achieved with artificial somnambulism.'

'And what is that, pray?' Sheridan dug into another potato.

'To delve into the farthest reaches of the human mind.'

'The human mind. Well, yes, that is a mystery.'

'Monsieur Sheridan, you are a man of the theatre, a writer, so you too will comprehend that all men must wear some disguise. A mask, behind which to a greater or lesser extent, we hide our true selves from the world. The earl, for instance, it is a mask, monsieur, of such refinement that I have not encountered before.'

Cardonnet nodded to himself with a look of profound appreciation. Whether this was for the veal pie or for Cannock, or both, Sheridan was not entirely sure.

'There are very few who can resist my ability to entrance. But the earl will not let me into the mind.' Cardonnet tapped his own head and laughed slyly. 'I have my theory about the earl. It is most outrageous.' He laughed again softly to himself, and it was clear that he was not going to share whatever outrageous theory he had arrived at with Sheridan.

Sheridan had lost his appetite and certainly his taste for the conversation. He braced himself to say *adieu* and quit the table, but the Frenchman was not quite finished with him.

'We all of us present a face that will be accepted by those we wish to be accepted by. Yourself, Monsieur Sheridan, your dearest wish is to be accepted as a gentleman.'

Sheridan stiffened at the veracity of this insight.

'To this end you will consort with the highest in the land; you will entertain them and partake in all their debauchery.'

Sheridan swallowed hard and reached for his beer, which he dearly wished to tip over the doctor's head for his impertinence.

'It is the disguise of an interloper, *non*?'

There was a pregnant pause. Did the rogue expect a response to the insult? Well, Sheridan refused to be goaded.

'Perhaps in your true self you long for a New Order entirely.' Cardonnet eyed him keenly. 'To sweep away the Old Order.'

'I am commonly known as a Reformer, sir. That is hardly something which I feel the need to disguise. Indeed, I am proud to be so; only this year I have been party to founding The Society of the Friends of the People.'

Cardonnet sneered. 'But every day there is another nail in the coffin of your Reform, Monsieur Sheridan. Being a *gentleman*, you espouse moderation, but I think you would like something…' He clenched his hands and then puffed them into an explosion. 'A little more dramatic! *Non*? You are a man of the theatre, after all. To see these men of ancient privilege, before whom you must scrape and bow, reduced to the level of their miserable merit.' Cardonnet's eyes narrowed and Sheridan toyed with the few crumbs on his plate to avoid the intensity of their glare. 'You might even be tempted to become a traitor.'

'Traitor? That is not a charge to be bandied about lightly, Doctor, not at this time.'

'You are right. Pardon, monsieur.' Cardonnet held up his fork in a gesture of apology. 'This is not France, where even a king — a former king, should I say — may be called a traitor by any man in the street, *n'est pas*?'

Sheridan felt an urgent need to redirect the conversation. 'And you, Dr Cardonnet, what is your true desire?'

Dr Cardonnet smiled crookedly. 'Never to be caught in a lie, monsieur.'

Was the fellow trying to be witty? With all his talk of masks and disguises, he concocted a world in which living itself was a continuous act of subterfuge. Well, perhaps he did speak truthfully. And Sheridan was no nearer to understanding the fellow than he ever had been.

He scraped his chair back. 'You must excuse me, Doctor, I have —'

'Pressing business. Of course. You are never idle, monsieur.'

Sheridan forced a smile. Was Cardonnet being sarcastic, having heard the slur in government quarters?

'*Jusqu'à ce que nous revoyions.*'

'Likewise, Doctor.'

Pleasant days of snatched romantic whispers in the nooks and crannies of the villa followed with his secret betrothed. Sheridan was pleasingly reassured of Pamela's ardour. She had made her promise, and her affections were genuine — quite as sincere as his own. But on the Friday evening Sheridan again returned to town. The pressing reason for the dereliction of his duties as host in Isleworth was the appointment which Isaac Fethard had the following morning with the hangman. Sheridan felt that he could not be at the villa whilst this event occurred. He could already sense the creeping edge of a melancholy which was descending on him. The black humour which few of his acquaintance were ever permitted to witness. He certainly would not allow it to cloud the precious days of perpetual sunshine with his dearest Pamela. Those days would be over all too soon. Passage had been booked from Dover and the party would be sailing mid-week. He would instead sit at Grosvenor Street and draw down his copy of Mr Dryden's poetry, which he always found a solace, and allow himself to give way to this gloomier aspect of his nature.

Amongst the correspondence waiting for him at the town house he found an invitation to attend a soiree in Mayfair at the home of Lord and Lady Cannock on the following evening. He would attend, he decided. He would be interested to meet with them now that the reward had been posted for Lucy Webster. He wondered how Lady Cannock was coping with the decision to reveal the incriminating missive.

CHAPTER TWENTY-SEVEN

The executions were to be early, which Sheridan thought a blessing. It was many years since he had ventured near such an event, and he hoped that at Newgate there might not be the crowds and carnival atmosphere which had so often been found at Tyburn a decade before. He had no desire to watch a man die. And not this man. Isaac Fethard was a wretch and a villain who could probably be sentenced to hang on half a dozen charges of theft and assault, but of this one charge of murder, Sheridan felt certain he was innocent. The wheels of justice turned, however, and would not be delayed once set in motion. The same wheels would trample over Lucy Webster soon enough, unless by some miracle yet another suspect presented for Edward Stretton's murder.

He had mulled over the circumstances of Isaac Fethard's verdict. According to Constable Nicholls, the judge had accepted a sworn affidavit from the purported witness, who wished not to appear in court in case doing so would endanger his life. Sheridan's testimony at the magistrates' hearing at Bow Street that Fethard had been one of a party which had attacked the watchmaker's shop and his own person earlier on that fateful evening had also been weighed in the balance — as evidence of the man's violent nature.

The prosecutor had even suggested that Fethard had slipped into the theatre in Haymarket not only for the purposes of theft but to exact some obscure revenge on Sheridan for the earlier incident. The prosecution case was all flimsy hearsay.

For the reward, any man might swear to anything. Or hold a grudge. The witness might even have been paid to give such evidence. In order to protect the real perpetrator? Sheridan's mind wove through a myriad of permutations.

Once Ned Cribbins' alibi had disintegrated, there had been nothing to save Isaac Fethard. Nothing, Sheridan reassured himself. The verdict tugged at his conscience nevertheless. Should he have mentioned the discovery of the dragonfly on Daniel Webster's clothing? Sheridan sighed. This would have been laughed out of court. The White-faced Darter! The very name of the insect would have been cause for hilarity, not only in the court but also in the Grub Street press. He imagined that some would even suggest it was a prank of some kind on his part to embarrass the Old Bailey or the particular judge, who was a dyed-in-the-wool government man.

Isaac Fethard would hang and there was an end of it. He looked at his fob watch. It would take place in little over an hour. He could not sit still. For ten minutes he paced the room and then he called for his hat and coat.

The rising sun was a faint glimmer through the morning mist and had yet to dispel the black cloak of night, but already the streets were beginning to throng. The workforce that fuelled the engine of that great city was abroad and setting about their industry. Clerks scurried to their offices. Kitchen servants ambled to the marketplaces with empty baskets that would soon be loaded and cumbersome. Two beggars squabbled over their claim to a stretch of pavement. Carters and wagons from the surrounding countryside laden with autumnal produce dominated the roads where later carriages and sedan chairs would prevail.

The bustle increased as Sheridan drew nearer to the older parts of the city where the streets were narrower and the houses and shops tumbled one on top of another. He knew that his feet were briskly steering him in the direction of Newgate. What was driving him there? A forlorn hope that at the last Fethard would receive a pardon and his sentence be commuted to transportation? Would that it might be so. It grieved him that a man's life hung by so thin a thread.

As he made his way up towards the Old Bailey and Newgate Street, debating whether or not to risk cutting through one of the back streets, he became aware that others were also heading towards the scaffold. A man was selling copies of *The Newgate Calendar*, with its lists of the recently hanged, accounts of their lives, their confessions and dying words. Taverns had opened early, selling porter and ale to the prospective spectators, some of whom, Sheridan suspected, were still inebriated from the night before. Food vendors carried trays of pies or fruit. Games of chance of various kinds had been set up en route.

Sheridan slowed his pace. He had come far enough to acknowledge and bear witness to the man's passing without viewing the lurid show itself. He could not imagine the anguish of facing that noose as an innocent man, with no one to believe it. He felt that his presence was in some small measure an act of atonement.

Sheridan halted and, stepping back into shadow, drew out his watch. Twenty minutes. He stood against the wall to guard against the pickpockets who would be out in force and began to peruse the crowd. It was only a matter of moments before he picked out Mrs Fethard, supported by a woman of a similar age — her sister, he would hazard, from the family resemblance.

Clearing a path for them was a tall, broad-shouldered man with the scarred and calloused hands of a smithy. And in their wake were three girls, not above thirteen or fourteen. All were accompanied by a fellow Sheridan recognised as the thick-necked ruffian who had sung so lustily for King and Church. The man placed a consoling hand on the youngest child's shoulder. A wave of murmurs and exclamations rippled out from Mrs Fethard's party as she was recognised as the wife of one of those to be hanged, a woman soon to be widowed. The information was relayed with prurient zest to those behind.

A gang of young apprentices laughed and made playful wager amongst themselves on the length of time it would take for the victim to die. In the jostle, one of them nudged against Sheridan. He pushed the fellow along and afterwards checked his pockets. Nothing taken. It was a larger crowd than he had anticipated. He felt uneasy and began to wonder at the wisdom of his presence. But the crush of people in the narrow streets was such that to turn against the flow would be foolhardy.

Events unfolded and he followed their narrative course through the rising crescendos of noise and the sudden troughs of silence. Sheridan imagined that by these particulars of sound a blind man might know the arc of a tale. He judged the moment that Isaac Fethard dropped and the point thereafter at which his life expired. He sighed wearily.

From the dispersing masses he overheard more details of the scene, the plaintive sobs of the convicted man, his pathetic cries claiming innocence, which many in the departing crowd found a cause for great mirth, and his final bloodcurdling oaths against his accusers, which passers-by repeated with obvious relish. Sheridan listened as a rumour solidified into an assertion that Mrs Fethard had resorted to promises of payment to various associates of her husband, urging them to rush forward and scale the podium to pull at his legs in order to cut short the final jig. What change to her circumstances would widowhood bring to her and her fatherless daughters? Sheridan felt his sentiments pricked and he resolved to send some small sum in charity. His thoughts were thus engrossed when he caught sight of a man whose narrowed eyes were fixed on him with deadly intent and who pushed a path toward him.

The weasel-faced youth, Ned Cribbins.

Sheridan felt a lurch in his stomach. The scene at the magistrates' court when he had sabotaged Ned's testimony for Isaac Fethard returned to him. His back was against the wall. The crowd, which seemed to have swelled of a sudden, pinned him to the spot. It would be a simple matter for Ned to stick him with a blade and then lose himself amongst the swarm before anyone should realise what had happened. He locked eyes with Ned to let him know that he was seen, in hopes of forestalling his murderous approach. But he saw no hesitation there.

'Let me pass!' he shouted into the surging tide. 'Let me through, I pray you!' With a shove he heaved into the swell and felt the press of bodies around him. Now he could no longer see Ned nor the direction from which his assailant might be coming. He felt a rising panic and struggled for breath as he tried to keep himself upright and in motion within the jam of human traffic. Sharp elbows dug into his ribs. His toes were stamped upon. His face was pressed up against a dirt-encrusted jacket. The smell of beer and sweat assaulted his nostrils. He must cling to his hat or lose it.

'Mr Sheridan!' a booming voice rang out.

With a jolt of relief, he cricked his neck to see who might be calling him.

'Mr Sheridan! Stay fast!'

And then he was plucked from the throng by two uniformed officers of the militia. A row of fellow officers was blocking a passage and had thereby funnelled and herded the crowd into the current gridlock.

A hand was laid on his back and Sheridan found himself siphoned behind their lines and brought in front of Mr Biddulph.

The Bow Street officer clapped his shoulder. 'Well, sir, you look quite discountenanced!'

Sheridan inhaled deeply. 'Thank you, Officer Biddulph. For a moment there I thought to be crushed.'

And worse, he could have added. He bowed to the corpulent gentleman, inwardly bemoaning that he seemed to be perpetually beholden to the official.

'I wonder you don't go about with a manservant, sir, to protect your person.'

'That would seem to be a sensible precaution.'

'You were here for the hanging, of course.'

Sheridan winced.

'If I had known you were going to attend, Mr Sheridan, I would have provided an escort and you might have joined the dignitaries.'

'It was a decision of the moment, sir. Foolish, as you see, and I did not watch the actual…'

'Justice was seen to be done, I can assure you, sir — though some ruffians knocked a way through to pull at the assassin's legs and hastened his end.' He grimaced. 'We have them in custody, you'll be pleased to hear.'

'Officer, there is something for which I have meant to petition you.'

'Whatever that may be, sir, we are here to oblige.'

Sheridan had come to a decision whilst he had kept vigil over Isaac Fethard's demise. As the person who had put up the reward for the capture of Daniel Webster's killer, he would insist on meeting the witness who laid claim to that thirty guineas before he would hand over a single penny. He would look the man straight in the eye and he would know.

CHAPTER TWENTY-EIGHT

He had gone afterwards to Wanstead, where Mrs Canning greeted him warmly and remarked on his return to the fullness of his health.

'Yes, I am quite restored, Hitty. You must know I was a very fortunate invalid to be cared for by so many darling angels.'

Mehitabel raised an eyebrow. 'A household of beautiful ladies. I still wonder at the extraordinary circumstances of their arrival. But how very pleasant for you, Richard, to be at the centre of their ministrations.'

'Now, Good Sister Christian, I have had to share a large portion of that stage with my son. Young Tom has enjoyed the ladies' favour most hugely and practised all manner of gallantries in their company.'

'Well, that is good, I think. The boy sadly misses the feminine influence of his good mother. May God bless her memory.'

They both nodded at that sad reflection and Mehitabel sniffed back a renegade tear.

'That we do, Hitty, the dearest creature that ever there was.'

Mrs Canning squinted at Sheridan. 'There is still a little pallor in your complexion, Richard. Have you been abroad too much?'

'My affairs are always pressing. And … I have this morning been to Newgate.'

'Dear God, it is the prison pallor then. I hope you have not caught some other vile infection.'

Sheridan shook his head. 'I did not enter. There was a hanging.'

Mehitabel shuddered. 'I know it to be a necessary evil, but that such a show is made!'

'It was the man charged with my scene painter's murder.'

'Well, there's an end to it.' She sighed. 'You must think no more on the sad business. I shall send for my own cordial; it will revive your spirits.' She rang a bell at her side.

'Only I think this man was innocent, Good Sister Christian.'

Mrs Canning frowned.

'And I beg you might pray for his soul.'

'If you so wish.'

'And now,' said Sheridan, leaping up, 'I must see my daughter!'

'The cordial…'

'There shall be plenty of time for cordial, Hitty.'

Sheridan kissed the cheek of his dear friend in passing.

'Where is my Mary?' he called out as he bounded up the stairs. 'Where is my dearest, most precious girl?'

By the time Sheridan had reached the upper landing the wet nurse had emerged from the nursery with the child on her hip.

Ensconced in the comfortable armchair used by the nurse, Sheridan spent the next hour amusing his protégé and she likewise entertained him. He blew raspberries and she blew bubbles. He twined his fingers in her soft curls and she pulled at his side whiskers. Then he held her out from himself so that her strong little legs dangled on his knees in an attitude of standing. He jiggled her up and down as though she were jumping and dancing on the platform which his thighs provided. She in turn kicked out, attempting to affect her own momentum.

'Who's a strong girl then? Who's my bonny Mary?'

Here was a jig that spoke of life, not death, and Sheridan felt his heart swell to embrace it.

*

As he changed his outfit in readiness for the visit to the Cannock soiree, Sheridan realised that his watch had been stolen. It had been a gift from the Whig leader Fox. Inscribed within the case were the words *To R.B.S. Time waits for no man. C.J.F.* — a teasing reminder of Sheridan's notorious timekeeping. He had treasured it. Its design was simple but it was a refined and exquisite object, with the mechanism crafted by a first-rate watchmaker in Clerkenwell. He had been a fool to carry it to Newgate. A fool to venture forth at all.

The reception in Mayfair heralded two events. The first was a private exhibition of the portrait of the earl and his wife with their son Sempronius. The formal individual portraits were not yet completed but the sittings were finished, and so the Cannocks planned to return to Sandbourne in the week following. The group portrait was much admired, not only for the likenesses but for the naturalness of the pose, the young boy playing with a hoop.

'Dear little Sempronius looks quite angelic!' one matron enthused.

'He is no angel, I can assure you!' his mother countered with a laugh. 'I wonder that Mr Hoppner managed to capture his likeness at all.' She nodded over to the artist. 'He fidgeted so! Is that not true, Mr Hoppner?'

The artist bowed politely.

Sheridan congratulated the younger man. He too had sat for Hoppner in years gone by and considered the artist captured something of his youthful intensity, though he had thought at the time he might look a little arrogant. But then youth was arrogant.

The other event of the evening, coming half an hour later, was the arrival of Emmanuel Stretton, recently released from Newgate. He was in the company of the earnest Mr Wilberforce and Mr Gustavus Vasso, an esteemed man of letters whose sensational narrative of his life as a slave in the Americas continued to be reprinted most regularly. The latter's new wife occasioned quite as much fascination and interest as the man himself, Sheridan observed. It was not merely that Mrs Vasso was some twenty years younger than her husband, but that she was an English country rose who hailed from the streets of Soham in Cambridgeshire. Together, they presented a striking couple.

Emmanuel was dressed as a gentleman. Sheridan noted that he wore his stylish new clothes very well, and no one could doubt the nobility in his demeanour. To the astonishment of the assembled guests, Lord and Lady Cannock introduced the former West Indian slave as their cousin. The gasps which circulated the room were strangled in polite restraint.

In his quiet, measured voice, the earl went on to inform the gathering that Emmanuel, rather than being broken by the condition of imprisonment, had used his time to read widely and at length. He had also begun to learn the classical languages, Greek, Latin and Hebrew — for which he had shown an exceptional facility.

This was greeted with a ripple of applause.

The earl continued. He and Lady Cannock, together with Sir Humphrey Barclay, who was sadly indisposed, had always believed in Emmanuel's good character and had been convinced from the start that he was innocent of the charges levied against him. The earl invited the company to share in their relief that justice had prevailed and Emmanuel had been exonerated. His Lordship then turned to the young man with a look of pride and announced that Emmanuel had expressed his desire to study law with the ambition of furthering the cause of Abolition.

'A place has been secured for this purpose at the university in Bologna and Emmanuel will be departing soon in the company of Mr Vasso and his wife, who are embarking on a tour of talks and lectures throughout the European continent.'

In the wake of this proclamation there came a further round of polite applause. Toasts were offered and glasses raised to the success of Mr Emmanuel Stretton's future endeavours.

'The earl, they say, is quite eccentric, as well as a recluse, and I may know it now for a truth,' one Whig lord murmured to another.

The company dispersed into small groups, but before anyone else could claim his attention Sheridan was drawn to one side by Lady Cannock.

'My dearest Richard, I am so glad that you have joined us this evening.'

'The pleasure is all mine, Lady Cannock.'

'You will appreciate how momentous a day this is for us. To see our dear Emmanuel acquitted and to be party, with my dear uncle, to his advancement.' She cast a beaming look of admiration towards the young man.

'I am certain that he will be a credit to you all.'

'Now, Richard…' She patted his arm and lowered her voice. 'You must tell me; do you know anything more of Lucy Webster? Samuel has confided to me that you have seen her.'

Sheridan started. 'I see. Yes, I have.'

'Sir Anthony and the magistrate here in London had to accept that an appointment was made with Edward on the morning of his murder and that he was lured to his death; there could be no case against our dear Emmauel. Now the hue and cry is all for Lucy Webster. Mr Hanley is most distraught. I believe he was once rather partial to Lucy. You know my thoughts. Were you able to convey that suggestion? A fresh start in the New World?'

A conspiratorial liveliness in Lady Cannock's expression spoke of her readiness to take action as soon as she should be given the nod.

For a moment Sheridan gazed at Lady Cannock in wonder. Was there ever a lady who so immersed herself in the lives and cares of her servants? He had always considered the Cannocks rather worthy but dull people. Now he felt that he must re-evaluate them. In their gentle and unassuming manner, they could nevertheless stand alongside the foremost revolutionaries of the age. Why, then, did he feel this disquieting sensation of subterfuge when in their company?

Perhaps it was all Cardonnet's talk of masks and disguises earlier in the week. He had found himself in the days since their luncheon encounter peering at more than one of his acquaintance, with the object of discerning the nature of their mask and what might lie behind. Even his darling Pamela presented a disconcerting plethora of disguises in her poses and attitudes. Life seemed all a game to her. A constant performance. He had to reassure himself throughout the week that her feelings for him were genuine and heartfelt.

'I am sorry to say, Ann, that Lucy has since disappeared from our last meeting place. So I have been informed.'

'By whom?'

'An officer of Bow Street.'

'Sent to apprehend her?'

'The offer of reward makes Lucy vulnerable, Lady Cannock, to snitches and the like.'

'I see.' Her bosom heaved. 'Lucy has evaded capture. That is good.' She turned her intense eyes on Sheridan. 'But did you tell her of my offer? A ship's passage? A new life?'

'There is much risk now, Your Ladyship. Now there is a hue and cry.'

'It can be done, Richard.'

'I talk of the risk to *you*, Ann,' Sheridan warned with urgency.

Lady Cannock pulled up straight. 'I must do what my conscience tells me.'

'Lucy seemed confused. Her wits…' Sheridan shook his head sadly.

'But will she think on?' Lady Cannock pressed.

'I cannot say.'

'If I, or Samuel, could only speak with her she would see the sense of it. Have you any notion where she might have been taken? And do you trust those who have her care — now that there is such a bounty on her capture?'

'I know not who to trust, Lady Cannock. And the girl is not well. I fear for her health and that of her unborn child.'

'Lady Cannock. Mr Sheridan. Is this not a truly remarkable occasion?'

It was the diminutive Mr Wilberforce who intruded, his face shining with enthusiasm. They broke away from each other to encompass his incursion.

'It is most gratifying, William. If you'll excuse me, gentlemen.' Lady Cannock nodded and moved away.

'I must say, Sheridan, it pleases me to see you here. I did not know you were acquainted with Lord and Lady Cannock. They see so few people.'

'Stafford.'

'Ah yes, you have your seat there.'

'And my mind presently in Haymarket whilst my heart resides in Isleworth, but I have quite lost track of my toes.'

The young politician looked bewildered for a moment. Sheridan recalled that he was of a very literal disposition.

'Ah yes, I see. Most amusing.'

Before departing, Sheridan approached Emmanuel and, clasping his hand, shook it warmly with admonitions to leaven his study with cheerful company and a good bottle of wine, both of which, he assured him, were readily available in Italy. The young man inclined his head and bowed graciously. Here was one neck that would not swing. That was a blessing.

CHAPTER TWENTY-NINE

It was after midnight when Sheridan returned to Isleworth, and all the household was asleep. But he was not yet ready to retire as he reflected on the course of the evening. He poured himself a bumper of brandy. That would ease his agitation. He quickly downed a first and poured a second. It had been an abstemious evening — the tone set by the Cannocks themselves — and to have overindulged would have been taken ill. They were unlike his usual company, the prince, Fox, Hanger and others, with whom he might very easily be drunk under the table by now. The brandy calmed his nerves. He told himself that he had done all that he could.

The demands of other guests being such, he had been unable to continue the conversation with Lady Cannock, but then he had sighted Hanley. The factotum was not of the party and yet he was clearly more than a servant as he hovered in the background with his eye ever watchful on Lord Cannock.

Not for the first time had Sheridan paused to speculate about Samuel Hanley. He had been treated by the old earl as a boyhood companion for his frail son, and the two boys had grown up together sharing the old earl's passion for the laboratory. Lucy had written that they spoke more like brothers than master and servant. Might there not be some actual relation? That evening Lord and Lady Cannock had shocked their guests by claiming Emmanuel as a cousin; could the same also be claimed for Samuel Hanley? He had the same fair hair and high brow of Lord Cannock. And, whilst he was older, broader and with a darker eye colour than the late Edward Stretton, one could yet see some clear resemblance in their physique. Sheridan shook his head; he was allowing his fancies into a gallop. Of one thing he was certain: Samuel was loyal and trusted by both Lord and Lady Cannock. Tearfully, the manservant had professed his affections for Lucy. He would have a care of the young lady's maid, despite Edward Stretton's success as the rival suitor. Sheridan determined he would find an opportunity to speak to Samuel.

On the pretence of needing to refresh himself, Sheridan drew the manservant from the room. Samuel was quick to grasp that Sheridan wished to confer with him and they slipped into a small parlour. Lucy had evaded capture, Sheridan informed him, possibly to the lodgings of an Irish coal heaver by the river. He reiterated his concern for her health and that the reward now made her vulnerable to any who might be so tempted.

'That is my worry also, sir. There is no time to be lost.'

Sheridan nodded. 'Also, there may be others who look for her, thinking that she may hold the key to some *great secret*.'

'How so? Did Her Ladyship not think that Lucy's note was merely a lure for Mr Stretton? Is that not what has been accepted?'

'Stretton believed the note,' Sheridan stressed.

'He was a desperate man.'

'But I rather think he had some inclination of his own that was revived by it. In any case, I have reason to believe that he imparted its contents and his own conjectures to another gentleman. A rather dangerous gentleman, unfortunately.'

Samuel studied Sheridan narrowly. 'The man who holds his debts, Mr Greaves?'

Sheridan did not deny.

'You think this man may hunt for Lucy?'

'I do.'

'This gentleman believes that Lucy knows some means to blackmail my lord?'

'Does she?'

Samuel shrugged. 'There are no secrets.' He laughed softly. 'What secrets might there be? We are very quiet and dull at Sandbourne.'

'Samuel ... I believe Lucy does know something; she intimates...'

'What does she intimate, Mr Sheridan?' Hanley demanded, as though he were speaking to an equal.

'I think you know, Samuel. I think you know all there is to know.'

Samuel was silent then, his brow furrowed as it seemed to Sheridan he grappled with his conscience.

He heaved a sigh. 'Can I trust you, Mr Sheridan? Trust in your discretion?'

'I believe you can.' Sheridan straightened as though to accentuate his probity.

'Lucy came to me some while ago... Her mother, Mrs Webster, had let slip something of the circumstances of my own birth. Undisclosed circumstances which Mrs Webster had been privy to as a young maid — one of the very few to know the particulars of my origins. I know not why Mrs Webster broke my mother's confidence, but she did. I imagine she sought to warn Lucy of what miseries might befall a young servant woman.' Hanley took a deep breath. 'My mother was abused sir, forcibly, by Mr Francis Stretton.'

'Edward's father?'

Hanley nodded curtly. 'I was the consequence of that violent encounter. I believe Lucy's mother feared the attentions of that man's son, that he might be cut from the same cloth as his father.'

'I see. So you are the natural son of Francis Stretton.' It was as Sheridan had begun to suspect; Samuel was a bar sinister cousin to Lord Cannock. And half-brother to Edward, the man who had cruelly seduced the object of Hanley's own affections. Well, here was a spider's web of secrets.

'I made Lucy promise, indeed swear, that this was a knowledge that must not be shared — for my good mother's sake, for her honour and reputation.'

'Naturally, that would be most distressing for Mrs Hanley.'

Hanley rubbed his brow. 'Perhaps it was because we had shared this intimacy, but it must have set Lucy thinking on the subject of family secrets and illegitimacy. She had ever a quick and lively mind. And then she came to me the day before those tragic events in the woods, with her ridiculous suspicion that the earl may be no legitimate heir to Sandbourne!'

Sheridan's brow creased. His mind flew to the portrait of the beautiful young woman who had died giving birth to twins, only one of whom had survived. Had she been unfaithful to her husband? Why should young Lucy Webster, a mere servant, make such a claim after some forty or more years?

Hanley pressed on. 'Edward Stretton should have the title, Lucy said. Mr Sheridan, I thought it was a jest.' He shook his head in bewilderment. 'Now I begin to suspect that her wits were already astray; she may have truly believed it when she wrote that note which was found on Stretton's person. Edward was constantly impugning the virility of the 3rd Earl in contrast to the military prowess of his own vile father. He should have been delighted to imagine that some proof existed that confirmed the impotence of the present earl's father.'

'But why would she then murder Edward?'

'Because, later that evening, she discovered his engagement to Miss Wentworth in Shrewsbury. I believe that is when Lucy lost all sense and killed Stretton in a jealous rage.'

'There is no proof then of what she "imagined"?'

'Because it is all ridiculous fancy, sir!'

'Mr Greaves will be disappointed. He is not a man who likes to be disappointed. As I revealed to you, Lucy claimed to be wedded to Edward Stretton. There may very well have been some sham of a marriage — the man was an utter scoundrel — but in her maddened state she is convinced that her unborn child is the true heir to Sandbourne.'

Samuel looked ashen. 'We must find her.'

'Or the Runners, anyone but Mr Greaves.'

Sheridan had then suggested that Samuel try to find The House of the Swan, attempt to speak with Tilly and persuade her that Lucy could be helped to a ship before it was too late. Tilly might trust Samuel and, more importantly, Lucy would trust him.

Sheridan's reflections were interrupted by a light rap on his bedroom door. His heart skipped a beat. Surely it could not be Pamela? Would she be so bold on the promise of marriage to seek him out in his private chamber? She was a creature of impulse, so it was not beyond imagining. And how he longed to give full rein to his passions.

He would be a gentleman, of course. Must be a gentleman. For a moment he recalled his young ardent self. Having married Eliza in the course of their flight to France at a church near Calais, he had yet refrained from consummation until they had returned to England and begged the necessary permission and blessing of their fathers to legitimately marry again. His own father had refused, had stubbornly declined to reconcile for many years. But he and Eliza had finally married at Marylebone with Thomas Linley's blessing. Well, but here was Pamela. He would be as gallant again in the face of passion. She would esteem him all the more.

Sheridan moved silently to the door and took care that it should not creak as he half opened it.

Tom stood on the threshold in his nightshift. 'Pa.'

'Tom?' Sheridan was taken aback.

'May I speak with you, Pa?'

'Of course, dearest boy, do come in.'

Tom moved swiftly into the room.

'What troubles you? Sit down. Have a glass of brandy.'

'Thank you, Pa, I will, but I do not know that I can sit.'

Sheridan regarded his son as he poured two large measures of brandy and they raised the glasses.

'Your good health, Pa.'

'And yours, my boy.'

Tom did not look unhappy or troubled, but rather he seemed flushed and excitable. His eyes were wide and glittering.

'I seek your advice, Pa.'

Sheridan nodded and sat down in the chair near his bed. 'What is so urgent that you seek me out at this hour, Tom?'

'It is urgent, Pa, because if I am to speak, I think it must be tomorrow. Our time is almost over.' Tom paced rapidly to and fro.

A smile twitched at the corners of Sheridan's mouth. Was his son enamoured with the young mademoiselle? He had fancied there was some youthful flirtation with the duc's daughter. Tom was lately seventeen. It was only natural. Nothing which could be serious.

'I am not practiced in matters of the heart, Pa…'

'Plenty of time for that, my boy.'

Tom stopped and plonked himself on the end of the bed. 'I fear there is no time to be lost at all!'

Tom's expression of sudden distress prompted a surge of paternal fondness in Sheridan. His poor boy, grappling with his uncontrolled passions.

'I wonder how to let her know my feelings, Pa? How would you advise? What must I say? There is so little time before they are to depart, and if I declare myself then she may wait and will not be tempted by the suit of some Frenchman.' Tom slammed his fist into his palm. 'She must know the strength of my feeling. She must be made to wait for me. What must I say, Pa?'

He did not want to dampen his son's spirits. And for all he knew, having been so much out of sight being ill and then on business, the young Mademoiselle Adéle may be consumed by an equal flame. But Sheridan had a duty and a responsibility to the duc whilst his daughter stayed under his roof. He was *in loco parentis*. And mademoiselle was a princess of the House of Bourbon. That must never be forgotten.

'You must say that you will write. That you will both write to each other, long letters full of chat and gossip and fun, and if in time your feelings —'

'Pa, unless I speak now I fear she will see me as a boy and not the man I am become. I know she is a little older, Pa, but only by a year or two, which is not a great deal and will seem nothing at all before long.'

Sheridan felt the blood drain from his face. Tom spoke not of Mademoiselle Adéle. His son's ardour was all for Pamela.

His son was right. Pamela was scarcely two years the boy's senior. They were near contemporaries, whilst Sheridan was a man of forty-one. For a moment he floundered, but then regained his bearings. Yes, he was a man in his prime. A man of standing, who had wooed and won Pamela's heart. The dear girl loved him quite as much as he worshipped her. But how could he ask Tom to accept this young woman, for whom it was now evident Tom was also possessed of strong feeling, as his stepmother? Well, thinking on that would have to wait. His poor boy. Tom's young heart would break, but being youthful it would mend quick enough and by Christmas there would be some other fancy.

'You must forget her, Tom.'

'Pa?'

'You must put Miss Syms quite from your mind in that regard.' He looked Tom straight in the eye. 'She loves another.'

The boy's face dropped, overcome with anguish. 'Then I am already lost.'

'I promise you, my dearest son, that there will be one that is for you. And what a fine heart you will have to offer her.'

It was little enough to ease the pain. They sat in silence for some moments, both consumed with thoughts of Pamela Syms.

'Goodnight, Pa.' Dejected, Tom rose and crossed the room. At the door he turned. 'Thank you, sir.'

Once Tom had departed Sheridan buried his face in his hands. This was ill. He blamed himself. He had not kept watch over Tom. The boy's emotions were in the turmoil of youth. His sweet mother had passed away in June. He had been taken out of his schooling. A wild and carefree summer with a sorry lack of any routine or discipline had followed, and then the boy had been plunged into the company of some of the most alluring and exciting women of the present times with little else to distract him. In acting as their escort, Tom had begun to fancy that he was already a man of society. But he was still a boy and Sheridan had been neglectful in pursuing the furtherance of his education. He must find a tutor, someone who could channel the energies of his son before Tom lost the inclination to study at all. It was now a matter of the utmost urgency. He would set his mind to it on the morrow.

CHAPTER THIRTY

The next morning Sheridan did not rise much before noon. No one would remark. It was not unusual. When he came down it was to find the household in any case all dispersed. Tom was calling on a friend and the French party had been invited for luncheon with his neighbours the De Quinceys. Mrs Tucker had an omelette produced and Sheridan settled down with the post, which had just been delivered. He cast all missives aside save one. A letter from Paris.

It was from the radical reformist John Stone. Stone wrote to inform him that he had for the moment blocked a proposal from the National Convention to confer honorary French citizenship on Sheridan. He had prevailed on Monsieur Brissot to delay the announcement. Stone had thought it expedient to confer firstly with Sheridan. Stone hoped that he had made the right decision and waited to be advised.

Sheridan was grateful for Stone's caution and his intervention with the chair of the proposing committee. At this present time such an honour might be easily misinterpreted. There were others, including young Mr Wilberforce, who had earlier in the year received just this same honorary citizenship as a mark of his 'high ideals' from the National Convention in France. But Wilberforce was an undoubted friend of Mr Pitt, loyal through and through, to the point where he increasingly supported Pitt's repressive regime.

A matter of six months or so and the climate had become altogether different. One could almost taste the rising fear in the air. It was palpable. Informants and agents were everywhere, as Sheridan had learned at first hand. Events in

France had unsettled Mr Pitt's government — not least the Revolutionaries' treatment of Louis XVI. Now that a Republic had been declared, Louis' position was ever more precarious. The outbreaks of violence in Paris and the steady trickle of émigrés, which threatened to become a flood of refugees escaping from Madame la Guillotine, had roused a spread of anti-Jacobin mania. In 1789, Sheridan had embraced the Revolution as many had. He had helped to found The Society of Friends of the People in the previous year in part to oppose Burke's anti-Revolutionary influence within the Whig party. He saw himself as a leader amongst Reformers. But here was the rub: he was an Irishman by birth. That enthusiasm for revolution abroad might credibly translate into a support for revolution in Ireland. A revolution which would be sure to have the backing of the French. Sheridan could well see how this might endanger his position.

The recent ncounterr with Dr Cardonnet came vividly to mind. The mesmerist had named him a traitor. A jest? A provocation? He had begun to realise how much Dr Cardonnet enjoyed toying with people's minds. The letter to the prince had certainly been evidence of that. But perhaps Cardonnet had been offering him a judicious warning? Hinting that the genial Sheridan mask might slip and then others would be all too ready to see a traitor, whatever he protested.

He must be on the alert. Yet he must appear as nonchalant as ever. What a fine line he walked; only tip one way and not the other and he might be arrested for treason. How that would delight his enemies across the floor of the House. These were treacherous times. He must tread warily. But oh, how exciting were these days! What a time to be alive! When the whole world presented the possibility of a new order with the overthrow of all that was arcane and calcified. And yet for all his support of revolutions, he played with princes. As he scraped his luncheon plate clean, he was moved to ask of himself, *Sheridan, who are you?* And a reply came.

I am first one man and then another, and frequently both at the same time.

The morning for departure had arrived. Tom insisted on accompanying the party down to Dover. Sheridan could hardly protest. His son had proven himself a very gallant escort and all the ladies professed their great affection for him. The addition of his son to the company put Sheridan on edge and meant that he must be guarded in his attentions to Pamela. It was clear that she sensed a change of atmosphere as she cast bewildered eyes towards him. He knew he was not acting as a lover should. But he could scarcely tell her the reasons why he behaved so offhand and cool. He tried to distribute his charm and favour equally amongst the party. Indeed, he directed a large part to reassuring the countess that this time there would be no incident on the road to Dover and that if they were waylaid, then he and Tom and the various footmen would see the brigands off *tout suite*.

It being November, it was a long and miserable journey. The rain was relentless and as the day drew on the two carriages negotiated the worst sections of road with a care for ruts and muddy potholes. A chill that heralded the arrival of winter meant that they were wrapped in shawls and covers against the draughts and pressed tightly together in a soporific fug. Sheridan abandoned the imperative to entertain and allowed himself to doze.

At every stop en route he sensed that Tom had eyes only for Pamela. The soulful eyes of one who had lost in love but had not yet shaken free of its spell.

His son pulled him aside at the halfway tavern and whispered urgently, 'Can you not tell me who it is, Pa? Then I may know for certain that all is lost. Else I shall wonder if it is some passing fancy and I may yet prevail.'

'In matters of the heart, Tom, you will learn that discretion is all. I have not always been as discreet as I should have been and others have been hurt in consequence. I do not excuse myself. There are painful lessons here.'

Sheridan knew he spoke in part to deflect his son's enquiry, but he also recognised that he shared a truth. He had been careless of Eliza's heart. He had seen many with whom he consorted leaping from one bed to another with barely a passing thought for the sanctity of marriage. But so many of the *bon ton* had married for property, alliance or advancement. He had married for love and Eliza had loved him. For her he had been disowned by his father — a rift which had been long and painful to him. She in turn had given up her celebrity and risked poverty to be at his side. His dalliances, his affairs with Lady Crewe and Lady Duncannon, had been too careless of her feelings. He would have a better care of Pamela. Indeed, he firmly resolved to be a faithful husband.

'Do I find two conspirators?' Pamela appeared behind them. 'Have I found Belmonte and Pedrillo, and are you plotting to abduct us before we are even taken by pirates to the seraglio of the Pasha? Mademoiselle Adéle is already practiced in the part of Constanza, and Tom would make a very pretty Belmonte!'

'Or Pedrillo!' Tom interjected, casting his hopeful eyes on Pamela. 'And wasn't Pa the old buffoon? What's his name?'

'Osmin. But I may play another part now, I hope.'

Pamela took both of their arms and led them back to the table. 'I think that I shall abduct you! And stow you both with our luggage below decks.'

'Let us hope it is a smooth crossing then.'

'Yes, Pa gets mighty sick on the water. But I should make a very happy stowaway!' Tom glowed, basking in the warmth of Pamela's regard.

With the slow progress of the day it was near midnight before the carriages clattered through the streets of Dover. The party were aching and weary when they descended at the dockside. The ship would leave on the early morning tide. Madame de Genlis was anxious to board straightaway and settle herself and her charges in their accommodation. Sheridan and Tom would stay at a nearby hotel. As the brig's captain descended the gangplank to greet his distinguished passengers, the moment had come to say a final adieu. Sheridan allowed himself to gaze as meaningfully as he could into Pamela's eyes.

'Parting is such sweet sorrow,' she sighed.

'It will not be for long,' he whispered urgently.

'Do not forget me,' she whispered in response and then turned to bestow wide smiles on Tom, who hovered close and looked near to tears.

'Never,' Sheridan promised under his breath.

CHAPTER THIRTY-ONE

The venue chosen was a tavern off the Strand, a small room at the back. The informant, who had given his name as George Hodgson, did not wish to be seen entering the Bow Street Magistrates' Court. He had been told that the gentleman putting up the money for the reward desired to thank him in person for effecting the arrest and eventual execution of Daniel Webster's murderer. Sheridan had ordered a bottle of port to steady his nerve. Whilst they waited, Mr Biddulph offered up a toast to their success in the case.

'It was thanks to your generous reward that we secured the arrest so swiftly, Mr Sheridan.'

'The courts seemed satisfied to take this fellow Hodgson's word. What manner of man is he?'

The officer guffawed. 'He is a villain like all of them, sir!'

'And yet he is believed?'

'Who else would know Fethard's business?'

Biddulph's logic defied Sheridan's comprehension but he must accept that thus were the wheels of justice oiled and be prepared to pay out to this snitch.

'Strange business altogether is it not, Mr Sheridan? For it appears now that the sister of your scene painter is herself wanted on a charge of murder! This Daniel Webster was harbouring her at that very time that he was stabbed. I rather think Mr Webster got what he deserved — and had you known his character, sir, you would not have been so generous with the reward, or even offered one at all!'

'Daniel Webster was a good young man, Officer, and I believe his sister may have fallen foul of a conspiracy.'

'Oh. Have you information, Mr Sheridan, that we should know?' Mr Biddulph eyed him eagerly.

Sheridan sighed. He had said too much, as he was wont to do. 'Nothing yet that might save her.'

'Well, she is not found. Constable Nicholls had knowledge she was in a brothel in St Giles, which seemed a promising avenue, but that proved not to be the case. There will be someone that will give her up nevertheless, you mark my words. Rewards. That brings them out.'

There was a rap on the door then and the publican announced Mr Hodgson.

He stood at the entrance, hat in hand. Sheridan did not have to look hard to know this man. It was the thick-necked fellow with the raucous singing voice. The same cove who had acted as escort to Mrs Fethard and her daughters on the way to the scaffold to see hanged the very man for whom he was to receive his thirty pieces of silver.

Sheridan smiled broadly. 'Well, Mr Hodgson, you have brought an assassin to justice. Allow me to shake your hand, good sir!' He moved forward with his own hand extended in readiness. 'But do I not know your face already?'

The man shifted uncomfortably as Sheridan grasped his hand in a firm grip and then peered about his features ever more closely.

'Why! Were you not at Newgate with Mrs Fethard?'

'As may be,' Hodgson grunted.

'Now tragically widowed, her daughters orphaned. What a horror to find she had been married to such a villain, poor woman — she is no doubt in need of comfort?'

'Aye, a villain, sir.'

Sheridan continued his perusal of the man's face, his own expressions alive with first puzzlement and then exaggerated astonishment — a performance he was sure his celebrated actor Kemble might have envied.

'But — were you not of that party that attacked Monsieur De Lubac's shop a month or more past?' Sheridan released his grip as though he had touched a stinging nettle, and took a step back. 'My memory holds good for that event, as I was somewhat tumbled in the fray!' he exclaimed dramatically.

Even as he spoke Mr Hodgson's eyes darted from Sheridan to the quizzical Bow Street officer until, doubtless suspecting a trap, George Hodgson turned tail and ran from them.

Sheridan turned back to face Mr Biddulph with a shrug. 'It seems that Mr Hodgson's need for the reward is not so pressing as we might have imagined.'

As Sheridan was in the vicinity of the Strand en route to Haymarket, he decided to pay a visit to Dr Cardonnet's new premises on the pretext of a friendly inspection. He had also been running through a prospective scenario to deal with Dr Cardonnet and the prince's little problem. He might savour the dramatic irony of such an encounter, knowing what he now planned.

A request for a consultatIon would be sent to the Frenchman from a very grandly titled noble, the sort of approach Dr Cardonnet could not fail to accept forthwith. He would ask George Hanger to arrange the use of some suitably grand apartment and then the trap would be set. Mrs Jordan had been absent from the company on tour in the time since Cardonnet had arrived and appeared at The King's Theatre. They had not met. In any case, Mrs Jordan had a great relish for disguise and comic acting and could transform her features in the most mercurial manner. As a louche lady of title, she would entertain Dr Cardonnet and then once her maid had left the room, confide her understanding that his mesmeric 'treatment' included a promise of all manner of intimate sexual cures and healing.

Whether he protested or not, Mrs Jordan would then secure hold of the good doctor in a compromising clinch, at which point the screen would drop. It had always been a high point of his play *The School for Scandal*, and in this instance a very irate elderly lord, the husband, possibly played by that old trojan Mr Deverill Gardener, would thunder into the scene, with a factotum or even a son in tow, hurling accusations of adultery or anything else of a criminal nature which came to mind, etcetera, etcetera. Mrs Jordan would meanwhile scream and add to the clamours with her own accusations of molestation. The lord would challenge Dr Cardonnet with ruin in the courts such that no decent person would consort with him again or believe a word that he might say.

At which point Dr Cardonnet would flee the scene and likely the country too before any such criminal suit could be taken against him. Never to be heard from again and so on. Mr Sheridan, please take a bow. Inestimable gratitude of His Royal Highness the Prince of Wales. Any favour that might be returned, etcetera, etcetera. He could knock the scene up in an evening. Mrs Jordan returned on the morrow and was always game for any prank, so he could set the stage within the week, all being well.

He arrived at the building on the Strand to find that the landlord was within on the first floor.

'Good afternoon, sir. I had hoped to find Dr Cardonnet already installed. I believe he means to establish a practice here?'

'Did, sir.'

'How mean you?'

'Dr Cardonnet has had a change of mind, it appears.' The landlord grimaced, his mouth a thin line of discontent.

Sheridan looked around the entrance room, and those beyond, with an appreciative nod in the direction of the fittings and décor. 'I think your premises perfectly splendid, sir, and in the most favourable of locations. I fail to understand what might have caused such a change of heart.'

'He informs me he has left the country, sir! Well, good riddance, I say. This is the problem with foreigners. And the French in particular! They are not to be trusted! We were due to sign the contracts on the premises this very day!'

Sheridan stared at the landlord. 'Left the country? Are you quite sure of that?'

The landlord waved a letter in the air. 'I have it by his own hand, sir!'

'Did he offer a reason?'

'None that I can fathom, curse the man!'

'Perhaps I might…?'

The landlord thrust the letter into his hand. 'Make sense out of that, Mr Sheridan.'

Sheridan scanned through the letter. All reasonably businesslike and intelligible, Cardonnet even offered to forward some small recompense for any inconvenience caused. And then the last line, which was indeed a puzzle:

There are wild animals on the loose and I must seek a safer shore.

'Sir, I cannot make any sense of it at all.' Sheridan returned the letter.

'Frenchmen, sir, they are all gone mad!'

*

Sheridan continued to the theatre at Haymarket, still reeling from the news of Cardonnet's sudden and unexpected departure. What had caused so unheralded a flight? He stopped in the street. Could it be that the scene which he had concocted in his imagination might have already occurred in reality? The idea delighted him, for it was not beyond the bounds of possibility. It might even go some way to explaining the strange last line of the letter. If only he could know for sure. Then he, George Hanger and the prince could all rest easy on the matter.

It occurred to him that a thing did not need to be true in order for it to be believed so. The object of his planned ruse had been to discredit the doctor, or at least to make Cardonnet believe that he could hold no standing in anyone's estimation and therefore would lose all leverage in any attempt to blackmail the prince. Now that Cardonnet had flown in suspicious haste, Sheridan could simply orchestrate rumours of impropriety and criminal suit to spread in that wake. The outcome would be the same.

Sheridan arrived at the theatre satisfied with this revised plan.

Old Fletch accosted him at the door.

'Mr Sheridan, sir.'

'Yes, my dear Methuselah?' Sheridan beamed cheerfully at the old man, for his day was becoming brighter by the hour and it was not yet noon.

'There is a man that wishes to speak with you. I said I thought you would be back before long and so he waits for you at the coffee house yonder.'

'Did the fellow give a name?'

'No, sir.'

'Did he look like a creditor or a dun?'

Old Fletch chuckled. 'Oh no, sir, I give those types short shrift. Those vultures will not nab you, Mr Sheridan — not whilst I am on the door!'

'Good man.'

'He was a Scots man. Red hair. Very tall. Very broad. Near enough a giant. He said you would know him by this description.'

'Indeed, I do, Mr Fletcher.' Sheridan turned to leave, then whirled back. 'Tell no one where I am gone.'

'Right you are, sir.' Old Fletch tugged his forelock and chuckled again.

'I am sorry for our last farewell, sir.' Tam stirred the thick, sugar-sweetened coffee.

'As am I. It was not well made, being full of lumps and bumps.'

'I pray that you will forgive me. Aye — it was our caution in the circumstances.'

'My crown will not bear a repeat performance.'

'Of that you can be reassured, sir.'

Sheridan leant across the table and lowered his voice. 'You have Lucy safe? She has thought about the offer of passage from Lady Cannock? Did Mr Hanley —'

Tam cut across. 'Aye, yon Mr Hanley found me at The Swan and I had near persuaded the lass, but now it is all for nothing — she is gone! Last night. She has been taken!'

'By the Runners?'

Tam shook his head violently. 'These were rough, low men and one of them wielded a pistol. My daughter was injured trying to prevent them and might have fared worse had my son-in-law not returned and given one rogue a hefty blow to his nose that he will not forget in a hurry. But they got what they came for.'

Sheridan paled.

'It is the damn reward, I'll wager,' Tam continued. 'Someone has spied her arrival. It is a place alive with river rats.'

'Then they will hand her over for that money; we must pray she is unharmed.'

Tam eyed him keenly. 'Tilly believes this girl to be innocent. Most assuredly so. I fear that Tilly's mind is clouded by the feeling she had for the brother; she had hopes in him, poor wee lass, and Daniel Webster seemed a decent fellow that was gentlemanly. But the sister, that is another matter. Tilly will hear nothing against her and has listened to all her talk of marriage and secrets in some great house in the country and the girl's fear that there is someone sent to kill her. That is why I am here, Mr Sheridan, for Tilly's sake. She will not rest easy. Tilly fears that Lucy has been taken for some malign purpose.'

'And why do you come to me?'

'Tilly has a notion that you may yet save the lass — whether it is from the gallows if it falls that way or if these are villains that have taken her...' Tam shook his head. 'Then I do not know what — but she has a great regard for you. And so, I am here, sir.'

Sheridan nodded. *Look after Lucy* had been Daniel Webster's dying wish.

If he had known then what his promise might cost!

CHAPTER THIRTY-TWO

Sheridan had sent a message to Samuel Hanley, expressing his fear and stating they could do little now but wait to see whether Lucy would be handed over to the authorities in return for the reward. Lord and Lady Cannock were due to return to Sandbourne the following day and he presumed that Samuel would go with them. If there was no news of Lucy's arrest, then the time may have come for Sheridan to call on Mr Greaves. It would not be without some trepidation. If his instinct that Isaac Fethard had not killed Daniel Webster was correct, then the likely assassin might be one of this man's associates.

Samuel should perhaps warn Her Ladyship that some ransom for Lucy might be a necessity, particularly if Greaves had gained nothing of sense from her. Overnight Sheridan had determined that if the girl was in Greaves' 'safekeeping', he would offer his services to Lady Cannock as a broker in the matter. He trusted that she might lay hold of the kind of sum that Greaves would demand before the earl caught wind of the affair. She was a most competent woman and she would act to save Lucy, he felt sure. He set the matter to one side.

To various men of educational standing he fired off copies of his identically worded request to recommend a tutor for Tom. The sooner the better. The boy needed to be prepared for university before he lost all notion of Euclid or Homer. He spent the rest of the afternoon writing half a dozen love letters to Pamela. He even attempted some verses in French, although he had never been an adept student of the language and he wasn't entirely sure what his piece of doggerel might say in translation. But no matter. If it was sufficiently poetic she would be delighted, and if it was nonsense she would laugh. There had been nothing from her. No words of love or longing. No counting down the days before they might be reunited. Her silence preyed on his nerves.

Day by day he heard reports of the steps which Mr Pitt's government was taking, both openly and behind the scenes, to repress dissent. The panic was escalating in response to events across the Channel. Sheridan had begun to suspect that letters to him from France were being intercepted, and in all probability opened or kept back by the state authorities.

He prayed that his own missives would reach their object. Pamela must receive his words of love and adoration or else feel that he neglected her and was not serious in his affections. He worried that in Paris, in the company of her 'patron', the illustrious Philippe Égalité, there would be any number of young men keen to court her attention. That his son Tom had become so besotted no longer surprised Sheridan. It was only natural. One had only to be in her delightful company an hour to fall in love and lust! He must be a vigilant lover. He had none of the advantages of youth, he conceded.

He had caught his reflection in the mirror after a night of drinking hard and long and forced himself to see the effect. He looked aged, his eyes bleary and bloodshot, his face red, coarse and puffy. In his youth that red flush which came with excess had faded swiftly enough, but now he feared it was taking up more permanent residence, as some unkind caricaturists were quick to incorporate in their viperous cartoons. And yet he did not drink as much as Mr Pitt! Nor the princes! Nor many other gentlemen, like Grey! It was his damned complexion, his constitution that did not fare so well. If Pamela would marry him then he was resolved to rein in the excess. He would have less need for the company of those who drove him to it. He should desire only to sit at her feet. He felt the better for this good intention. All would be well. He was her Sherrie.

From the small window he could hear the clatter of carriages and the noisy crowds arriving for the evening's performance. He would amble forth to greet those of consequence and be that figure so universally applauded and admired. The sort of man it was only natural a young, intelligent woman such as Pamela Syms should seek out and wish to marry.

It was soon abundantly clear to Sheridan that his betrothal might not remain secret for much longer. The gossiping Lady Malmesbury had evidently heard rumours of a potential romance. She pounced upon him behind her box and badgered him to know if he had yet proposed to the Syms girl. Whilst he had attempted to quash any whiff of scandal arising from the sojourn at Isleworth, that such speculations would leak here and there should not surprise him. After all, he had openly sung Pamela's praises for months.

'Mr Sheridan! We have not seen you for an age!'

It was Mrs Buckberry, who had arrived for the evening's entertainment with her niece.

Sheridan bowed politely.

'We hear such insistences, Mr Sheridan. That you have been bewitched. Do tell us they are not true.' Mrs Buckberry leant in towards him with her attempt at an aside. 'My dear niece Cressida here will be quite heart-choked!'

'Artichokes, I do believe, may be pickled, Mrs Buckberry, and then Miss Cressida may consume as many as she likes at any time of the year.'

'Indeed. That is a sound piece of colander advice.'

'Sheridan!' Major Hanger slapped his shoulder and then bowed to the ladies. 'Mrs Buckberry, how delightful. You will excuse us, I hope. I am on His Royal Highness' business.'

Mrs Buckberry's eyes glittered. 'The Prince of Wales, of course. Do send our solipsis, if you please.'

'The prince would be honoured to receive them, madam.'

The ladies moved away, shivering with the excitement of their close encounter with royalty by way of the prince's equerry.

'Well, Sheridan, you are to be congratulated!'

For a moment Sheridan struggled to think what for.

'Dr Cardonnet, we hear, has taken flight to Switzerland.'

'Ah yes. Switzerland. So I believe.'

'The prince is exceedingly grateful and insists that you join him for dinner this evening at Carlton House — all very impromptu, family and a handful of other guests. The prince wishes that we might celebrate your achievement, all very hush-hush, of course.' Hanger put his finger to his lips. 'What did you do, by the way, Sheridan? We are agog to hear your account. The prince verily overflows with curiosity.'

Sheridan hesitated. 'This evening I —'

Hanger wagged his finger. 'The prince will brook no excuse. You must cancel all else. None of your *unexpected circumstances … I must entreat Your Royal Highness' indulgence … sincere attachment and devotion … blah blah…*'

Of course, Hanger would read his letters to the prince.

'No. You are commanded. And I am here to escort you, Sheridan.'

'First to Grosvenor Street. I must change, Hanger.'

He needed time to think what he might say to the prince. The truth — that he had done nothing? That would never do.

'No need. No need. Perfectly acceptable as you are. We are *en famille*, as I say. No ceremony. The prince's own words. An evening amongst friends.'

George Hanger, who always looked dashing in his uniform, smiled with that wicked glint he had.

It never failed to give Sheridan a frisson of excitement to walk up the steps into Carlton House, even though he was now a frequent visitor and had a bedchamber at his disposal. He felt that he had arrived, as it were, at the pinnacle of society. No expense had been spared by the Prince of Wales on his town residence. It was palatial. The prince had a penchant for extravagant interior decoration and the collection of fine artworks was a primary interest. A love of beauty and a restless yearning combined to indulge his creative fancies. A room might be no sooner complete than he would have some new inspiration and all would be superseded by the latest marvel.

Sheridan might, with familiarity, lounge in one room after another, recalling the games and japes of every kind which had been played there. Hiding behind curtains or pursuing the ladies into antechambers and capacious cupboards. Finding Mrs Fitzherbert quaking under the divan, the prince wielding a shooting gun to flush her out. Drinking and dancing until sunrise.

Sheridan bowed low. The prince was immaculate in his dress, a dusky pink. As usual he favoured the sound of his own voice.

'Ah, Sherry. Glad you could join us.' The prince leant in conspiratorially. 'Thought we could celebrate getting rid of that damned vulture.' He looked about the gathering. 'Hardly be much of a shindig without you anyway. We are only thirty or so but I've got some of the brothers here, so you may expect that we shall drink you under the table!' He laughed and nodded in their direction at the other end of the large reception room. Frederick Duke of York, William of Clarence and the young Prince Ernest, for whom Sheridan had never had much of a liking.

'Had to invite that damned Thiers-Auberet — tedious old macaroni, sticks to my brother York like a limpet these days. Has some ridiculous notion that he might be persuaded to lead the charge into France! Truth is, Yorkie has got a bit of an eye for the little wifie. I've warned him to be careful he don't catch something!' The prince chuckled and gave Sheridan a knowing look. 'Hear you've been plucking a French rose or two yourself, my dear fellow! Fine-looking girl, Pamela Syms. Interesting connections, shall we say. Although madame, I hear, is a step or two away from joining the fairies down in Bedlam.'

'Madame de Genlis is a woman ahead of her time. That is always to court madness, I fear.'

'Hmm. That's the problem with the French — no restraint. They are all excess. Only have to look at the way they dress!'

The prince was not one to recognise irony, Sheridan reflected.

'And in the bedroom, well... I've been hearing about this fellow the Marquis de Sade ... enough to make the mind boggle. As for their damned revolution! All well and good to begin with; no one could question the need for change, reform, that sort of thing, but why can they not be civilised as we are in such matters? No, they must be swayed by mobs, and before you know it men of sense are dropping like flies and there are common lunatics running the show. But the last thing we need is to get dragged into their bloody mess!'

Sheridan nodded, heartened to hear that the prince had not succumbed to the bleating of the warmongers.

'I do not think all is lost, sir. There are still good men to be found at the helm and despite this declaration of a Republic, many seem agreed that a monarchy, more akin to our own, is the way forward for France.'

'Quite right, Sherry. If we act too hastily, we may only push the French to further excess. Enough of politics! Let us dine!'

The meal, though of only five courses, was nevertheless sumptuous and finished with a marzipan swan floating in a pond of blue-dyed jelly fringed with various sweets made in the likeness of reeds or bankside flowers. The princely brothers were determined to out-drink each other and, Sheridan suspected, already half-cut when they came to the table. With his new resolve, Sheridan attempted to be more restrained.

York had placed himself next to the young marquise and was near drooling into her bosom already. Mrs Fitzherbert had remained at her house in Brighton, so the prince was free to distribute the largesse of his favours amongst half a dozen ladies at the table.

Sir John Lade, dressed as ever in riding breeches, and his wife Letitia were vying with each other in the coarseness of their language, goaded by Hanger and Fitzroy. Captain Stewart was also of the party. Sheridan had allowed himself a smirk of triumph when they had exchanged greetings in the reception room, only to watch his advantage slip away.

'I gather Mademoiselle Adéle has arrived too late in Paris. She is already listed as an émigré, having overstayed in England. Until the matter can be resolved, I believe our most delightful party of friends are to move to the border at Tournai. There they may hopefully move swiftly to safety, should the need arise.'

Pamela on her way to Tournai? Matters in France in a delicate balance? With a sinking heart, Sheridan would not dwell on the part the delay in Isleworth may have contributed to these present tribulations. His darling girl, what dangers might she face? The sooner Madame de Genlis and the girls should return to England, the better. Or he to France and, marrying her straightaway, he would carry Pamela back to safety in his arms.

'I hear from our sources in Paris that mademoiselle's father is most irate. The duc's position is weakened considerably. His cousin Louis' trial is imminent by all accounts. I doubt even Philippe Égalité can save him from the guillotine. I would not be much surprised if he does not sign the death warrant. He is in too deep with the Revolution now. When Louis dies, if not before, there will be war with England.'

'And you would welcome it, no doubt, Captain Stewart? But we are not there yet. Would we not do better to try and prevent such developments? There are men of reason on both sides of the Channel.'

It was the captain's turn to smirk. 'You damn Reformists! You cannot see the wood for the trees.' Stewart turned away then, and Sheridan had to swallow his rising gall.

After dinner the prince announced that the gentlemen would retire to his billiard room and re-join the ladies presently.

Once they were there, the prince offered a toast. 'To our dear Sherry for having rid us of a most confounded villain!'

The Duke of York paused the toast to enquire, 'And who might that be? Pray do tell.'

'Fellow called Cardonnet. French. Called himself a doctor! A thoroughgoing quack! Anyway, the rogue is halfway to Switzerland by now, I daresay. To Sherry!'

Before he could imbibe, however, the marquis interjected. 'Docteur Cardonnet, he has fled the country?'

'*Oui*, Monsieur le Marquis. He has most decidedly scuttled off, and good riddance!'

'It is most sudden, Your Highness!'

'Told you. Sherry here has foiled some plot of the scheming knave. To Sherry!'

'To Sherry!' Hanger and Lade echoed loudly, with a more muted response from others in the room as they downed their glasses.

'You'll tell me all the gory details later, heh, Sherry?' The prince chuckled and turned to have a word with his equerry.

The room broke into smaller groups but Sheridan could hear Prince Ernest on his older brother's coat tails, his enquiry punctuated with titters. 'That's the mesmerist fellow, isn't it, Georgie? Was he trying to blackmail you?'

Sir John Lade talked about horses, which Sheridan tolerated in a good-humoured way, and was offered a tip on a sure thing for an upcoming race meeting. Sheridan nodded his thanks but doubted he would find time to attend.

'The horse is Fair Game, if you do. Mark my words — Fair Game.'

Slapping his boot with the crop he customarily carried with him, Sir John turned to another acquaintance and, sizing up his shot on the billiard table, he offered advice on the best angles.

Stewart was heading towards Sheridan, who did not much relish another encounter that evening.

'It seems the tiger of revolution is on the loose,' the captain intoned slowly and distinctly, looking directly into his eyes.

At the words 'tiger of revolution' Sheridan experienced a strange sensation; his mind became hazy and his limbs began to act of their own volition. He found himself crossing the room to where the prince was showing the marquis one of his latest purchases, a still life painting by a Dutch Master. When he reached the two men, Sheridan found that his hands moved around the throat of the Prince of Wales and before he knew quite what was happening, they were both thrashing about and falling onto the billiard table, feet kicking and balls flying everywhere.

Shouts and clamours arose on all sides.

With a squeal the marquis leapt out of the way. '*Sacré coeur!*'

Major Hanger and Captain Stewart were quick to the scene. Sheridan's hands were prised from the prince's throat; he was dragged off the table and yanked violently to his feet, held fast by Hanger on one side and Stewart on the other, who wrenched his arm behind his back, yelling, 'Traitor! Assassin! In the name of His Majesty the King, Richard Sheridan, you are arrested for treason and conspiring with the French Revolutionaries!'

Sheridan blinked half a dozen times. Amidst the shouts and general melee, he heard the word repeated again and again: *Traitor!* Traitor. That was the word Cardonnet had used of him. *Traitor.*

Stewart twisted his arm even tighter and hissed in his ear, 'A parting gift from Dr Cardonnet!'

Visions of the looming Tower, ancient dungeons, scaffolds, the butchery of being hung, drawn and quartered all assailed Sheridan's mind in a phantasma of horror.

The prince was helped back onto his feet by Lade and Captain Fitzroy. Rubbing his neck, he looked dazed for a moment whilst he recovered his breath. And then he looked about at all the astonished faces gazing towards him. The room had gone deathly silent, save for Prince Ernest, who was cackling like a hyena. The rest waited with bated breath to see what the prince would do.

All of a sudden, His Royal Highness broke into laughter. 'I say, what a prank! Heh, Sherry? I think we had everyone worried there for a moment!' Then he paused as though in recollection and declaimed in stertorous tones, 'You were like a wild animal set loose!'

At those words a most extraordinary sequence of events occurred which, if related or recorded, would scarcely be believed. Stewart abandoned his grip on Sheridan and advanced, roaring like a lion, on the Duke of Clarence, tackling him to the ground. Howling like a wolf, the Duke of York let loose a volley of kicks on Captain Stewart. The Marquis de Thiers-Auberet in his turn set about Fitzroy, his little fists flying, his wig at half-cock and screeching like an angry cat. Given his superior stature, Captain Fitzroy had no difficulty in keeping the old émigré at bay. At first nonplussed, he then rather delighted in tweaking and pinching the marquis' nose, much to the amusement of the crooked son who rivalled Prince Ernest in his hysteria.

Hanger released his grip on Sheridan and patted his back.

The room had descended into madness.

A door was flung open. Lady Lade stood on the threshold.

'What the devil, you whorry dogs!' Letitia shouted as she took in the sight of grown men tussling like unruly schoolboys when the masters are away.

She clapped her hands loudly. It acted in the nature of a signal and the fighting parties all desisted at the sound.

Sheridan arrived home to Isleworth that night a little worse for wear to find a message had been delivered from Dr Cardonnet. He tore it open.

Monsieur,

I trust you enjoyed the spectacle. Perhaps you have seen into the true heart of men.

I am already in Switzerland when you receive this. It is a country, I believe, where a true man of science may flourish, as it is quite without principle — although of course it hides this very well.

My daughter found you a most charming man. Appropriately she sends you her felicitations.

I share with you one last observation; I know that in this you will act wisely, for you are in truth a wise fool, even though your disguise is most effective.

The earl — of whom we spoke and for whom my admiration is in every respect immense — is not an earl at all.

Your most obedient servant,
Dr Honoré Auguste Cardonnet

What in blazes did the man mean with his damnable riddles? The doctor had played them all for fools, that was certain. For his own amusement, no doubt. Sheridan crushed the letter in his hand and threw it into the fire.

CHAPTER THIRTY-THREE

Sheridan stood on the dim stage and looked out across the auditorium into the fathomless dark. He breathed in the smells of paint and wax and lingering body odours. What a world was here upon this small stage. Tragedy and comedy. Flights of fancy and grim death. But above all, wonder. Perhaps Lord Cannock was right. He had wasted his talent. His real life's work was in words and playmaking. In frivolity and frippery. In the antics of actors and not the deeds of men. All well and good. But now he must act. No one had come forward to claim the reward for Lucy Webster nor demand a ransom.

As he turned to leave, there came a sudden whoosh and deadening thump. There, where he had stood but a moment before, one of the weighted sacks used to lower scenery had dropped from the flies overhead. Sheridan's breath caught in his chest. That had been death for certain. He blinked with astonishment and relief.

'Mr Sheridan — are you all right, sir?' It was the gruff, one-eyed stage manager Mr Shaw, and in his wake one of the stagehands, a muscular brute.

'I am ... I am...' He was too much in shock to complete any sentence.

The man nodded and then shook his head. 'There's luck for you, Mr Sheridan. Rope must have frayed. I'll have them all checked. Right, Harry?'

'No accident, gaffer.' The stagehand held up the end of the rope attached to the sack. 'This has been cut!'

A scarpering sound came from high above.

Their eyes as one peered up to the heavens, but the darkness would not be penetrated.

'I'll have the filthy bastard!'

'Go at him, Harry!' the stage manager shouted before he too followed after the sprinting flyman, who, Sheridan noted, had exceptional speed for a man of his stocky frame.

The two members of the stage crew returned, dragging a squirming, struggling man between them.

'You had better let me go or it will be Hell for you!'

'It's Hell for you now, you devil's spawn!' Harry slapped the man's head.

'Shall we call for the Runners, Mr Sheridan?' Shaw asked.

'Leave the murderous rogue to me, sir — I would wring his chicken neck right now! Say he fell from the flies in the chase!' Harry slapped the man again.

Sheridan could see that there had already been some violent scuffle in the man's capture. He peered closer in the gloom, and despite the blood that trickled down the villain's face he could see that it was Ned Cribbins.

'So, Ned, you would kill me, would you?'

'I ain't killed no one!'

'And the sack flew down of its own volition?'

'I'll not hang!'

'No? Perhaps you'd prefer I have you transported to the new prison colony and see how you like that rough place!'

A look of horror rushed across Ned's features. 'It were meant only to frighten yer.'

'That was a deadly aim.'

'To warn — that was my instruction. You are one to give offence and the gentleman was wanting you to know it.'

'Liar.'

'I swear on my life.'

'That's worth a dog's turd!' Harry laughed and shook his captive.

'On oath. A gentleman came to me that knew of the grudge I held against you, Mr Sheridan, because of Isaac.'

'Who was this gentleman? Did he give a name?'

Ned half grinned. 'What do you think?'

'Has he paid you?'

Ned hesitated.

'He would want to see the deed done first. So, you must meet him again. Where and what time is your assignation?'

'He said he would find me.' A look of cunning came to Ned's eyes. 'We might lay a trap, sirs. And then you may have the real villain. If you will let me go about my ordinary business —' Ned made to move.

'Not so quick, you lying jackanapes!' Harry tightened his grip and Ned winced.

'I have a better plan.' Sheridan turned to the stage manager. 'Tell Old Fletch to have my carriage brought round. Harry, I will need your assistance, and yours too, Mr Shaw.'

Ned had been squeezed between Harry and Mr Shaw for the journey, both large men so Sheridan fancied it had not been a comfortable ride for the weaselly youth.

'Where are you taking me, good sirs?' Ned had whined throughout, becoming increasingly concerned as they left the city streets behind and entered more rural parts. Perhaps he fancied that he was to be disposed of in some woods, buried in some quiet ditch and otherwise dispatched in such a way that he would never be discovered. Sheridan took pleasure in watching him squirm, although Ned had very little room in which to do so. When they pulled up beside the carriages lined up along the course, Ned's worry increased.

'What do we do here? We are at some races, are we not?'

Horse racing was not a regular pastime for Sheridan, but there were many amongst his acquaintance who spent a good deal of time and effort in studying form and pedigree. For the most part to little advantage, as far as he could see. The weather was overcast but the rain had held off, so there was a fair turnout at the meeting.

'Ned, before we disembark, there is a question I would ask. I shall know if you answer truthfully, and it would be in your best interest to do so.'

'Depends what it is you want to know, Mr Sheridan?' Ned looked suspicious. 'I do not want to increase my danger.'

'Believe me, lad, your greatest danger is here!' Harry shoved his fist into Ned's shoulder.

Sheridan softened his tone. 'On my honour, Ned, it may help your fate.'

Ned nodded reluctantly.

'Did Mrs Fethard have a proper care of her husband? Might there be another? You may answer either way, only tell the truth.'

This was obviously not a question Ned had expected. He shrugged and relaxed a little. 'Well, yeah.'

'Yes, which?'

'Isaac. She always stood by him whatever, though in truth at times he led her a merry dance.' Ned's face brightened. 'But he was good to her in his way, and he loved them girls!'

Sheridan digested this information. 'Do you know Mr Hodgson?'

Ned racked his brains.

'George Hodgson,' Sheridan repeated. 'Sings for King and Church.'

'George? Well, there is a George Robson — nah, hold on! I think he does go by Hodgson sometimes, by way of an alias.'

Sheridan nodded. 'That sounds about the limit of his imagination. Now, hold tight, Ned. We would not want you to stray.'

He was bundled out of the carriage, with Sheridan leading the way.

Sheridan then headed to where the owners and men of means were gathered with their own tents. They passed all the other gaming that might be found at such an event. The sparring booth, gambling stalls, the three-card trick, beer and food sellers. From within one tight circle they heard the familiar squawking of a cock fight. Ned strained his head about, trying to see if there were any who might assist him. Harry shoved him onwards.

Sheridan spotted Skiffy Skeffington, who waved a silk handkerchief. By his side stood Sir John Lade, looking perfectly at home for once in his riding rig. He raised his whip in salute and ambled across Sheridan's path.

'That was a rum do the other night, Dick! Thought you was going to be clapped in irons and thrown in the Tower! Eh what!' Sir John gave Sheridan a friendly tap with his whip. 'Captain Stewart, they say, is being considered to accompany the marines on the next fleet to Botany Bay. He's quaking in his boots, I should think!'

Sheridan allowed himself a small smile.

Sir John chuckled. 'Wife made a good show, putting a stop to all that nonsense. Pity, I was rather enjoying myself. Of course, the prince talks of it all as a great jest now, but he wouldn't want it spoken beyond our circle.' Lade winked.

'Hanger seems convinced this Cardonnet played the lot of us for fools and the fellow is some revolutionary after all. Says the whole masquerade was an elaborate revenge on the marquis!'

'Rather too elaborate for my liking.'

Sir John grinned. He then nodded towards Ned. 'Caught yourself a snatch-purse? Want me to give the villain a good thrashing?'

'Thank you, Sir John…'

Ned looked aghast at the whip, which Sir John was now flexing in readiness.

'…but I have other plans for Ned. Good day.'

And there at last was the man he was in search of and had felt certain would be in attendance. Mr Acton Greaves, within a tight circle of his henchmen. One of whom, he noticed, had recently suffered a great injury to his nose.

Sheridan strolled over with Ned and his own bodyguards in tow.

'Mr Greaves. Our paths cross again. There is no murder done today, however.'

On seeing Greaves, young Ned was visibly shaken. Whether or not he knew Acton Greaves by sight, he certainly knew of him by reputation.

'A word, I pray, in private.'

Greaves nodded warily.

'Mr Shaw, Harry, do make sure you hold Mr Cribbins fast. We would not want to mislay him, would we? Who knows what might happen to him.'

Ned was fairly trembling now, which made Sheridan smirk.

'What is it you wish to talk about, Mr Sheridan? I don't have all day for idle chit-chat.'

'Don't worry, Greaves, you will not feel that your time has been wasted.'

'You are interceding on someone's behalf?'

'One might fairly say that, although not for any debt.'

'Then you may very well be wasting my time.'

They had moved to a point beyond the tent but still in sight of their respective parties.

'I confess my earlier thoughts were that in your fury you exacted a murderous revenge on Edward Stretton, he not having found the funds to pay you his debt.'

Greaves was about to object.

'Hear me out, Greaves. You know I have something of interest to say or I would not presume to approach you.'

'Very well, but be careful in your suggestions, Sheridan.'

'The method of Stretton's killing was far from ordinary. Poisoning by syringe. The instrument used was quite outside the common.'

'A valuable commodity.'

'Indeed, it may prove so. The killer had some access to these syringes and some rudimentary knowledge of how these instruments might be applied to the business of murder.'

'Why do you tell me all this, Sheridan, fascinating as it may be?'

'Because, Mr Greaves, it led me to the realisation that you were not responsible for the death of Edward Stretton.'

Greaves snorted. 'That is very generous of you, Mr Sheridan.'

'Murder would not be your instrument of choice. Only *in extremis*.'

'I would like to see any man prove it.'

'First and foremost, you are a man of business, Mr Greaves. Your business is to make money off the backs of others' misfortune.'

'I merely collect, Mr Sheridan, from those foolish enough to wager.'

'Even when you know it is beyond their means?'

'More fool they.'

'Blackmail would be far more to your taste and better serve your business interests.'

'Have a care, Sheridan. You make yet more unsavoury suggestions.'

'Let me rephrase then. You collect information and if that assists you in the collection of the debts owed — with interest — it is merely a pressure to lubricate the wheels of your operation.'

'That is delicately put. I own one may discover a little something which persuades the debtor that it really would be in their best interest to place me first in the line of their creditors.'

Sheridan nodded. 'Edward Stretton received a note on the evening before his demise. I have seen it.'

Greaves raised a brow of interest.

'The informant promises information which will make his fortune. There is more, more specific as to how.'

Greaves pursed his lips.

'This is familiar to you?' Sheridan eyed Greaves keenly. 'I believe that you received a letter from Stretton on the very morning of his appointment with you. That missive begged for your patience for another hour or two, with the promise of great reward and various hints as to how it would be obtained. And where will that fortune come from?'

A flicker in Greaves' eye confirmed to Sheridan that they were of one mind.

'There was only one source of great wealth to hand. Sandbourne. But Edward is merely second in line to inherit. In his youth, when he thought his cousin a confirmed bachelor, he got into the habit of betting on his future inheritance. Then the earl, much to everyone's astonishment, married and had a son. Poor Edward, how the vultures began to descend. And like most inveterate gamblers he continued to chase his tail, hoping that his luck would change. He tried to keep you at bay with small payments, but you were ever-circling overhead.'

'You have a way with words, Sheridan.'

'Edward was not a man to be trusted. He was desperate, at his wits' end. But something in the letter which he sent convinced you that he might have indeed found a way to get at this fortune at Sandbourne. Blackmail might spring to mind, and you were deliberating whether or not to risk an extension on his period of grace.'

'You tell a good story, Sheridan.'

'For a man who likes to control his universe, it must have been more than an inconvenience to learn that Stretton had been murdered. The flip, however, was that you yourself began to speculate; perhaps Stretton had not misled you. He had been assassinated for some reason of import. The more details you learnt, the more certain you became that there was indeed a great secret to be uncovered. One which might make you an even wealthier man than you already are.'

'You really should return to your writing of plays, Mr Sheridan,' Greaves sneered.

'Sadly, this is not a comedy, Mr Greaves, but has all the makings of a tragedy. You were informed that in the wake of Stretton's assassination Lady Cannock's maid, Lucy Webster, had mysteriously disappeared. Here might be the key, you surmised. You may not retrieve Edward's debt as such from the earl, but you may have the means to open his purse, shall we say. You began to search high and low for Lucy. You discovered that her brother, Daniel, lived in London and worked as a scene painter. In my company.'

'You are quite entangled in this story yourself, it would seem.'

'I take it personally when one of my own employees is fatally stabbed.'

'You have my condolences.'

'Whoever did for Daniel played with him; there were little scratches about his throat. They wanted him to give up the whereabouts of his sister.'

'Now you have me quite agog. Did he?'

Sheridan shook his head solemnly. 'No. He would give his own life for hers.'

'It was careless of the assassin to kill him before obtaining that information.'

'I believe he was disturbed by sounds of approach. I live with that likelihood.'

Greaves raised an eyebrow. 'You disturbed the villain?'

'I suffered only a blow to the head, thankfully.'

'This is all very interesting, Sheridan. But what has any of this to do with me?'

The field on the racetrack was thundering towards the finish, and all about there were shouts and cries for one horse or another.

'If you will bear with me, I have an interest in this race.' Greaves nodded towards the track.

'Of course.'

It was no surprise to Sheridan that the way opened before them, as if Moses were come to part the Red Sea. And more than simply the common sort appeared to touch their forelock to Acton Greaves as he passed.

'Again, I wondered whether yours might be the hand behind these events.'

Greaves sighed and leant against the rail. 'I see you are a man who likes to take risks, Mr Sheridan. I wonder that you are not on my books.' He nodded towards the approaching horses. 'Would you care to place a wager?'

'The White-faced Darter.'

Greaves frowned. 'I do not know that nag. It is not one of this field.'

'No. Actually, it is a type of dragonfly.'

'You have a fondness for riddles, sir.'

'It is this peculiar insect which has convinced me you had no hand in that assassination either.'

'You are very free with your insinuations, sir, to consider me for murder. Have a care I do not take offence.'

'Should I consider you for burglary?'

'Damn it, Sheridan, where are you leading?' Greaves asked impatiently as the roar began to crescendo. The jockeys in their garish colours whipped their steeds to the finishing line, the crowd shouting encouragement to their chosen horse; but Fair Game had it by a nose.

'Fair Game it is.' Greaves slapped the rail.

'A win for Sir John. And for you, I daresay.'

Greaves twitched a smile, then pushed away from the rail. 'Well, here is one satisfactory conclusion. Do you have an ending for *your* tale, sir?'

'I think we may near the climax. The reward for Lucy Webster under accusation of murdering Edward Stretton revived your determination to find this most interesting young woman. And with the aid of your informants I believe that you have found her.'

'If, for the sake of argument, I had her, would I not be handing her over to the authorities? She is wanted now for murder.'

'Neither of us want to see that eventuality.'

'And why would that be?'

'I, because whether or not Lucy has murdered Edward Stretton, she has been ill-used, and you because she has value. More than the hundred guineas' reward. And if she has knowledge of a secret which would unlock Sandbourne's riches to you…?'

There was a silence.

'What might that secret be?' Sheridan continued, eyeing Greaves. He felt instinctively that Greaves had yet to discover it. 'I come to you, Mr Greaves, because I think we may be able to assist one another.'

'How so?'

'Lucy has claimed that she was married to Stretton and the child she carries is legitimately his. Not only may she be carrying a secret, but also an heir. Perhaps more than that. You need to know if their marriage is valid and potentially of value in any dealings with Lord Cannock, else there is but a disgraced servant and a bastard infant.' Sheridan paused. 'I have the details of the marriage.'

Greaves turned to Sheridan with a quick flash in his eyes. 'And what is your object, Sheridan, in this scenario?'

'I want to know who stabbed Daniel Webster and why.'

'That seems little enough when you speak of fortunes to be had.'

'And I want to keep Lucy safe. You have Lucy.'

Greaves flicked his head slightly.

'You want to know for what great secret Stretton was killed. But Lucy's wits are gone and whatever she may say, Greaves, without proof, she will not be believed.'

'I can't get any sense out of her.'

'Let me speak with her.'

The winning horse was returning in triumph along the course.

'Fair Game. It seems you have a winning streak, Mr Sheridan. I shall send a carriage for you. Tomorrow evening at the theatre. You will come alone.'

Sheridan nodded quickly.

'Do not cross me.'

Sheridan shook his head equally quickly. 'One more favour, Mr Greaves.'

Greaves looked exasperated.

'That young fellow we have yonder. Give him a devilish look when we return.' Sheridan grinned charmingly.

Greaves shrugged. 'I think it all a play to you, sir.'

As they approached Sheridan could see that whatever look Greaves did direct at Ned, the lad was clearly terrified by it.

'So, Ned, I am sure we are all agreed that there's no good in a snitch and not one that does it for reward.'

Ned was quick to respond, his eyes never leaving Greaves. 'I ain't no snitch, Mr Sheridan! I ain't no snitch, Mr Greaves!'

'Good, Ned. But I will tell you who is.'

'And who is that?'

'George Hodgson, otherwise known as George Robson.'

'George?' Ned's eyes narrowed in comprehension.

Sheridan looked to his stage crew. 'You may let our friend go now.'

Ned glanced nervously at Greaves and his henchmen and then cast pleading eyes towards Sheridan. 'I would come with you sir, Mr Sheridan.'

'I am sure you will make your own way, Ned. Look after Mrs Fethard's interest, won't you?'

CHAPTER THIRTY-FOUR

Sheridan had not been dissembling when he had told Greaves that he had details of the marriage. He had received the information that very morning. From the moment that he had grasped there might be some truth in Lucy's claims of a wedding, he had begun to make discreet enquiry through one of his political supporters in Stafford. He had a notion and followed it through. It was the tutor Mr Cray who had first drawn his attention to Edward Stretton's proclivity for maidservants.

Like father like son. For had not Francis Stretton assaulted Mrs Martha Hanley when she was lady's maid to the previous countess? Martha had been betrothed to the earl's butler, Josiah Hanley, and he had kept his promise to marry her despite knowing she had been despoiled and carried Stretton's bastard. The scandal had been quashed. It had occurred to Sheridan that Lucy's predecessor, Miss Dickens, had left service to marry a curate.

The enquiries bore fruit. The curate in question had a weakness for gaming and was one of the few men in the county to have found himself in debt to Edward Stretton. With a certain amount of addition and subtraction, the equation which Sheridan arrived at was that Stretton had called in a portion of the debt when he had suggested the benefits to this curate of marrying Edward's discarded lover, Miss Dickens. Some recompense for her, to be a curate's wife. He had then called in the rest of the outstanding debt when he arranged for this curate to 'marry' him to Lucy Webster. There had, however, been no Banns and no record of the marriage in the church register, and therefore no material evidence. Furthermore, at the time of the marriage, Lucy had not yet celebrated her twenty-first birthday and had therefore married without consent. Poor Lucy, how thrilled she must have been on that day and how easily duped.

Having secured the information, Sheridan must now tread carefully. Greaves was not a man who liked to lose and Lucy was in a fragile state. It was her safety and future which must be paramount. She knew something which was dangerous. He was convinced of that now. Daniel had been murdered because of it. Whatever scandal it was, someone was prepared to kill for it. Possibly with assistance. That seemed likely. And there were only two persons who could have so great a secret: Lord and Lady Cannock. Were Greaves to uncover that secret, then who knew what might ensue?

Near midnight Sheridan had almost given up on the arrival of the carriage. The theatre building had emptied and the night watchmen were arriving.

'You work late, Mr Sheridan?' It was Mr Shaw at the door. 'Everything all right? We have our eyes peeled for that little weasel Ned. I still wonder you let him go, sir.'

'I have a generous nature.'

'Too generous, sir.'

A lad called up the stairs then. 'Seems I am to tell you a carriage has arrived. Go careful, Mr Sheridan.'

'I will, Shaw. Tomorrow we must discuss the pantomime! I am thinking of *The Goose that Laid the Golden Eggs*!'

'Oh, that is a favourite, sir.'

The man with the broken nose sat opposite Sheridan. The curtains of the carriage were drawn and would remain so, he surmised; he was not to know whither they were headed.

Sheridan attempted conversation. 'You are a pugilist perhaps, sir?'

The man grunted.

'I have a man, Harry, you met at the races. He is very handy with his fists and sports at Marylebone Fields. But you have not fared so well in your last engagement?'

The man grunted again and that was the extent of the banter to be had.

Unless the carriage had been going about in circles just to confuse him, Sheridan deduced that they must be somewhere near the edge of the metropolis. It was a dark night with a thin crescent of a waning moon, and that fleeting behind the roiling clouds. He wondered how Constable Nicholls would fare on horseback in following their trail. He had deliberated over whether to approach the police officer. The risk was great should Greaves discover that Sheridan was not alone, as he had promised. The plan was simply that Nicholls would follow so that he could locate the hiding place and then return on the morrow with sufficient force. Nicholls was right. The safest place for Lucy now was in custody.

At last the horses clattered to a stop.

The pugilist extracted a thin black scarf from his pocket and held it out to Sheridan with a grunt. Once blindfolded he was handed out of the carriage to another henchman, who manhandled him across a yard and through a door. It was only when he had climbed a set of stairs that the precaution was removed.

'Your master is very thorough, I will give him that.'

Greaves emerged from a room. 'Sheridan, you are here. And do you have that information for me?'

'All in good time, Greaves. First I would like to see Lucy.'

Greaves glared at him.

Sheridan sighed. 'Very well. A curate, Mr Cox, in a parish near to Stone. He is the one that has married them.'

Greaves' eyes gleamed. 'Good. Good. She has been asleep but wakes now. I have a woman with her. Her health fails. If she can only have the child, I may at least have recompense from Cannock. And you may yet prise sense from the girl. I think her delirious; all she will say is that the earl is not the earl.'

Sheridan nodded. 'That is strange and speaks of madness.' And yet Dr Cardonnet had used very nearly the same words in his letter.

An old woman at the bedside looked up with beady-eyed suspicion when Sheridan was ushered in.

'Come to visit Mr Greaves' poor niece, have you, sir?'

Lucy turned and blinked in recognition when she saw Sheridan.

'Lucy … I am sorry you are still so poorly. May I sit with you a little while?'

Lucy nodded weakly.

Sheridan turned to the old nurse. 'Good woman, perhaps you might fetch a warming broth or tea?'

From behind him, Greaves evidently nodded because the woman laboured to her feet and shuffled, grumbling, across the room.

Lucy smiled wanly. 'Mr Sheridan, I had thought you were my friend.'

'I am, Lucy, I am.'

'You would hand me to the police, I think.'

'I wish you to be well.' He sat by the bed and leant towards her.

Lucy shook her head and winced, evidently in some pain. 'I feel I shall never be well again. All is lost.' With a sigh she closed her eyes.

Greaves shook his head. 'I have done with her, Sheridan. This is a damnable business!'

'She has worsened since last I saw her. Damn you, Greaves, have you no feeling?'

Greaves sneered. 'I lost that a long time ago, sir.'

'Let me stay with her awhile.'

'Do as you please.' Greaves turned on his heel.

Sheridan took a deep breath and gently picked up Lucy's hand. He sat in silent contemplation.

The old woman returned with a bowl of broth. 'And now she sleeps again, and I am up and down them stairs for nothing!'

'Let me watch over her. I see you have a cot over there. Take your ease.'

'Happen I will.' She waddled to the low bed and with much huffing and puffing lay down.

After a while Sheridan heard a low snore.

'Sir.' Lucy's voice was so low it was little more than a whisper. 'You would look after the child?'

The girl scarce looked older than a child herself, he thought, as he clasped her hand and whispered in return, 'I would look after you, Lucy.' He nodded. 'Mrs Stretton.'

There was a flicker of a smile then. 'He would be a great lord.'

'Who?'

'My son.'

'Because … the earl is not the earl?' Sheridan hazarded.

Lucy nodded and her face creased with despair. 'Do not let them kill my infant.'

'No, no. On my honour.'

She seemed content with this reassurance and closed her eyes again.

'The earl is not the earl…' Sheridan repeated under his breath. What did she mean by that?

'It is my curiosity… Dan always said it would get me into trouble…'

Sheridan strained forward to catch her words.

'…I did not mean to… I know I should not have been there, and when I heard an approach, I hid…'

Minutes passed. Sheridan stroked her hand.

'And you heard something or you saw something?'

'I do not know how to say it.'

'I am listening.' He patted her hand. 'And I will believe you.'

'I slipped from the room when I could … but Lady Cannock had sight of me and called me to her… I was shaking, I… She must have known what I had seen.'

Sheridan waited.

'Then Mrs Smethurst came to her and Her Ladyship let me go.' Lucy squeezed his hand tight and gasped. 'Only Edward, I thought, would know what to do … to bring it out.'

'Bring what out, Lucy?'

'The earl is not a man. I know not what … but not a man.'

Suddenly Lucy screamed. It was a sound that made Sheridan's blood run cold. He leapt to his feet. When Lucy opened her eyes again, they were wide with fear.

'It comes! My baby comes!' she yelped and then cried out again, a sound more animal than human.

The old woman stumbled from her cot, bleary-eyed. 'What's what? What's amiss?'

'The child — there is something wrong.' Sheridan looked frantically at the harridan. 'You must help her. Please, you must help her.'

Lucy writhed on the bed.

The old woman pulled back the cover. 'Her waters are broke. That is ill; it is too soon.'

'We must send for a doctor!'

The old woman shook her head. 'Mr Greaves won't want that, sir.'

'Damn Mr Greaves!'

Greaves appeared at the threshold and took in the scene.

Lucy screamed again, long and primal, with one hand clutching her pregnant belly. Sweat beaded on her brow.

'Damn you, Greaves! You must send for a doctor!'

Greaves said nothing. In his eyes Sheridan could see that he calculated the odds as he might with a horse race.

'If you won't, then I will!'

Greaves barred the way. He had not completed his deliberations.

There were shouts below. Men's voices, raised and violent. The whole household, it seemed, had suddenly woken to clamours in the middle of the night.

It was a night that Sheridan would not forget in a hurry, he reflected, when he crawled into his own bed the next day.

On hearing the commotion downstairs, Greaves pulled out a pistol and listened hard. He would not rush out. He was a cautious man and would trust to his henchmen before he would place himself in any danger. The shouts continued and were coming up the stairs. Sheridan was at last able to make out a voice he recognised. Constable Nicholls. And he was demanding that the other men stand back.

Sheridan's heart jumped. He must warn the officer. Greaves had a pistol at the ready.

'Constable Nicholls! We are here. Have a care!'

Greaves glared at him. 'A constable?'

Sheridan held his stare.

'You have crossed me!' Greaves hissed, but even as he spoke, he was putting away his firearm.

Nicholls backed into the chamber, his eyes darting all the while. He held the pugilist in his grip with a pistol to his head as hostage.

'Constable, you are most opportune.' It was Greaves who spoke, his hands splayed open and with a smile which was perhaps as welcoming as a viper might manage.

Nicholls ignored Greaves. 'Mr Sheridan, I heard the screams.'

'It is Lucy — the child, it is early.'

Greaves had meanwhile been calling his men to desist and now turned back to the constable. 'As you may see, sir, I have found that murderess you have been hunting and gladly hand her into your custody, which has always been my intention. Forgive my men. They have not recognised a Runner under your cloak and may have thought you an intruder.'

Again, Nicholls ignored Greaves and addressed Sheridan. 'How does she fare?'

Sheridan shook his head.

'I shall send straightaway for a doctor.' Greaves hastened to the doorway and called instructions downstairs. Then he again addressed the constable. 'As you see, I have a woman here that is practiced as a nurse and midwife. Every care has been taken of —'

The old woman was mopping Lucy's brow. 'There, there, lovey. You must be a brave girl.'

Nicholls shoved the pugilist aside and advanced towards Lucy's bed, calling for clean cloths and hot water, brandy and laudanum. He set about propping Lucy up with pillows, speaking softly.

He turned to the old nurse. 'In what position is the infant?'

The woman pressed around the belly. 'It is part breeched, poor thing.'

Greaves paled. 'Do what you can for the child.'

Sheridan turned on Greaves, keeping his voice low so as not to alarm Lucy. 'The child is likely dead already, no thanks to you. We must do all to save the mother.'

Greaves stared hard. 'I will not forget your deceit.'

'Be glad the constable is here that you may squirm out of an arrest for abduction, sir!'

At another piercing scream Greaves backed out of the room with his man.

Memories came to Sheridan of his own stillborn son, a grief that had tempered his joy at the triumphant opening of *The School for Scandal* a few days later. For years that sorrow at the loss of their child had swept in waves over Eliza and himself, and they had treasured their son Tom all the more.

With assistance from the nurse, Nicholls prodded at the belly to move the infant around as best they could. Then they had Lucy out of bed and half-walking, half-carried about the room, whimpering and crying out at intervals. An hour passed in this way, with the constable keeping up a stream of soothing words.

'It comes, sir, it comes. Lord A'mighty.' The old crone tutted.

Nicholls called to Sheridan to take over the support of Lucy whilst he coaxed her to delivery.

In the end the child slipped out bloody and limp into the world. A tiny thing, not brought to full term.

Sheridan marvelled at the way Nicholls took the babe and, sucking mucus from nose and mouth, he rubbed and breathed life into the still form until a mewling sound brought tears to Sheridan's eyes and a gasp of joy from Lucy. She had collapsed within his arms and he laid her back on the bed. Nicholls quickly wrapped a clean cloth about the infant and handed the swaddled bundle into Lucy's waiting arms.

'My son…'

Nicholls looked at Sheridan and raised a brow.

Lucy gazed with wonder at her child and then at Sheridan.

'You will look after him when I am gone, sir?'

'I will look after you both!'

Lucy smiled weakly.

The nurse meanwhile was all a panic. 'She is bleeding, sir. There is too much blood!'

And at the growing bloodstain, Sheridan felt his legs go weak.

A sharp-looking doctor arrived at last, but there was nothing that could be done to save Lucy.

'We must get the child to a wet nurse and to better care.' It was Nicholls. 'My sister will do it.'

Greaves made ready the carriage to take them. 'You will look after the boy, Sheridan?' he asked.

'The boy is a girl, Greaves.'

Greaves looked momentarily disappointed. 'Of some value, nevertheless.'

'To me. But not to you. That marriage of which I spoke will have no validity. She is a bastard child. Thank God!'

As a dawn light stole in at the window, they had left for the little house in Marylebone where Nicholls' sister resided.

'You have delivered a child before, Constable?'

Nicholls nodded. He cradled the newborn girl with surprising tenderness for so strong and broad a man. 'I am the eldest of fifteen, sir.' He smiled. 'And none lost.'

CHAPTER THIRTY-FIVE

Winter descended fast and furious. There had been frost and ice in London, but as Sheridan's carriage left Birmingham on the second day of his journey the first flakes of snow began to fall. Their progress was slow and arduous, and by Stafford the snow lay thick upon the ground. The early night sky was pitch dark and studded with stars. Ice hung in the air and promised that the freeze would stick. Sheridan shuddered as the sharp chill slapped his face.

He was thankful for the roaring fires which greeted him at The Stafford Arms. He was ushered by the landlord to a table close to the heat and promised a hearty supper of mutton stew and dumplings at the double.

'We are glad to see you, Mr Sheridan. You are not usually a visitor at this time of the year. Oddsboggart! I am afraid this weather is coming in on us. There will be more snow tonight.'

'Well, it will make a pretty picture.'

'That it will, sir.'

Sheridan warmed his hands at the fire and stamped the cold out of his boots before sitting down to a welcome and hearty repast. He felt swiftly revived by the wholesome fare and almost drawn from that despair which had beset him since the death of Lucy Webster. He was conscious that he had failed in his promise. All through the journey he had struggled to know how to proceed.

If he believed Lucy, which he allowed himself to incline towards, despite the bizarre nature of her assertion, then Lord Cannock was what? Some form of eunuch? An accident of birth or childhood? A eunuch could not be a father;

Sempronius might not be legitimate, but Cannock might still be an earl. Or, and this seemed too incredible, perhaps he was not a man of any kind, but a woman. It stopped his breath. How could it be? The deception. The disguise. That mask of rare refinement to which Dr Cardonnet had alluded would have begun to be moulded from the day of birth. Such a thought was almost too far beyond imagination to be countenanced. And yet... *The earl is not the earl.*

Sheridan reeled. He must allow himself to imagine the unimaginable, as if it were some fable of ancient legend. A girl raised as a boy.

Let him gather the facts as he remembered them. Cannock's mother had died in childbirth. It had been a difficult delivery for her. There were twins: a boy, John, and a girl whose name he could not recall. The girl had died with her mother. But what if it were not the girl but the *boy* that had died? The 3rd Earl, mad with grief, might have refused to accept that his son and heir to his title had died along with his beloved wife. Sheridan could tentatively believe such a possibility. But to sustain this belief! That was the rub. There would be the wet nurse, the maids, the doctor. Dr Burton, in fact. As a young physician he had delivered the infants. Why would so many others support this deception over so many years? And the child? Had she been accepting of her fate?

And where would Ann, Lady Cannock stand in all of this? Here was a secret so great, a deception so immense — why, it would be the scandal of the age! One which, if it were true, would destroy the Cannocks utterly. And ruin the future prospects of young Sempronius. No longer legitimate but a bastard child. And who, then, was his father?

Sheridan shook his head in disbelief. No. It could not be. It was outlandish. Lucy was mistaken. That was the simple answer. An easy enough mistake to make if the hiding place should limit her viewpoint. A lively, curious girl, prone to be fanciful and besotted with a lover whose fortunes might be transformed by such a revelation. Yes, Lucy was mistaken in what she had seen.

By the time he had reached Stafford, Sheridan had resolved that he must abandon the fantastical tale and set his mind to the express purpose of the visit. Mrs Webster. Such griefs she must have. First her son Daniel fatally stabbed, and then her daughter Lucy accused of murdering Edward Stretton and dying giving birth to his child. This was real life — real agony and real pain. To have lost all her children and those last in such circumstances. He must offer comfort and help the good woman look to the future. He would discuss what might be arranged for the child, her granddaughter. In his own mind he had already named the Infant Lucy, for her mother. He had charged himself to *look after Lucy*, and he would see it done.

Mrs Webster lived in a small tithe cottage at the edge of the village which straddled the southern edge of Sandbourne. A curl of smoke escaped the chimney. It was neatly kept with a small garden of herbs, and there would be flowers in the spring. The views across the lane were of the pasture and woodland of the estate, all frosted and pristine in the fresh snowfall. One might be content here, Sheridan surmised as his carriage drew up outside. Enough to satisfy Mrs Webster. Both her children, however, had held larger ambitions and they were now tragically turned to dust. What a house of sorrows must be concealed by this picturesque façade.

Mrs Webster was a handsome, lean woman, somewhere well above fifty he would judge. She divested him of his cloak and greeted him solemnly before inviting him into her small parlour, promising to make tea. There were biscuits freshly baked, the enticing aroma wafting from the kitchen. Whilst she was in preparation, Sheridan took in the simple, solid furniture, the sparsity of decoration and the Bible prominent on the table. It was not without comfort, but had the serene atmosphere of a monk's cell. A horse and rider passed outside, wisps of breath trailing in their wake but no sound, the snow muffling all in a deep quiet.

The tea was poured and biscuits proffered. Sheridan felt a desperate urge to cut through the pervasive silence, yet here in this room all was restraint, and to break that spell felt a sacrilege.

'Madam, I hope you will accept my deepest condolences.'

Mrs Webster nodded gravely. 'Thank you, Mr Sheridan. It is good of you to call on me.'

'It was ever my intention after your son Daniel's tragic end. I was with him at the last. He was not alone.'

'We are never alone, Mr Sheridan, if we accept the Lord Jesus.'

'Your religion must bring you comfort, Mrs Webster. I believe you are a Methodist?'

'I do not ask for comfort, only the blessing of God's word.'

'Madam, I have a small chest of Daniel's belongings in the carriage which my man can bring in, and I took the liberty of having this drawing reframed.'

Sheridan presented the picture wrapped in a cloth. Mrs Webster slowly opened it out to reveal the mother and daughter portrait in a silver frame.

'Daniel had it on display in his lodgings. I think it a good likeness, although your daughter was at a young age when Daniel left here.'

Mrs Webster rewrapped the portrait and put it aside.

'His talent is a great loss to our company. As I wrote you, Mrs Webster, Daniel was held in high regard.'

'The theatre, sir, it is all profanity. Daniel was lost to me many years ago now.'

'That is a sadness, Mrs Webster. He was a good and honest young man.'

In the silence which followed Sheridan picked up a biscuit. The brittle crunch seemed to echo back to him from the bare walls.

Mrs Webster sighed. 'I did not want Lucy to go into service at Sandbourne. There is an elderly gentlewoman nearby, Miss Hinckley, who would have suited her very well as an employer. But Lucy was always a wilful girl.'

Sheridan could well imagine that young Lucy would have wanted to escape the narrowness of this house and then would have been reluctant to share any confidences with her mother.

'You worked at Sandbourne yourself, did you not, Mrs Webster?'

'I was a chambermaid before I married Mr Webster, who was coachman.'

Sheridan nibbled at the biscuit, indicating with his expression his enjoyment of her baking.

'I was glad to leave.'

'I gather you are a seamstress now, Mrs Webster?'

'Simple mending. Nothing of fashion.' She hesitated, but the urge to confide evidently overcame her diffidence. 'There is bad blood in that family, Mr Sheridan, unnatural proclivities.'

He nodded earnestly. 'Mr Hanley acquainted me with the circumstances of his birth, the assault on his mother, which I believe you were privy to.'

'It was me, sir, that found poor Martha. Wicked, it was, what he did to her.' She shuddered involuntarily. 'Mr Francis

Stretton was a brutal man. I was ever afraid of him; I was but a girl of fourteen then, and the way he would look at me…' Mrs Webster's cup rattled in its saucer. 'The old earl would not have his brother in the house after that. And his lady was in a fury. They would not have his name spoken. Francis Stretton went off to the Americas then. He married there — an heiress, they say — but everything was lost in that war.'

A misfortune in more ways than one, Sheridan mused, for that war for independence in the American colonies had eventually brought the son, Edward, over to England by way of the Indies.

'And you were then at Sandbourne when the present Earl Cannock was born — that was a tragedy for the 3rd Earl, was it not? To lose both his wife and a child. It was fortunate it was the son that survived. Else Francis Stretton or his son Edward would have had Sandbourne…'

Sheridan watched Mrs Webster closely, but she would not look up at him and clasped her hands tight in her lap.

'If it had been the girl who had lived,' Sheridan continued, 'well, I daresay the 3rd Earl might have married again.'

Mrs Webster shook her head ever so slightly.

'I daresay he would do anything to stop his brother gaining the inheritance.'

'It was kind of you to call, Mr Sheridan.'

She looked at him directly now.

'I was with Lucy, too, at her end, Mrs Webster.'

'There is no need to speak of Lucy.'

Here was a hardened heart indeed.

Sheridan softened his tone in response. 'But I believe we do need to speak of her infant daughter.'

Mrs Webster bridled. 'She may go to a Foundling Home, may she not?'

'I thought perhaps that you —'

'I'll not have Lucy's bastard here, and none of Edward Stretton's flesh and blood!' Mrs Webster stood.

Sheridan followed suit and bowed. 'Beg pardon, madam, for having presumed on your time.'

The visit was over.

CHAPTER THIRTY-SIX

When he spied the figure in the cemetery, Sheridan asked his coachman to stop and wait at some little distance so he might not be observed. Even at this point he was undecided. Curiosity got the better of his judgement. What a damnable thing it was, that desire to know how the story would end.

The snow deadened his approach as he picked his way carefully across the graveyard. Lord Cannock did not hear Sheridan until he was by his shoulder.

'Mr Sheridan?'

'My lord.' He bowed. 'My visit with Mrs Webster has been long overdue on Daniel's account, and now…'

'Her daughter too is gone, I hear.' The earl nodded sadly. 'Such tragedies.'

'Death casts a long shadow.'

Sheridan looked at the names inscribed on the headstones. 'Susannah… I was trying to recall the name of your twin. Susannah. It is a pretty name.'

'For my mother — she was Henrietta Susannah.'

'There are those who would say you cannot miss what you have never known. But I do not agree. You miss Susannah?' Sheridan pulled his cloak tighter.

'More than I can say.'

'I was baptised Thomas — for a brother that had died the year before I was born. That earlier Thomas was but three years old; my parents had doted on him. Evidently, however, I did not pass muster as a Thomas; the family name, you see — my father, my grandfather. So, my second name, Richard, was used from near enough the start and I was free to be a disappointment. Little Thomas, his ghost lingers still. I am sure that you never disappointed your father, Cannock.'

'I hope not. I loved him with all my heart.'

'And you would do anything for him. Be anything for him.'

'You have an interest in human nature, Mr Sheridan. That is the province of the playwright.'

'At my last meeting with Dr Cardonnet, before he left so abruptly for Switzerland, he talked of how all men wear a disguise. I won't repeat what he discerned behind mine, it is not flattering, but he remarked that yours was such a mask of refinement as he had never encountered before.'

'Ah yes, Dr Cardonnet. A most interesting gentleman. I began to suspect I should not stay in his company long or he would know me. Such piercing eyes.'

'Your meeting led him to an outrageous theory, Cannock, which he confided only to me — for reasons which I am yet to fully understand.'

'And what was this outrageous theory?'

Sheridan allowed himself a small smile. 'Cardonnet is a man who likes enigma. *The earl is not an earl at all.* Now, what the devil did he mean by that, do you imagine?'

Cannock turned towards him, and it was only then that Sheridan noticed the shooting gun by his side, a double-barrelled fowling piece, the muzzle pointed to the ground.

'I suspect you know what he meant, Sheridan.'

'But am I right in what I suspect?'

Cannock sighed and inclined his head towards the gravestone of the infant Lady Susannah Stretton. 'I have been dead all my life.' He shook his head. 'There, it is said.'

'And forced to play another's part.'

'More than that, Sheridan. A play will have an ending, a final curtain call. The actors may divest the drama's character along with their costumes.'

Sheridan paused to admire Cannock. What an achievement! Oh, there were plenty of breeches parts in the theatre. Shakespeare alone abounded with them. Cesario, Balthazar and Ganymede. Mrs Jordan had built her celebrity on playing male parts. The audience loved such farces. And he had heard of the notorious women pirates and other rare women who had taken the disguise of soldiers and fought on battlefields. But this? A whole lifetime in another sex?

The high cravat was something of fashion, of course, and would disguise the absence of an Adam's apple. Cannock's style of clothing was all designed to cover his shape, and Sheridan now conjectured that those who supported the deception had padded the shoulders. Cannock had teased hair around the cheeks to suggest side whiskers and must shave to have a man's smoothness and be rid of any fine down on the chin. But when one knew the truth of it, there were signs. Aside from not being tall, Cannock's hands were fine and long, but nevertheless small for a man, and there was a delicacy in the facial features which, on closer observation, became apparent.

'I am weary, Mr Sheridan. I observe myself in the mirror and I do not know who I am.' Cannock looked at him with sharp, intelligent eyes. 'I would talk with you. I have need to confess and you have a kind and forgiving face, although I require no absolution. Shall we take a walk through my woods?'

Sheridan felt he had little choice while Cannock held a loaded firearm.

*

The trees were bare of leaves but heavy with snow. It was a walk which on any other occasion Sheridan might have relished despite the cold. At various points along the path the woods would open to allow a vista of the landscape. They paused at a particularly magnificent view and Cannock at last broke the silence.

'I have loved Sandbourne. I have loved its hills and fields, its woods and its pastures. I have loved its springs and river and the lake.' Cannock nodded to the lake below, glittering like a mirror under its sheen of ice. 'Above all, I have loved its people that are a part of it. The servants, the tenant farmers, the villagers. I have sought to have a care of them.'

Sheridan waited.

'My father had just such a love for Sandbourne. That is why he did what he did.' Cannock paused. 'Even though it was wrong.'

'It was a great wrong he did you, Cannock.'

'Yes — but he was also right. My uncle should not inherit. It righted a greater wrong.'

'Mrs Hanley, you mean? And that is why so many — the Hanleys, Dr Burton — have kept this secret?'

'Each had their own reason. After my father died, I accepted that my life would be a lonely one without true intimacy or companionship. I would devote myself to the study of medicine and the service of others. In this I was fortunate to be guided by Dr Burton.'

'I would have more readily accepted Dr Cardonnet's insinuation but for one fact that unsettled the theory. You did marry.'

'Yes.' Cannock's features creased in amusement. 'I had not reckoned on Miss Ann Cooper. She is a truly remarkable woman, Sheridan, you may have noticed.'

'My admiration for her increases on each and every meeting.'

'Admiration, heh? She is a match for any man.'

Cannock tapped the gun against the ground. 'To those who have vision and intelligence, poverty may be a great blight. You may know that yourself, from your own youth. And if one is a woman — how much more cruel! Ann and I were always fond of each other as children. We played in these woods and rowed on the lake.'

Cannock looked about, as if conjuring those childhood scenes.

'But being a boy, I received all the advantages of education and wealth to allow my ambitions full rein, whilst I stood by and watched Ann's world narrow into that of a spinster with no dowry or means of her own. She was a dependent, first caring for her aunt and then fated to be little more than a glorified helpmeet for her uncle, Sir Humphrey. Such a piteous waste of talent.'

'I can imagine that would have been galling.'

'She came to me one day and very boldly proposed that we should marry.' Cannock chuckled. 'I laughed. And then had to apologise for the impression that I might be insulting her with my laughter. "If the earl were to marry," I said, "it would be to no one but Miss Ann Cooper!" "Then it is settled," she replied. "I know why you do not marry. I have known since we were children. But you may marry me in confidence, and together we will educate and we will heal." The hospital was all her inspiration, and the schooling for girls and so many other improvements around the estate. And her friendship — that was the most prized of all the gifts she gave to me.'

'I see. She married you for your money then?'

Cannock bestowed a broad, open smile. 'Without a doubt!'

'That was an honest arrangement.'

Cannock nodded.

'Your honesty stopped short of your cousin, however; he should have been the rightful heir, should he not?'

Cannock's face looked pinched. 'When my cousin Edward first arrived, he was a young man, a rather callow youth of nineteen or so, but I hoped that with time and my guidance he might be a worthy successor to Sandbourne. I was ever conscious it was his due —'

'Of which you had deprived him.'

'Believe me, Sheridan, it was my dearest wish that Edward should inherit Sandbourne...'

'But he proved to be too much his father's son?'

Cannock sighed. 'Ann worried that should I die, Edward would destroy everything we were building.'

'It was still his birthright, already stolen from him.'

'I know. I know. I own that has been a great, great wrong. And I allowed it. That has been my sin. I lived with it.'

They were silent. The scudding clouds were all in retreat, the sky above blue and clear, the winter sun bathing the landscape in a snow-reflected glow.

'The boy has been a great joy. I do not know who Sempronius' father is. Ann begged that I never ask but assured me that I would not be disappointed. It would pain me deeply if Sempronius were ever to know the truth. I hope there will never be a need to tell him.' Cannock eyed Sheridan keenly. 'The burden of these lies is a very heavy one.'

'And the danger of exposure?'

Cannock nodded. 'The circumstances of Edward's death have troubled me greatly. I have seen that note which the maid Lucy had written. Ann assured me it would be read by the Justice as nothing more than a devious lure to get Edward to that temple, but it was too close, too close.'

Sheridan halted. 'You believe Lucy Webster killed your cousin?'

'Is there any doubt?' Cannock looked bewildered.

'I doubt. Yes, I doubt. And I believe that whoever killed Edward Stretton also slew my scene painter.' There, he had voiced what he truly believed. This confessional could work in both directions.

Cannock frowned. 'But who else, if not Lucy Webster? And a man has been hanged for the murder of poor Daniel.'

'I fear the assassin was someone who believed the danger of exposure to be real and imminent.'

'No. No. There is none that would murder.'

'I was told that you are honest and decent, Cannock, that you put your faith in justice. I want justice for Lucy and for Daniel and yes, even for Edward Stretton — and, God's teeth, for Isaac Fethard too.'

Sheridan backed away, his arms spread wide in what he knew was an overly theatrical gesture, and looked heavenward. 'You should want that justice. Or, if you would silence me, you had better do it now.'

A shot rang out.

The noise shattered the winter stillness, so loud and close it could only have been aimed at him. If he had not stumbled in the thick snow it would have got him. Had it got him? He half-staggered to his feet.

Another shot rang out in deafening assault, and a third followed almost immediately. With it came a stab of pain. And then Sheridan was certain that he had been hit as he crumpled into the snow.

CHAPTER THIRTY-SEVEN

When he was at last able to prop himself up, Sheridan was aware first of the blood seeping from his left thigh, spreading and marring the pristine white of the snow. Secondly, he became aware that Cannock was at a further distance, kneeling in the snow and cradling the raised head of Samuel Hanley. Cannock smoothed the fair Stretton hair from the manservant's brow and murmured the diminutive of his name over and over. But it was Cannock's features that were creased with pain. Samuel Hanley felt no more. He was dead.

'You saved me, Cannock.'

Cannock glanced across to Sheridan. 'He was like a brother. An older brother who always protected me…' A sob escaped.

Sheridan nodded. 'And he loved you as a brother. What one might do for love, he did. He would kill anyone that might hurt you. He would have killed me too.' The shock sent a spasm through his body and the shivering would not abate. 'But you saved me, Cannock,' Sheridan repeated.

Cannock straightened and gently lay Hanley down. 'You are bleeding, Sheridan. But you are alive. I thank God.'

Cannock came towards him, removing a cravat, and examined the wound on Sheridan's thigh with trembling hands. Gulping back sobs, Cannock bound the cloth tightly about the injury.

'It is only a flesh wound but must be cleaned very thoroughly to prevent infection. Dr Burton will do it.'

Sheridan winced as the knot tightened.

'Come, you may lean on me. I am stronger than I look.'

Cannock picked up the gun and used it as a crutch as they slowly made their way through the deep snow down the slope towards the lake, now sparkling under that winter sun. The orange glow lit the facade of the great house rising up from the other side.

They paused to rest by the lake which, though completely frozen over, was not yet thick enough to be safe for skating. Cannock lowered Sheridan gently onto a fallen tree trunk which had been stripped of its roots and branches. He felt numb with the cold, or perhaps it was the blood that he had lost.

'Sheridan, I know now what I must do.'

'Cannock?'

'Samuel's actions were all for my sake. I can see that now. That does not make them forgivable. Nothing warrants taking a life. Poor Samuel, he was all misguided, for the safety of my secret. He would never have committed such crimes were it not for that. He was a good man.' Cannock straightened. 'I would take those deeds on myself. You are right. Lucy Webster should have no stain on her name, and her brother and my cousin deserve some justice.' Cannock looked steadily at Sheridan. 'You will say that I have committed these crimes and confessed all to you. That I might have been provoked to murder my cousin will not be contested, I fear. You may say that Lucy witnessed the assassination and that is why she fled, and I tracked her down and killed her brother and so on…'

'The note?'

'The note … I knew her writing, and its purpose was to cast suspicions away from myself. Samuel…' Cannock hesitated. 'Samuel had found me out. He loved Lucy. Did you know that?'

Sheridan nodded.

'He challenged me and I… This is my confession. It was all by my hand. There. You will have your justice.'

Sheridan shook his head, his heart torn in first one direction and then the other. 'Cannock…'

'Only promise me one thing, Sheridan… I pray you will not reveal that other story, my story, for Ann's sake. For my son, Sempronius. I feel that I may trust you, Sheridan.' Cannock stepped to the edge of the lake and looked out across its expanse.

'When you are arrested, I fear your sex will be revealed, whether you want it or no.'

Reaching into the snow, Cannock picked up a sizeable stone from the pebbled lake shore and felt its weight.

'I shall not be arrested.' Cannock dropped the stone into a pocket and picked up another, and another. 'Who can tell from bones that have been picked clean if they belong to a man or a woman? If they are found at all.'

Sheridan had a sudden knowledge of Cannock's intention. 'Cannock, no.'

'Susannah. I should have liked that name.'

'No!'

Sheridan winced and struggled to rise to his feet, but before he could even limp to the edge of the lake, Cannock was already striding with purposeful haste towards its centre.

Sheridan could only watch on in horror as Cannock lifted the fowling piece and fired the remaining shot into the ice. Within moments Cannock had slipped through the spreading cracks into the frozen waters beneath.

The shot had been heard. As Sheridan stumbled painfully towards the house, he could see servants heading towards him and Lady Cannock emerging onto the terrace, her face alive with dread. What must he say? He needed time to think. This was all too swift. One misery following another. And was this justice? For the murders, perhaps. But for Cannock to embrace such ignominy? Who, after Edward, would succeed to Sandbourne? Who would be the 5th Earl? Not Sempronius. There was likely some cousin. He felt sure of it. What must he do? Persuade Ann to retire on a stipend, purportedly out of grief and shame at Cannock's actions? Yes, that might be plausible — and Sempronius could relinquish all title, for the same. He nodded to himself. That would be his course. He must persuade Ann to give up Sandbourne, for Cannock's sake, and for her son. From this day must come some good; wrongs must be righted. A manservant arrived at his side and took his arm.

As they neared the terrace Lady Cannock saw that he was injured and commanded another footman to assist whilst directing other servants to search for the earl.

'Mr Sheridan! Richard! What has happened? There has been a hunting accident? I did not know you were here. My husband? Where is my husband?'

Sheridan was half-carried inside and seated by the roaring fire. One of the servants was directed to send for Dr Burton straightaway.

'Richard! What may we do for you?'

'Brandy. I would have some brandy. And you should too.'

When they were alone, Lady Cannock sank into the chair opposite and all colour drained from her face. 'You have come to tell me that my husband is dead.'

Sheridan nodded. 'Drowned, in the lake, by his own hand.'

Lady Cannock clasped a hand to her mouth, stifling sound.

'I have come to share his confession, but also to tell you the truth.'

'I may not wish for it.'

'No. But you will hear it out.'

The brandy arrived and Lady Cannock dismissed the servant. Sheridan relayed all that had transpired that day and more. Lady Cannock listened attentively and he marvelled at her composure. The earl was right. Ann truly was a remarkable woman.

'You are saying that John was not my husband but a lie. A lie which I have supported. That makes me a pretence too, does it not, Sheridan? We must all know what will happen next. My son needs to know what will happen next.'

'Justice, Lady Cannock. That is what must happen; you must see that. I shall keep this secret — but right must be done.'

'Let me tell you a real truth.' Lady Cannock stifled a sob. 'There was no finer man than John Stretton, Fourth Earl Cannock. No one of greater probity or worth in my whole acquaintance. No one who has done so much for the good and asked for so little in return.' She cast her eyes about and indicated the magnificent vista through the windows. 'John was gifted this estate, Sandbourne. It was not ever sought but rather it was accepted, and not to do so would have injured others who had made that decision for him.'

They started at the sound of the door opening. To Sheridan's surprise, Mrs Hanley entered the room without asking for admittance.

'Mrs Hanley —' Lady Cannock stood.

'His Lordship they say is drowned, and no accident.'

Lady Cannock nodded. 'It is so.'

'And my Samuel, he is found.' The elderly housekeeper held herself stiffly, an effort at composure.

Ann placed a hand to her brow. 'We are all bereft, good Mrs Hanley.'

Mrs Hanley's eyes narrowed as she turned to Sheridan. 'You have heard a confession, have you, sir?'

'His Lordship —'

'No.' Mrs Hanley shook her head vehemently. 'I won't have His Lordship take the blame, him that would not hurt even a fly.' The housekeeper moved further into the room. 'I have held my tongue, but Samuel is gone now. It was him that did it all, and he must pay that price even in death. I did not care about Mr Edward; he was his father's son and no mistake! But killing Daniel — that was ill. He said it had not been his intention but... My poor boy. He was ever at war with his own two natures, the good that was in him and the blood of that same brutal father, Francis Stretton. No, I will have no blemish on His Lordship's name. I suckled those two babes, and that poor motherless child was as much mine. But we shouldn't have done to that poor little mite what we did. Who knows what Lady Susannah's life might have been if we had let her be?'

'You are shaken good, Mrs Hanley. Pray take a seat.'

'No, thank you, Your Ladyship. I will stand.' The housekeeper straightened. 'My poor Samuel. I never loved him as a mother should, not with the manner of his begetting. He only wanted for a mother's love and would do anything to please me. He has done these murderous things for my sake so my sins might not be found out. It was me that begun it all. I said, "How would anyone know if it was the girl or the boy that has died?" Such a small difference it seems when they are so tiny. I knew the old earl could never marry again. It wasn't in his nature; there had only been Her Ladyship. And she in a great fury for what Francis Stretton had done to me, his wicked violation. No one present in that room would countenance that devil having Sandbourne. But it was a wrong.

I am punished now with Samuel's loss and the infamy which his name will bear.'

Mrs Hanley took a deep breath. 'You will let it be known that Samuel did all for jealousy and love of Lucy Webster, a love that went to the bad and hate for her betrayal with Edward Stretton. Young Daniel died protecting his sister from that wrath. There's a story for you, Mr Sheridan; you may make a tragedy out of it. I am gladdened Emmanuel was freed. That did weigh heavily.' Upright as ever, Mrs Hanley nodded and departed.

Lady Cannock sighed. 'Good Mrs Hanley.'

Sheridan eyed Lady Cannock and drained his brandy. He should not ask, but he must know.

'I presume it was you, Lady Cannock, who told Samuel that Lucy had seen more than she ought?'

'Yes, Richard.' Ann looked him squarely in the eye. 'And I knew what I did. Samuel understood what must be done. That Lucy must be silenced, that our secret should not spread to Edward's ears.'

Sheridan caught at his breath. Did she admit to ordering these killings? No, she wished to silence Lucy, that only. Not to kill, surely? He would not believe that. He dared not. Lady Cannock had meant that Samuel would offer a bribe to Lucy. Yes, that was all that she had meant. The murderous actions had been all Samuel. And yet…

'I know that you would do anything for your son, Lady Cannock.'

'Our son.'

Sheridan blinked. Had he heard that right?

'Our son,' Lady Cannock repeated, and there was a challenge in her eyes.

'My son?'

'You were rather drunk, very drunk in truth, and you have your reputation with married women. I confess I led your seduction, allowed you to play the gallant. I often wondered if you remembered anything of our tryst or if it simply merged with a dozen other such escapades in your mind.'

He could not think. He could feel a flush rising on his face, and not just from the brandy or the heat of the fire. Flashes of memory assailed him. Was it seven years ago? Yes. The images came to him. Their snatched moment in the night and the tumbling on a chaise longue.

'I chose you nonetheless, Richard, for your better qualities.'

He fumbled for words. 'I had begun to think the child might be Samuel's.'

'No. There has only been you, Richard.'

Sheridan felt himself on shifting sands. Here was not some abstract moral dilemma. Here was his own flesh and blood.

'There is one final argument I would put to you in our case. There is man's justice and there is natural justice. That is your choice. If you would see my son disinherited, then Sandbourne will go to a distant cousin: one James Stretton, a planter in Barbados. He is unmarried and childless, save for the slaves he has begot to profit from their labour and their sale. You may recall that Emmanuel was one of that progeny, as was his mother. If your conscience does not prick to have such a man as earl and master of Sandbourne, to have the care of the local tenants, the interests of the new hospital and the poor of the parish, then by all means promote his claim and the title will die with him. Or you might rather see the man that Sempronius promises to become, with a fine and noble heart like his two fathers, the one that has raised him and the one who gave him life.' She looked pointedly at Sheridan. 'We are in your hands.'

Lady Cannock was indeed a force to be reckoned with. What a politician she might have made, if women were allowed. There was a thought. What must he do? What was just? What was right? But — he had already listened to his heart.

'I have one condition, Lady Cannock.'

'I am listening.'

'Two conditions,' he added hurriedly.

'Acquaint me with your terms, Mr Sheridan.'

'There is a newborn babe that needs a home when she is weaned. Lucy Webster's daughter. She is after all a Stretton, though it may be a curse for her to ever know that. Were the child to become your ward, she should have all the opportunities Your Ladyship can offer her.'

'I agree most readily.'

'I had liked to name her Lucy.'

Lady Cannock thought a moment. 'That might be a little painful for me. Let us say Lucy Jane, and I shall call her Jane.'

'Very well.'

'And your other condition?'

'Your son.'

'Our son,' Lady Cannock corrected.

'What might be the full list of his given names?'

'Sempronius Severus William —'

'William! That will do very well. Let him be plain William.'

Lady Cannock managed a smile. 'As you wish, Richard.'

'Then I shall keep my counsel.'

Some secrets, Sheridan had decided, were best left to rest in peace.

CHAPTER THIRTY-EIGHT

In mid-December Sheridan finally returned to Westminster. He had been absent since April, since the period of Eliza's illness. It was timely, he determined, to throw himself fully back into the cut and thrust of the House and the hurly-burly of the political fray. Fellow Whigs embraced his return; his wit and oratory had been sorely missed, they insisted, as the opposition continued to fracture and lose ground against the government of Mr Pitt. Even his enemies, or a large number in any case, greeted him warmly in the corridors of power. All were solicitous. He was well known as a man of feeling, and grief at the death of his dear wife was an accepted reason for his long absence.

A sense of looming crisis and foreboding was palpable. Louis XVI, or Louis Capet as his prosecutors insisted, was on trial in Paris. Few now held out much hope for his acquittal, or that of his wife, Marie Antoinette, whose own trial would surely follow. They would face exile or worse, Madame la Guillotine. The world then was on the brink of a great conflagration. And in the name of war, Sheridan shuddered to consider, tyranny was like to follow as night follows day. How would all those dreams for liberty and reform fare in such a dark climate? He must hold firm to his highest ideals.

How much easier that would be when he had the love and support of Pamela Syms at his side. She would embolden him to the future, and what fun they would have! Whatever his other cares in the world, life would be a merry round with Pamela on his arm, for she was all light and gaiety. As family and friends gathered at Wanstead for the Christmas festivities,

Sheridan endeavoured to be jolly and lively in entertaining all his guests, but in his room at night he sighed over Pamela's absence and longed to hold her at last in his fervent embrace. As the days passed, he comforted himself with the prospect that they must soon be reunited, and he sat down to write yet another letter.

I must delay my coming to Paris, which I meant however to delay only to the present time, when parliament will adjourn for three weeks.

Had she received any of his letters? There was the rub, for he had received nothing from her. And yet he knew full well in his heart that she would have written. Lovers should not be kept apart by the affairs of states; it was a cruelty that should not be endured! If the authorities opened this letter, they should hear it from him.

That they have opened here all letters to us from France I have known for some time, but there has been a fatality in their withholding letters which could answer no purpose to them.

No purpose to them at all! How he had longed to read her notes to him, sweet inconsequential nothings. And how his dear girl must think he neglected her. If only she knew the truth of it, that she was now in his mind both day and night.

How inconsistent and unfeeling you must have thought me, and now, when I hoped to have surprised you at Tournai, war and public folly are raising new obstacles.

War would be an obstacle indeed to his travel plans, but he would not let the follies of others prevent him from marrying Pamela Syms.

On the final day of the year, he spoke in the House on the Alien Bill by which the government was attempting to stem the flow of refugees fleeing from across the Channel. Sheridan rose to propose that ladies should be exempt from the restrictions of the bill, to show all that the Age of Chivalry was not gone in England, whatever may become of it elsewhere! He was roundly cheered, and not only by his Whig friends. All his thoughts whilst he spoke had been of darling Pamela and carrying her with him from France to London.

As his carriage trundled into Wanstead that evening, Sheridan reflected on the year that was soon closing. It had been a momentous year which had wrung out his heart in more ways than one. But on a personal level he could look forward to 1793 with the open prospect of new joys and pleasures.

There were two letters awaiting him when he arrived at his home.

The first brought a warming smile: an invitation to the wedding of Constable Louis-Pierre Nicholls to Mademoiselle Thérèse-Madeleine De Lubac. The watchmaker's granddaughter. Well, here was a happy ending, and there would no doubt be many children in the future if Thérèse-Madeleine had the constitution for it.

The second letter was also on the subject of marriage. Sheridan had to read it two or three times over to allow the contents to make the journey between his heart and his head. How could he believe or comprehend what had taken place? But that it was a true account he could not doubt. The duc, Philippe Égalité, had been in attendance with his son.

Pamela had married in Tournai.

Married. When only the previous month she had accepted his proposal. He felt a lurch in his stomach. She must, after all, have thought him in jest. His courtship a mere play of gallantry. Another of his silly games. Never to be taken seriously. How would his heart survive the blow? Not when he came to read the name of his rival, the man who had succeeded where he had failed. If it were a fiction the critics would laugh aloud, for it could not be more incredible! Lord Edward Fitzgerald. Eliza's lover. The father of his little Mary.

The account told how they had met at the Paris opera on November twenty-first, soon after Madame de Genlis' party had arrived in the city. Lord Edward had been overwhelmed by Pamela's likeness to Eliza and sought her out. He had pursued the party to the border town of Tournai and once there, laid siege to Pamela's heart. Edward Fitzgerald, son of the Duke of Leinster, could never be mistaken for a prankster. He was all seriousness, with impeccable revolutionary credentials. Now dubbed by Parisians *Le Citoyen Eduoard Fitzgerald*! The newlyweds were to move to Fitzgerald's home in Dublin, and no doubt they would go on to lead a heroic revolution in Ireland.

Sheridan imparted the news to Tom as they retired upstairs. There were few with whom he felt he could share this surprising information.

Tom was sanguine. 'I see now, Pa, why you felt that you could not tell me the name of Miss Syms' lover. You were afraid, were you not, that I would be distressed to know that my mother had been so easily replaced in that young lord's affections. That perhaps he trifled with Mama all along and I would be angry and act foolishly. Is that not so?'

Sheridan squeezed his son's shoulder. He felt himself old and tired, and he had drunk far too much port. He wanted to cry but he would not let himself, and then another cry was to be heard. Mary.

'Well, Tom, there is a wail that must be answered!'

Sheridan ascended to the nursery to find the infant lying in her cot, red-faced and crotchety. He lifted her up into his arms.

'Ah, that bold Signor Incisor! He is come to bring you yet more sharp little teeth!'

Sheridan settled himself into the comfortable nursing chair with his baby daughter and began to jiggle her about. When he had her attention, he pulled funny faces and blew bubbles into her cheeks, whilst tears slid down his own. Mary squealed with delight and then began to calm. With drooping eyes, she nestled her head into the crook of his neck.

When the wet nurse, Mrs Wilkins, lumbered up the stairs just before dawn and entered the small cosy room, it was to find both father and daughter sound asleep in the easy chair.

A NOTE TO THE READER

Dear Reader,

The naming of fictitious characters has all the potential to be an enjoyable task for an author. They may reference friends or acquaintances or even be auctioned for charity. My Sheridan novels are littered with real historical figures, the likes of Laetitia Lade, George Hanger, Skiffy Skeffington and so on, but at the centre of the fabricated mysteries are characters of my own devising. Having an interest in family genealogy, I realised that I had a store of names reaching back hundreds of years and decided to use them as a well from which to draw inspiration.

You will understand that I could not resist the temptation to use the name of an ancient cousin, Sempronius Stretton. My Sempronius is the young heir to the Sandbourne Estate, but the real Sempronius was a near contemporary born in 1781 in Nottingham who served in the military during the Napoleonic Wars. Colonel Stretton appears in the famous banquet portrait of the Duke of Wellington with his officers following the Battle of Waterloo painted by William Salter. An earlier posting for Sempronius saw him at York Barracks in Canada, the site which was to become the basis of the City of Toronto, and evidenced his artistic streak in some of the earliest sketches of that area and its indigenous peoples. There is a pleasing symmetry in that I dedicate this second novel to my writer friend Ellen Fox, who hails from that city. Our common Stretton ancestor was Sempronius' grandfather Christopher Stretton, who came from Staffordshire, and I chose Christopher to be my First Earl Cannock. I hope that

Sempronius would not mind my using his name for my purposes, but it also strikes me that he may merit a novel of his own.

I hope you enjoyed reading the novel, and I thank you for taking the time to do so. Reviews are really important to authors, and if you enjoyed the novel, it would be great if you could spare a little time to post a review on **Amazon** and **Goodreads**. Readers can connect with me online, **www.facebook.com/rosiewriter1** on Facebook and **@rosiewriter** on Instagram and you can find out more about my writing via my website: **https://rmcullenauthor.wordpress.com**

Thank you!

Rose M Cullen

Sapere Books is an exciting new publisher of brilliant fiction and popular history.

To find out more about our latest releases and our monthly bargain books visit our website:
saperebooks.com

www.ingramcontent.com/pod-product-compliance
Lightning Source LLC
Chambersburg PA
CBHW031939110426
42744CB00029B/176